GEORGE HERBERT: SACRED AND PROFANE

GEORGE HERBERT: SACRED AND PROFANE

edited by

HELEN WILCOX
RICHARD TODD

VU University Press
Amsterdam 1995

VU University Press is an imprint of
VU Boekhandel/Uitgeverij bv
De Boelelaan 1105
1081 HV Amsterdam
The Netherlands

Layout by: Sjoukje Rienks, Amsterdam
Cover by: Neroc, Amsterdam
Printed by: Wilco, Amersfoort

isbn 90-5383-368-4

CONTENTS

PREFACE AND ACKNOWLEDGEMENTS

In the short poem 'Superliminare' that prefaces 'The Church', the central section of his masterpiece *The Temple* (1633), George Herbert quotes Virgil, *Aeneid* 6: 258 ('procul este profani'):

Avoid profaneness; come not here ...

The address is not to the reader but to profaneness itself, 'Avoid' here carrying the imperative sense to the profane: 'Be off with you.' Both Herbert's injunction and its echo of Virgil remind us, as does Diane McColley in Chapter 3 of this book, of the etymology of 'profane' itself, that it refers to everything in front of (*pro*), and thus outside, the Temple (*fanum*).

The theme of this book may therefore initially seem puzzling to readers of George Herbert, even though Mario di Cesare, in Chapter 1, does approach 'Superliminare' from a liturgical perspective. Yet if one considers the book's contents as a whole, one is forced to conclude that many worldly, profane things do indeed feature inside *The Temple*: these are not just such obviously worldly things such as food (Heather Ross, Chapter 9) and wit (Helen Wilcox, Chapter 10), but equally challengingly, relationships with the secular world as well, such as sacred parody (Elizabeth Clarke and John Ottenhoff, Chapters 2 and 4 respectively). The lyrics, in other words, may be sacred but they clearly exist in relation to the ordinary secular world: to its money, its proverbs, its emblems, its politics. In one of his best-known poems, George Herbert describes prayer as 'Heaven in ordinary', and we can understand the constituent lyrics making up *The Temple* as experience of the sacred in secular dress.

Perhaps the 'profaneness' that is told to 'avoid' is an attitude that lacks sympathy with the activities of *The Temple*: there is no sense that the profane items and traditions, and even rhetorical skills, such as bargaining, which occur in the poems themselves, are to be excluded. It is in fact the mingling of sacred and profane that is one of the fundamental characteristics of Herbert's writing: it is part of that approachable quality that marks these lyrics out even among other religious texts. The chapters that follow explore the interplay of secular and devotional elements in *The Temple* from a wide range of perspectives: from overview, whether liturgical (Mario di Cesare, Chapter 1) or analogical (R.V. Young Jr, Chapter 7) to such captivating details as the lyrics' titles (Matthias Bauer, Chapter 8);

from the contemporary seventeenth-century context (Ted-Larry Pebworth, Kay Gilliland Stevenson and Robert Wilcher, Chapters 11, 13 and 14 respectively) to our own present (Cedric Brown, Chapter 15); from verbal rhetoric (Robert Cummings and Judith Dundas, Chapters 5 and 6) to visual (Bart Westerweel, Chapter 12) and musical (Diane McColley, Chapter 3) impact. Taken together, it is our hope that this collection of essays will enrich our sense of the complexity, wit and vision of George Herbert's lyrics.

Owing to circumstances beyond the control of all concerned, Chapter 9 (Heather Ross) appears in shortened form with limited documentation. The editors do not feel that this fact detracts from the interest and comprehensibility of the essay, which is why they have included it in this form.

The editors are indebted to the English Department at the University of Groningen for financial support and for hosting the conference out of which the volume has grown. They would further like to thank Alasdair Mac-Donald for support, inspiration and good humour, and Jeroen Kans and Arina Vermaas at the VU University Press for friendly and efficient co-operation.

Helen Wilcox
Richard Todd

Amsterdam/Groningen, April 1995

A NOTE ON EDITIONS AND ABBREVIATIONS USED

Unless otherwise stated, quotations from *The Temple* itself are taken from the modern-spelling edition of John Tobin, Penguin Classics (London: Penguin Books, 1991). This applies to George Herbert's other poems in English, including the modernized texts of 'To the Lady Elizabeth Queen of Bohemia' which Tobin, following the claims of recent scholarship (see Ted-Larry Pebworth, pp. 141, 150-51), has added to the canon. Page numbers from Tobin are given only for quotations from poems not in *The Temple*. Quotations from the Latin poems and from prose works including *The Countrey Parson* are taken from F.E. Hutchinson, ed., *The Works of George Herbert* (1941; Oxford: Clarendon Press, 1959). Where applicable, these sources are cited as 'Tobin' and 'Hutchinson', respectively, in the text that follows. English translations of the Latin poems are those given in Mark McCloskey and Paul R. Murphy, *The Latin Poetry of George Herbert: A Bilingual Edition* (Athens: Ohio UP, 1965), unless otherwise stated.

The following abbreviations have been used:

AV:	Authorized or King James version of the Bible (1611)
B:	Bodleian MS Tanner 307
BCP:	Book of Common Prayer
CQ:	*Critical Quarterly*
DNB:	*Dictionary of National Biography*
EC:	*Essays in Criticism*
ELR:	*English Literary Renaissance*
GHJ:	*George Herbert Journal*
MP:	*Modern Philology*
N&Q:	*Notes & Queries*
OED:	*Oxford English Dictionary*
PL:	*Patrologia Latrina*
RQ:	*Renaissance Quarterly*
SP:	*Studies in Philology*
W:	MS Jones B 62, Dr Williams's Library, London
1633:	First printed edition of *The Temple*

Abbreviations of books of the Bible and of works of Shakespeare conform to MLA usage. Quotations from the former are modernized from the AV;

quotations from the latter are keyed to Stanley Wells and Gary Taylor, eds, William Shakespeare, *The Complete Works: Compact Edition* (Oxford: Clarendon, 1988).

INTRODUCTION
HISTORICISMS AND GEORGE HERBERT

RICHARD TODD

In the decade that has passed since the commemoration of the 350th anniversary of the death of George Herbert (1593-1633), our shared conversa-
tions about this extraordinary figure have continued and grown. It is the
celebration of Herbert's quatercentenary in 1993 that has given rise to the
papers collected in this book. This introduction is not intended to try to
summarize these papers on George Herbert's 'Sacred and Profane', but to
rather to set them in context. That context is a brief discussion of three
forms of historicism—all of them, I suppose, revisionist, or 'New'. I shall
term them (a) sacred or religio-political historicism, (b) secular or 'cultural'
historicism, and (c) textual historicism.

To scholars not primarily engaged with the study of *literature* in the
Renaissance or early modern period, the term 'historicism' would be fairly
innocently recognized as a standard procedure, whereby what is stressed is
history's importance as both conferring value on a form of discourse, and
providing that discourse with emphasis on those events that have determined it. Yet the interests of literary and historical scholarship are often at
odds. Leah Marcus has suggested ways in which the old and the new historicisms complement each other, or fill in each other's gaps;[1] and historians
of mid-seventeenth-century England, that unique period of crisis, revolution
and Civil War, as Conrad Russell has recently shown, are faced with monu-
mental difficulties of self-definition all their own. Indeed, Russell despairs
of the English Civil War ever being explained in terms which the event
itself has not distorted.[2]

One simple fact with which we are faced is that George Herbert died
before the seventeenth-century English Church became polarized with
William Laud's appointment to the Archbishopric of Canterbury. We know
from Amy Charles' biography that Herbert's successor at Bemerton,
Thomas Laurence, was charged with various forms of 'deliquency'. But
these show an odd mixture—on the part of his accusers—of Puritanism (on
the one hand Laurence is said to have encouraged bowling and skittling on
Sundays and to have tolerated alcoholic intemperance) and of Laudianism
(on the other hand Laurence's doctrinal and theological practice within his
church building itself came under criticism).[3] Charles refrains from drawing conclusions about Herbert's own ecclesiastical practice other than those

we can deduce from *The Countrey Parson*, but Izaak Walton's nostalgia for pre-Civil War Laudianism has stuck. The title of Herbert's poem 'The British Church' notwithstanding, it really is impossible for us to guess how he would have responded to Laud's 'Bishops' War' of 1639 and the events that followed, even though the title in itself does lead one to speculate that he might have been inclined in support of Laud.

Yet even in suggesting this, one is falling victim to the treacherousness of 'historicism' as literary scholars of the early modern period have come to understand it. Claude J. Summers and Ted-Larry Pebworth, as well as Sidney Gottlieb, have written perceptively of the political aspects a poem such as 'The British Church' raises.[4] Both Nicholas Tyacke and David Norbrook have reminded us of the tumultuousness of English political and ecclesiastical life during the 1620s and 1630s,[5] and we can only speculate about Herbert's own decision to stand for Parliament in 1623/4. Amy Charles suggests a short and stormy period lasting from February to March 1624, and the evidence available—including a celebrated passage in *The Countrey Parson*—indicates that Herbert considered it a duty rather than an ambition.[6]

As we look back to the tercentenary commemorations of Herbert's death in 1933, it is as though we now inhabit a different world. In 1933, the presiding genii were those of T.S. Eliot and F.E. Hutchinson: the life of Herbert was still a hagiography, the only collocation matching 'New' was 'Criticism', and the approach to text was unquestioningly eclectic. Our historicisms of sixty years later display what Thomas Healy has recently termed 'anxiety about order':[7] they insist that individual and social identity are constructs, and that the consequences of regarding them as such include paying unprecedented attention to the ways our discourse are, or can be seen to be, 'gendered'; they privilege non-literary discourse as highly as 'literary', and in addition to asking awkward questions about what *is* 'literary', they make awkward points about 'text' as hostile to print culture or even to its own stability as an existential monolith.

'Anxiety about order': sacred or 'religio-political' historicism

The major acts of revisionism on this front predate the practice of new historicism, but new historicism has drawn strength from them. I have mentioned Walton's nostalgic Laudianism, and the co-existence of Eliot and New Criticism in the 1930s. To Eliot's must also be added the name of William Empson. With the prolonged argument between William Empson and Rosemond Tuve as to the values of the apparently rival practices of

New Criticism and an older (medievalist) historicism during the 1940s and 1950s, and the institutional endorsement of Herbert's achievement as a major lyric poet by a doyenne such as Helen Gardner, a duly anachronistically 'Anglican' or 'Anglo-Catholic' George Herbert had been constructed and established by the mid-1970s. Although it was one of several, this was the 'official' discourse for the first three-quarters of the present century. The quaintness was forgiven: George Herbert was more than a pious proto-Caroline Divine. He had become an English *poet* first and foremost.

Dissent from this position was of course tolerated—there was, after all, a disturbing amount of work being done in the United States that it would sooner or later become necessary to start taking account of. On the whole, though, institutional authority was claimed by Oxbridge (principally Oxford) and by the reactionary Anglo-Catholic hegemony within Oxbridge Renaissance English. Tuve's position as a medievalist of frightening erudition, along with her Ivy League credentials, admitted her to a position of authority within this hegemony. Empson was a Cambridge-trained maverick, but his work was 'brilliant' (a description that remains a cliché even today). Let me be quite clear: Empson's discussion of Herbert's 'The Sacrifice' was (I believe) an undertaking of such genius that the Oxbridge Anglophile institution was prepared to overlook his atheism in a way it was not when Empson later published *Milton's God* (1961). All the same, the British tendency to kowtow to Empson's later eccentricities must puzzle American scholars deeply.

Then in the second half of the 1970s two books appeared that blew this cosy institutional consensus apart: Helen Vendler's *The Poetry of George Herbert* (1975), and Barbara K. Lewalski's *Protestant Poetics and the Seventeenth-Century Religious Lyric* (1979). For present purposes the chief interest of the former lies in its secular nature, and in the frank admission it provoked from the then elderly I.A. Richards, Empson's own tutelary genius, who, reviewing the book in the *TLS*, affirmed his devotedness to Herbert and denied that his lack of religious belief should be considered 'disabling'. I have mentioned Richards' sympathetic response to Vendler elsewhere: my purpose in repeating it here is to claim that with it one pillar of the Oxbridge Anglo-Catholic hegemony collapsed.[8] Further, and this time irreparable, damage was done to that hegemony with Barbara Lewalski's thesis proposing that an unremittingly Protestant—indeed Calvinist—confessionalism underlay the poetry of George Herbert and indeed of many of his contemporaries. Lewalski's work has been much discussed, supported and disputed. My purpose in mentioning it here is to suggest that with its publication an act of cultural *enablement* was achieved.

For current orthodoxy could now be seen to hold that avowedly secular commentators were not just institutionally tolerated by the hegemonic forces they had dislodged: they would now set the terms for the debate, which would increasingly be fought out—not incidentally, but *principally*—on American ground. There is an attractive mythopoeia here, whereby Herbert's celebrated lines in 1633 about 'Religion stand[ing] on tip-toe in our land, / Readie to passe to the *American* strand' (*The Church Militant*) take on genuine prophetic force.

As it now stands the orthodoxy, or ideology, of a 'Protestant Poetics' is institutionally in the hands of Richard Strier, whose *Love Known: Theology and Experience in George Herbert's Poetry* (1983) is a work I greatly admire but one in which I nevertheless find much to disagree with. On the one hand I applaud the sheer intellectual poise that lies behind its synthesis of Lutheran theology and George Herbert's poetic practice; on the other I am disturbed by Strier's inclination to hypostasize a conception of Protestantism in such a way that indubitable patristic and medieval sources cannot be apprehended by Herbert other than through the filter of sixteenth-century Protestantism. Whereas we find Strier (rightly) showing scepticism concerning the unhistorical yet often-voiced split in the English Church prior to the Synod of Dordt as one between '"Puritans" and "Anglicans"' (p. xv), just over a page later (p. xvi) he is criticizing Tuve's and Louis Martz' revival of an 'Anglo-Catholic' Herbert. This time, Strier appears to be using the term 'Anglo-Catholic' without any qualification whatsoever, apparently unaware that it has no conceptual relevance within the Church of England before the middle of the nineteenth century. As Thomas P. Roche Jr, has asked, where does this strategy put the Protestant, and extremely English, propagandizing of Edmund Spenser?[9] This aspect of sacred historicism seems to be to be symptomatic of a real anxiety about order. One way out of a problematic historicist maze seems to lie in the more modest programme proposed by Gene E. Veith Jr (*Reformation Spirituality and George Herbert* [1985]).

I shall pass over the rather sterile 'nearer Geneva or Rome' debates that the work of Lewalski and Strier have galvanized, pausing only to mention that over against 'Protestant Poetics' there persists another—I use the word with no pejorative intent whatever when I say 'reactionary', and for present purposes interestingly Anglophile—strand of opinion, represented in the work of critics such as Heather Asals [Ross], A.D. Nuttall, and Paul Stanwood that may or may not be responding to one of Helen Gardner's worthier insights, that the Elizabethan settlement permitted more eclecticism in the English Church than elsewhere. This is a caveat we would do well to continue to bear in mind.

Identity as cultural construct: secular or 'cultural' historicism

Under this heading I can best consider one or two aspects of what I regard as one of the more intelligent exercises of the new historicism as applied to George Herbert under what I may term its 'secular' aspect. Michael C. Schoenfeldt, in *Prayer and Power: George Herbert and Renaissance Courtship* (1991), explores some of the ways in which Herbert's poetry can be related to the various forms of social discourse that prevailed in the early modern period. Schoenfeldt excavates a great deal of fascinating material, not just from courtesy books, but from less expected (but when one comes to think of it, perfectly reasonable) places such as forms of epistolatory address. Schoenfeldt's opening positions are that poetry can be an exercise of power because it can bend the hierarchy to one's own will; nonetheless, it comprises—in Herbert's hands—a vocabulary of affection as well as power.[10] A sceptic might point out that the hypostasized structure of Richard Strier, in which Lutheran theology accounts absolutely for Herbert's poetry of love, comes under strong secular challenge from Schoenfeldt, and although Schoenfeldt's equation of power and love is attractive, there seems to be a difference between these two new historicists that Schoenfeldt's claim cannot quite account for:

> Where Strier tends to stabilize the poems by reference to the Lutheran doctrines of justification by faith and of the irresistibility of grace, I attend to the lingering instability and moments of political resistance in Herbert's devotional performances (Schoenfeldt, p. 11).

Herbert's 'performances' presuppose the construction of a social persona: this is a position from which Schoenfeldt starts. I shall cite a couple of examples of 'lingering instability' and 'political resistance' as Schoenfeldt exfoliates these in what has proved to be his most controversial chapter: that on sexuality and acts of gendering in *The Temple*. There are some provocative and challenging readings: for instance, on the onanistic, self-directed discourse of 'A Wreath'; or on the complaints of poems such as 'Dulness' expressed in terms of a perceived lack of physical virility. Schoenfeldt's justification for this ingenious quarrying of sexual innuendos seems to be that Herbert's language works mimetically: it enacts its own imperfect, sullied state. This seems a fine insight, but as Stanley Stewart, reviewing an earlier version of this chapter, remarks, where does one quit?[11]

Schoenfeldt makes a point of saying that he goes further than previous commentators in commenting on the erotic charge of 'quick-eyed Love,

observing me grow *slack*/From my first entrance in' ('Love (3)', 3-4; emphasis added). I do not doubt this, and I respect his courage and integrity. It
seems inconceivable now, but I was taken to task as late as 1981 by an
anonymous reader for a British press shocked at my endorsing the late John
Mulder's 'insensitive importation' of detumescence into the poem. (That
press and I soon parted company.) Perhaps rather more credit should go to
Mulder (who was after all the first to *say*—in 1973—what was evidently
unsayable) than Schoenfeldt admits.[12] My problem here lies with the
extent to which we are still to consider the language of 'Love (3)' as
mimetic of a sullied and imperfect state of mind (even though the soul is
now—we are to assume—very much in a state of grace), or whether a state
of grace legitimates the use of such highly-charged and very self-conscious-
ly gendered eroticism (a position that would open up a direct line between
Herbert and medieval commentators on the Song of Songs)—or whether,
perhaps, both discourses are functioning simultaneously (which would of
course be the smart thing to say).

Whatever the case may turn out to be, the eroticism Schoenfeldt
provocatively sees, not just in *The Temple* but perhaps more so in the non-
vernacular, Christ-as-Mother tradition of the Latin poems, is a quality he
has no hesitation in tracing directly back to the Middle Ages, and in so
doing he blows the strictures of Lewalski and Strier right open. No-one can
now legitimately claim that this return to medieval mysticism is distilled
through any kind of Reformation sensibility. We have here a difference
between two intelligent new historicists of another order altogether from
that claimed by Schoenfeldt in the passage just quoted concerning Strier's
and his approaches to George Herbert.

Literary and non-literary discourse: textual historicism

George Herbert, unlike Donne, was not a coterie poet, and for many
scholars there is no textual 'problem' with *The Temple*. To what extent are
we to believe Izaak Walton that the fact that the poems have come down to
us is a result of studied good fortune? Recent scholarship suggests that
many of the lyrics may be earlier than we think, but what are our grounds
for considering *The Temple* as complete as Herbert would have wished it to
be, given Walton's deathbed mythography? We are now as good as certain
that Herbert never saw either Bodleian MS Tanner 307 (*B*) or any printed
edition, despite two of the latter appearing in the very year of his death. We
infer that the earlier William MS Jones B 62 (*W*) contains some of Herbert's
own corrections and (in certain cases) second thoughts.

Recently Janis Lull, *The Poem in Time: Reading George Herbert's Revisions of 'The Church'* (1990) has given the relationship between the two extant manuscripts more sustained consideration than they have received hitherto. I cannot rehearse Lull's case in the time available. I have reviewed her book more favourably than have others: Harold Toliver, for example, is troubled by what he terms 'a supposed text-of-the-authorial-mind hover[ing] somewhere between' the two manuscripts.[13] Yet I want to use the variety of responses to Lull to highlight briefly one or two points concerning new historicist scholarship as it concerns manuscript and print culture. George Herbert's *The Temple*, I suggest, offers us more than one kind of historical precedent: it is not simply the case, for instance, that Herbert is one of the first poets writing in English by whom titles of individual poems were clearly thought of with care. That *The Temple* was printed so quickly and carefully after his death, and revised again immediately, suggests that the cultural locale (a favourite among new historicists) in which the dissemination of manuscripts prevailed (with all the variants in transmission these inevitably lead to) was simply not at issue. These were private poems, and someone (whether Herbert or Ferrar) was anxious to get them into a form which we are now surely (in contradistinction to neo-historicist orthodoxy) forced to recognize as monolithic. To contextualize once more: recent Shakespeare editors have been at pains to show how their 'text' is not a final monolithic entity but represents what a given play was at one particular stage in its existence. Although Lull's analysis of Herbert's revisions suggests that this particular stage can be 'imagined' into existence (*pace* Toliver), that stage does not seem to have existed meaningfully other than as a readerly text available only to its author.

The same year, 1633, saw an execrably printed text of John Donne's *Songs and Sonets*, many of which poems already existed in several MS variants. Herbert's *The Temple*, in Thomas Buck's careful printing, is near-impeccable by contrast: the second edition perhaps even more so. These seem to me intuitive grounds for regarding the first two printed editions as having greater authority over Bodleian MS Tanner 307,[14] but I am well aware that Mario di Cesare, whose essay heads this collection, is one of several influential voices who disagrees. Matthias Bauer's essay on Herbert's titles also implicitly makes strong claims for *B*. However, it is not logical to dismiss my own postulation of a lost fair copy, as does Lull, on grounds that it offers a less 'parsimonious' explanation of the crowded pre-publication calendar that I am still compelled to regard as inconceivable.[15]

I conclude this brief survey of distinct but overlapping, at times rival, at times truly complementary, historicist discourses concerning George Herbert by admitting that I sense some real clashes among rival historicist discourses, and some serious internal contradictions. These various historicisms, for all their willingness to ask radical and timely questions about 'what it is to textualize', have at times nevertheless led to an *undecidability* that may not be so vastly different from that thrown up by the rival discourses within the hermetically-sealed New Criticism, or between that criticism and an older, archival, historicism.

Notes

1   Leah Marcus *et al.*, 'Historicism, New and Old: Excerpts from a Panel Discussion', in Claude J. Summers and Ted-Larry Pebworth, *'The Muses Common-Weale': Poetry and Politics in the Seventeenth Century* (Columbia: U of Missouri P, 1988), 207-210.

2   Conrad Russell, 'John Bull's Other Nations', *TLS*, March 12 (1993), 3-4.

3   Amy M. Charles, *A Life of George Herbert* (Ithaca & London: Cornell UP, 1977), 228-233.

4   Claude J. Summers and Ted-Larry Pebworth, 'The Politics of *The Temple*: "The British Church" and "The Familie"', *GHJ* 8/1 (1994), 1-15; Sidney Gottlieb, 'The Social and Political Backgrounds of George Herbert's Poetry', in Summers and Pebworth, *'The Muses Common-Weale'*, pp. 107-118.

5   Nicholas Tyacke, *Anti-Calvinists: The Rise of English Arminianism, c. 1590-1640* (Oxford: Clarendon , 1987), and David Norbrook, *Poetry and Politics in the English Renaissance* (London: Routledge & Kegan Paul, 1984) (both cited by Gottlieb). See also Norbrook's 'Introduction' to *The Penguin Book of Renaissance Verse*, selected and introduced by David Norbrook, edited by H.R. Woudhuysen) (London: Penguin, 1992), 1-67.

6   See Charles, *A Life of Herbert*, pp. 104-111.

7   Thomas Healy, *New Latitudes: Theory and English Renaissance Literature* (London: Arnold, 1992), 9.

8   Richard Todd, *The Opacity of Signs: Acts of Interpretation in George Herbert's 'The Temple'* (Columbia: U of Missouri P, 1986), 3.

9   Thomas P. Roche Jr, 'Typology, Allegory, and Protestant Poetics', *GHJ* 13 (1/2) (1989-90), 1-17, esp. pp. 8-12. Strier mentions Spenser just once, in a footnote to p. 34.

10 Michael C. Schoenfeldt, *Prayer and Power: George Herbert and Renaissance Courtship*, Chicago: U of Chicago P, 1991), 2-4.

11 Stanley Stewart, review of Elizabeth D. Harvey and Katherine Eisaman Maus, eds, *Soliciting Interpretation: Literary Theory and Seventeenth-Century English Poetry*, *GHJ* 15/1 (1973), 79.

12 John R. Mulder, 'George Herbert's *Temple*: Design and Methodology', *Seventeenth-Century News* 31/2 (1973), 43.

13 Harold Toliver, review of Janis Lull, *The Poem in Time: Reading George Herbert's Revisions of 'The Church'* (1990), *GHJ* 15/1 (1991), 92.

14   There is a case for regarding 1638 as perhaps the most reliable printed text of all.
15   Todd, *Opacity of Signs*, pp. 201-202; cf Lull, *Poem in Time*, p. 147.

SACRED AND PROFANE CONTEXTS

1

SACRED RHYTHMS & SACRED CONTRADICTIONS:
PROLEGOMENA TO A STUDY OF HERBERT'S
LITURGICAL CONSCIOUSNESS

MARIO A. DI CESARE

The sounding and lovely Greek word προλεγόμενα projects an apparent fullness and roundness and strength which, taken together, suggest something larger than this essay can hope to achieve. I use the word in its radical, modest sense: this is a very preliminary inquiry, a beginning towards a work in progress, an attempt to discover how to determine and talk about the presence of what I would like to call *liturgical consciousness* in Herbert's lyric poetry.[1] I am not dealing primarily with the documentary context—that is, verbal influence, liturgical texts, the feast-days, the saints, the liturgical year. I also want to avoid discussing devotion in general or prayer or liturgical doctrine or controversy.[2]

What does liturgy mean? How are we to understand *liturgical consciousness*? What are its implications? The etymology of *liturgy* is the Greek word λειτουργία from the verb λειτουργέω, which meant, at Athens, *to serve public offices at one's own cost*; thus, a λειτουργία was thought of as *a public duty*, which the richer citizens discharged (for instance in financing the chorus in the *Oresteia*). It could also mean *the public service* of the gods (in Aristotle) and *the service* or *ministry* of priests (New Testament).

For my purposes, liturgy can be thought of as rite and includes mainly song, communality, desire, worship, public prayer. More specifically: Liturgy is public and ordered rites, including mainly the Mass and the Office among Roman Catholics, mainly the Eucharist, Morning Prayer, Evensong in the Anglican Church.[3] Liturgy frequently is expressed in music and frequently includes psalms; often, the liturgy consists mainly of psalms and music. The saying of the Office (or Breviary) is emphasized in the *Rule of St Benedict*, where it is called the Work of God.[4]

The crucial words in this description are public or communal, ordered, and ritual. Not any public ritual, and not the spontaneous overflow of powerful feelings. The liturgical act must be a deliberate act, a conscious engagement, communal and public, proletarian and quotidian.[5] Institutionally, liturgy is limited to services and offices: for Roman Catholics, defined and expressed mainly by the Missal and the Breviary, supplemented by minor service books for lesser or specialized occasions; in the Anglican Church, the order for celebration and administration of the Eucharist as defined and expressed in the Book of Common Prayer (BCP), the official service book in the Church of England in Herbert's time. The full title as it was imposed in 1549 was: *The Book of Common Prayer and Administration of the Sacraments and Other Rites and Ceremonies of the Church, after the Use of the Church of England*; there were later versions and revisions, but it is from my purpose here to deal with those at any length. As the title makes perfectly clear, the BCP was intended to replace the 'services previously contained in the Breviary, the Missal, the Processional, and the Manual. ... [T]he only other book needed for the conduct of services was the Bible ...'.[6]

By way of the BCP, Cranmer attempted to impose substantive and far-reaching changes. He substituted English for Latin; he abolished the various Uses (Sarum and York mainly); he synthesized in this work the Roman Catholic missal, breviary, manual, and pontifical. Morning Prayer or Matins he compiled out of the Nocturnes of Matins, Lauds, and Prime, and Evensong he developed out of Vespers and Compline. The Order of Holy Communion comes from the Missal, the Sacramental from the Manual, and other services from the Pontifical—the consecration of priests, bishops, and deacons particularly.[7] His aim was not so much to streamline as to focus and order all these matters, imposing on them the new discipline of the Church of England and distancing them as far as possible from Rome. The decision to use English was nationalistic, obviously designed to give a new character to these hallowed rites and to encourage widespread popular participation as part of a system of naturalization and indoctrination. But all in all, the struggle for universal acceptance was a difficult one, for there was often stiff resistance to the new rituals even by those who otherwise accepted the new church without scruple.[8]

Thus Cranmer's reforms did not, could not, obliterate the central elements in the older liturgies, including the sense of liturgical participation and the traditions of song. Both are important to the study of lyric. By song I mean particularly plainchant, whether in Latin or English (both were used in the early seventeenth century), for that concentrates the essential qualities and nature of liturgy. While it originated at the end of the sixth century, after long years of development, this development continues into modern times.[9] The early Anglican versions of plainchant (the kinds of plainsong which Herbert would have known) maintain many of the original characteristics. I am particularly interested in the way chant exploits, while not abusing, rhythmical freedoms, and the way the melodies are adjusted to the words, rather than the words to the music. Chant has structure and form but seems improvisational; for an ardent experimenter in an age of prosodic experimentation, chant might seem ready-made.[10]

It is important to understand the free character of chant, lest we think of the relationship between the older chants and the developing music of the Middle Ages and Renaissance as like the differences between classical Latin verse and medieval verse. It is not: in the matter of verse, both kinds had distinct metrical structures and were carefully and tightly controlled. In the matter of chant and later music, I want to emphasize on the one hand the centrifugal, a-structural, a-metrical tendencies of the chant, which are no doubt resolved in most instances, but which still set up an environment quite different from, on the other hand, the measured and controlled and very regular rhythmicalities of modern (meaning post-Dark Ages) music.[11]

* * *

The question to be considered is the part which a consciousness of the rhythms and character of liturgical music (limited here to chant or plain-song) may have played in Herbert's creative life. In the course of his poetic career, Herbert transformed several conventional secular forms—such as the sonnet, the song, and the pastoral—into something new. However, he did not spend his main energies converting or metamorphosing the secular lyric but rather creating his own forms. The times he lived in invited such experimentation and creative action: in regard to rhyme alone, for instance, we know that Jonson struggled with rhyme—and condemned Donne for not keeping of number; Milton rejected it for his main work; Wyatt and Donne were not easy with it. Herbert's multiple experiments were his own way of struggling. Might he have found in the formal lack of fixity yet definable structures of chant the possibilities he most wanted—free rein for and yet control of the contradictions at the heart of his being, his belief, his feel-ings, his religion, his versing? Perhaps. Herbert's prolific inventiveness in stanza forms (he invented specific forms for each of more than one hundred of his lyrics) may well reflect what one inevitably notices after long immer-sion, the nearly limitless variety of chant. There are many modes, and these provided the base or ground within which chants developed.

Let me try to establish perspective here. Herbert's metrical structures include, though perhaps unusually, several long poems—'The Church Porch', methodically didactic with its 77 stanzas in *ababcc* rhyme; the neat and orderly 'Providence' with its iambic pentameter quatrains rhyming *abab*, the whole imitating the neat order of Creation; and 'The Church Militant' with its marching rhythms, expressed with grim certitude in the

heroic couplets. These major efforts would appear to offer little in the way
of liturgical possibility. But then there is that other long, metrically repetitive poem, 'The Sacrifice'. It is one of the least varied metrical forms in the
collection—iambic pentameter tercets with iambic trimeter refrain permeate
the 268 lines. In certain ways, 'The Sacrifice' represents a major departure
from the standard forms. Its firm assertive tercets are concluded by the
insistent refrain, 'Was ever grief like mine?' The tercets have the directness
and clarity and force of the *improperia*, with their plaintive opening,
Popule meus, quid feci tibi ... responde mihi—that final demand echoed in
Was ever, itself a demanding question, insisting on an answer and getting it,
twice, both times: *Never*, once in an outcry, and once, the final words, in a
plea: *Let others say ...* . The singularity of the prosodic organization has
been obscured by the edited texts. The poem has commonly been divided
into 63 stanzas since the first edition, but in fact it was written originally
with no stanza breaks whatever. The scribes of both *B* and the earlier *W*
wrote, exceptionally but unmistakably, twenty-four lines on a page, in *B*
inscribing the last line in what was marginal space almost everywhere else.
That is, they deliberately wrote the text as a continuous, unbroken unit. The
format highlights a profound aspect of the poem: the lament is immeasur-
able, not simply a string of *improperia*, and it ends only in death.

   The metrical glory of the collection is not only its inventive variety but
its constant capacity for surprise. In the rest of this paper, I would like to
suggest similarities, both extrinsic and intrinsic, between something like the
spirit that animates Herbert's lyric creativity and some of the elements of
liturgical functions, particularly the various modes of chant or plainsong. I
want to explore possible ways in which Herbert's ear and voice, memory
and imagination might have been nourished by the liturgy. For Herbert,
religious symbols and states and scriptures were mediated by the liturgy,
and dialectical structures of texts and rhythms and images and words and
phrases evolved out of liturgical substance.[12] He was not a theorist of or
commentator on liturgy, but there are nonetheless a few texts to ponder
before we turn to the poems.

   In *Musae responsoriae*, a set of forty poems written mostly around
1620, Herbert defended liturgy against the attacks of Andrew Melville,
even to supporting small points of detail. Melville's *Anti-Tami-Cami-Cate-*
goria was a long, vigorous rebuttal in Sapphics to the hostility expressed in
resolutions by Oxford and Cambridge against the Puritans' Millenary Petition of 1603.[13] Herbert's response is directed mainly at the first part, the
attack on ceremonies of the BCP, couched in 'language that was offensive'
(Hutchinson, p. 488). The poems are interesting both for the prosodic skill
and control they manifest and for their tone and use of imagery. Herbert

insists on the prosodic skill; the poems can hardly be called Latin exercises. Notably, Herbert emphasizes the variety of forms he has mastered and mocks Melville (gently, to be sure) for limiting himself to tiresome Sapphics. (Herbert was of course already experimenting widely in his English verse.) Notable too is the combination of temperate restraint towards Melville and the unequivocal praise of the beauty and importance of liturgy. Herbert not only passes up the chance to attack Calvinist theology; he sides with Melville on most points having to do with the Deity. What he is about, in Kelliher's perceptive phrase, is 'an imaginative justification of Anglican ritual' (Kelliher, p. 28). The defence of Anglicanism is often highly personal; the astonishingly smooth and varied *De musica sacra*, written in the difficult alcaic meter, expresses pain in the contrast between the harsh noisiness of Puritan attacks and the harmony that all nature expresses and adumbrates.[14]

In his preface, Nicholas Ferrar pointed out Herbert's commitment to Anglican liturgy:

His obedience and conformitie to the Church and the discipline thereof was singularly remarkable. Though he abounded in private devotions, yet went he every morning and evening with his familie to the Church; and by his example, exhortations and encouragements drew the greater part of his parishioners to accompany him dayly in the publick celebration of Divine Service.[15]

Herbert used similar words describing the country parson:

[He observes] the fasting dayes of the Church, and the dayly prayers enjoined him by auctority ... out of humble conformity, and obedience; [and] adds to them ... some other ... hours for prayers (Hutchinson, p. 237).[16]

But to the poems. No doubt the most famous liturgical poem in *The Church* is 'The Sacrifice', thanks in part to William Empson's notorious reading of one line which led to a long response and then a booklength study by Rosemond Tuve.[17] In its way, this is astonishing both as poem and as liturgical creation outside church liturgy. Barbara Lewalski, however, could not admit liturgy as an independent context for Herbert's poetry; she believes it isn't often 'possible or profitable to distinguish between general biblical influences conveyed through private reading, study, sermons and the like, and biblical influence conveyed through the liturgy'. I agree with Van Wengen-Shute that the special significance of a biblical allusion is often diluted or lost if its specifically liturgical context is not recognized.[18] A proper recognition of the biblical texts as situated in a liturgical context (whether or not including such special matters as typological elements) is essential to our understanding of many of Herbert's poems. Tuve pointed out that the Christ of 'The Sacrifice' is not the 'Christ we know in Luke's or Matthew's straightforward narrative—but He *is* the Christ of the liturgy of Holy Week'.[19]

A major theme in the poetry is the Eucharist, from the 'church's mystical repast' phrase at the entry to *The Church* to 'I did sit and eat' at the very end. Almost as important as the theme of the Eucharist is the presence of the Book of Psalms.[20] There are numerous poems which treat the spatial and the temporal aspects, or the physical and chronological aspects, of the Church's life.[21] Some celebrate feast days in the liturgical year, such as Christmas, Whit Sunday, Trinity Sunday, and Good Friday; attention to the liturgical resonances in these poems would be fruitful. Others deal with particular liturgical offices or events—'Antiphon', 'Evensong', 'Matins'.

In keeping with the liturgical spirit, these generally depend on some kind of counterpoint between metre and rhyme, like the liturgical counterpoint between melody and versicles. That antiphons work antiphonally comes as no surprise, but it is surprising that the serenity of an evensong should be disrupted, if ever so slightly, by contention *within* the already counterpointed rhyme. The rhythm of the verses of 'Evensong' is generally iambic, in varying metrics—3544 3445—whose overall rhythm is not far from the rhythm of plainchant. Supporting this curious rhythm and enhancing it, the rhymes of the poem vary in the second half of each octave: *abba cddc / abba cdcd / abba cddc / abba cdcd*. In each octave, the long second and eighth lines provide a kind of ordering balance in the rhythm and the final pentameter offers a kind of closure to the otherwise open rhythm.

In a recent essay on seventeenth-century devotional poets, Helen Wilcox addresses, among other things, their 'preoccupation with poetic *structures*', and notes that these poets were 'as a group great experimenters with the possibilities of expression through form. Herbert is the individual writer who probably springs to mind most immediately in this connection, with his shaped poems, pruned rhymes, and interwoven biblical text'.[22] Herbert was clearly the most adventurous of these poets in his 'attention to the formal potential of the lyric' (Wilcox, p. 14); one notes the astonishing range of Herbert's metrical, rhythmic, and rhyming experiments.[23] While the liberty of versing was relatively widespread in the early seventeenth century, patterned poems (at least in Herbert's work) are merely occasional, simply one articulation of the daring, lively, restless, constant kinds of experimentation that Herbert carried on. In some ways, in fact, the pattern poems may well be the most commonplace or conventional expression of the impulse to make it new.[24]

Now to more specific examples of what might be called liturgical in Herbert's poetry. 'Grace' is a poem resonating the Advent liturgy, not only in its language but also, and perhaps mainly, in its rhythms and prosodic structure. For one thing, the poem hauntingly echoes the minor-chord chants, the longings and incompletenesses, of Advent, not unlike the rhythmic and musical movements of 'Denial'.[25] The cry of the poem is the cry of hope and longing, subtly evoking the responsory common in Advent and based on the Introit for the fourth Sunday, *Rorate caeli desuper et nubes pluant justum*.[26] The plaintive tone of *caeli* must be heard for the rising tones and the outcry to be appreciated properly. The entreaty *Rorate* is, of course, a verb specific to *dew*, and *dew* appears in stanza 3 and dominates lines 9, 10, and 11. In line 11, by not calling for the *dew* and by wittily contrasting *grass* with *grace*, the poet utters again his own *Rorate*. You can't hear this stanza without hearing also the third and fourth lines of 'Virtue': 'The dew shall weep thy fall tonight; / For thou must die'.

This link evokes the contrary music of the liturgy, and not just in those instances where conveniently contrasting words, feelings, motions, are expressed. Whether or not 'Grace' has transmuted the universal theme of the Advent and Christmas liturgy into personal concern, the note of futurity also sounds richly, echoing, for instance, the Vespers antiphons of the Third Sunday of Advent.[27] Prosodically, the poem is different from most of Herbert's other poems. The verse form is *abab*, three tetrameters and a dimeter, but the dimeter is trochee followed by iamb, an unfinished and unresolved rhythm. The rhyme scheme resembles that of the preceding poem, 'Whitsunday', but with a signal difference. The stanzas of 'Whitsunday' consist of three tetrameters concluded and smoothly closed by an iambic pentameter. The stanza structure of 'Grace', however, is three tetrameters and a dimeter, with distinctly unfinished rhythm. It's worth reminding ourselves that an iambic pentameter is a finished line, one constantly capable of resolving sense or sensibility, words or rhythms, while tetrameter lines are delimited and require continuation. Helen Vendler observes something similar in the action of the poem when, discussing the '[seven] self-imposed conditions' of the formal pattern, she remarks: 'The marvel of the poem is that with all its iron conditions, "Grace" reads as pure colloquial spontaneity, unpremeditated meditation'.[28] Prosody and structure combine in a subtle evocation of Advent liturgy, of the *Veni veni Emmanuel* ('for thou dost know the way', line 21), enacting the speaker's spiritual condition as well as do the formal conditions set forth so crisply by Vendler.[29]

This Advent theme marks another unlikely poem, 'Denial', that poem with its own prosody of longing and incompletion imitating the incompletenesses of the Advent liturgy's longings.[30] As Mulder has pointed out, 'The speaker ... asks for Christ's reincarnation in man: "Come, come, my God, O come". This cry from the liturgy of Advent is followed by "Christmas" ...' (Mulder, p. 141).

A quite different example is 'Discipline'. This is actually Ps 38 (one of the Penitential Psalms) restructured, and then linked to the Litany.[31] The verbal echoes are not easily seen, but in this case that makes them more interesting. The simplicity and austerity of the lines do not deny the poem its power; conflicting emotions towards Deity are developed and then, finally and painfully, resolved. The unusual prosody—anapaest plus iamb in lines 1, 2, 4 of each stanza, and anapaest in 3—has all the marks of liturgical rhythms with its powerfully centrifugal impulse, just held in.[32]

That dispersed or centrifugal character of liturgy is felt also, in quite a different way, in 'Praise (1)', the poem immediately following 'Grace'. (Like many other of Herbert's titles, the word *praise* may be seen to articulate one of the major aims of liturgical functions, but I would be reluctant to seek liturgical relevance on such grounds.) This poem is driven by a rush of multiple images and phrases, variegated attempts to define by metaphor the object of our restlessness—*write a verse or two* (1), *estate* (3), *wings* (5), *Prince* (10), *sling* (11), *herb* (13), *poor* (15), *bees* (17), *work* (19)—and in this it is typical of many of Herbert's poems. 'Praise (1)' is restless in the way that liturgy itself is restless. To describe liturgy as a fully coherent, well-organized thematology of actions and gestures and verses is misleading at least and probably wrong in the end. Most liturgical events do maintain a kind of general coherence, but there is also an insecurity at the edges uncovering the attempt by the communal heart to reach to God—somehow. That *somehow* is the crucial word: the hymn-writers who gently but surely rubbed out the complexities and uncertainties of Herbert's poetry created exactly what they intended to create, verses which are clear and certain, with exactly the same kind of clarity and sureness that marked the highly structured hymns which replaced the liberation of chant. The creators of liturgy simply weren't so enlightened or certain, and that is why the ancient liturgies remain so attractive: they resonate the uncertainties of our own condition.

The images and metaphors of 'Praise (1)' constitute a restless series of successive approximations, which in the end turn back on themselves. The poem works through a problematic of song and harmony, and the pressure of multiplicity. These elements recur in a group of poems later, poems about restlessness and pain, grief and loss and contrarieties, as much as about singing. The group begins with 'Clasping of Hands', which itself climaxes in a splendid emblem of liturgy, the final expression of its object and purpose:

> O be mine still! still make me thine!
> Or rather make no Thine and Mine!   (19-20)

in which the reiterated *still! still* reaches out for some kind of stasis and immediately knows it is not available, the *mine* and *thine* disrupt it. The pervasive understanding of the individual in liturgy remains only so long as he or she is not wholly submerged (and one *almost* never is) in the community of worshippers.

The restlessness of 'The Search' reflects the marvellous but also unsettling variety of ways of knowing sought in the poem. The search is enacted in the inadequacy yet necessity of imagery—his 'daily bread' (line 3). The searches never 'prove', though the speaker's attempt to embody truth even if he cannot know it, in Yeats's famous terms, is multiple and earnest. Every stanza appears to have at least one metaphor of searching; some have more. A recurrent one is climbing, struggling upwards (see *growing and groaning thither* in 'The Flower', later in the sequence); another is tuning his sighs. In an adaptation of this poem, the adapter omitted many of Herbert's images, reducing the work from fifteen to twelve stanzas; as Vendler (p. 114) noted incisively, those 'conceits ... dwell speculatively on God's actions and his will. They seem to offend the adapter ... by their metaphysical daring'. It is difficult not to conclude that the adapter was trying, perhaps unwittingly, to get rid of the multiplicity of approaches, the inadequacies of human methods, the pain and restlessness of successive approximations.

The next poem, 'Grief' (perhaps taking off from 'Since then my grief must be as large', 'The Search', line 45) struggles with the theme of *absence* ('The Search', line 57) and points directly towards the *returns* in 'The Flower'. Note also the image of the winged arrow in 'The Search' (19), pointing directly to the *bent ... bow* ('The Cross', 25–26). The word *arrow* is used only here and in 'Artillery' (and in a doubtful poem, 'Psalm VII' [Hutchinson, 222]). The struggles suppress or oppress attempts at song, as is made manifest prosodically in the concluding lines of 'Grief':

> Give up your feet and running to mine eyes,
> And keep your measures for some lover's lute,
> Whose grief allows him music and a rhyme:
> For mine excludes both measure, tune and time.
>   Alas, my God!   (15–19)

The final line is an odd-numbered, isolated line, an unrhymed dimeter cry, counterpointed harshly against the regular iambic pentameters which precede in orderly alternate-rhyme quatrains and against the nearly-conclusive couplet which tries to dismiss the making of song. The rejection of secular poetry is not unlike that in 'Jordan (1)', but the difference here is that the final line is simply an outcry, not in any way a completion of a particular argument. Following 'Grief', 'The Cross' also engages the problematic of song; at the end (of a statement of uncertain syntax) the Son's 'but four words' become 'my words', which is of course one important end and aim of liturgical activity. Finally, 'The Flower' seems to end this loose sequence, with a moving enactment of the transitoriness of joy in its stunning chantlike prosody.

I have touched on several poems which do not seem liturgical at first glance. Let me turn now very briefly to a poem which, from the first line on, would seem to demand consideration in specifically liturgical terms, 'Aaron', a mimesis of the priest vesting for divine service. The poem is a good example of biblical matter—the evocation of Aaron—mediated through liturgical event, the *vesting prayers* as they were called in the Roman rite: the tradition of specified and prescribed prayers during vesting, by way of a definition of the priestly vestments in terms of the symbolism of virtues and graces (the white of the alb standing for purity of heart, for instance).[33] Like many liturgical hymns and sequences, the poem can be read across stanzas; it should be, for then the interrelatedness of movement and the paradoxes of meaning emerge more fully.

A seventeenth-century Dissenter revised this drastically, probably because of a compulsion to obliterate those old Romish traces, perhaps (or perhaps also) because of the distressing motions in the poem.[34] The essence of that adaptation may be seen in the penultimate stanza, which collapsed the third and fourth stanzas of Herbert's poem. Here are Herbert's third and fourth stanzas:

> Only another head
> I have, another heart and breast,
> Another music, making live not dead,
> Without whom I could have no rest,
> In him I am well dressed.

> Christ is my only head,
> My alone only heart and breast,
> My only music, striking me ev'n dead;
> That to the old man I may rest,
> And be in him new dressed.

By an alchemy that almost defies description, the adapter transmuted those stanzas to the following:

> And yet I have another Head,
>   Christ is my only Heart and Breast:
> He is my Musick causing Life;
>   In him alone I am well drest.

Herbert's penultimate stanza focused on being struck dead, centring on the remarkable lines: 'My alone only heart and breast, / My only music, striking me ev'n dead' (17–18), but the adapter omitted most of that stanza and converted music to source of life rather than death. The adapter kept three of Herbert's five recurring end-words, dropping *dead* and *rest*, and substituting *Life* at the end of the third line of this neat quatrain. In each of Herbert's *five* (not four) stanzas, the concluding word of the *central* line is *dead*. The adapter has in fact finessed the central focus on death almost out of the poem. The adaptation thus destroys the cunning shape of Herbert's poem, the whole *motion* of priesthood dressing, the liturgical evocation of particular symbolism in each garment. In that symbolism reside the variegated conflicts within Herbert's poem—contrarieties of holiness and profaneness, of physical and spiritual life opposed to physical and spiritual death, of serenity and noises, of light and perfections against darkness and restlessness.[35]

The attempted mischief is everywhere in the adaptations. 'The Flower' is troubled and ends uncertainly, but Wesley wanted it blameless for church singing, so he omitted the concluding warning against pride:

> These are Thy wonders, Lord of love,
> They mercy thus delights to prove
>   We are but flowers that bloom and die!
> Soon as this saving truth we see,
> Within Thy garden placed by Thee,
>   Time we survive, and death defy.
>   (quoted from Vendler, p. 285)

And here is Wesley's version of the last stanza of 'Virtue':

> Only a sweet and virtuous mind,
>   When Nature all in ruins lies,
> When earth and heaven a period find,
>   Begins a life that never dies.   (quoted from Vendler, p. 281)

While in both examples there is a kind of stab at paradoxical contrast, the blandness and smoothness stand out, the overwhelming desire for harmony and and fluency. One does not object to smoothness or harmony in themselves; the trouble is in the deprivation of content driven by the restrictive musical form. The rhythms are fixed and dominating, even domineering; they are roundly opposed to the fluidities and open generosity of chants, of those ancient melodies. What makes this (and post-Reformation hymnology generally) so different from Herbert's poetry or from older liturgical music like plainchant is just this harmony overriding and even destroying the exigent paradoxes and contradictions.

The priest is 'sacred intermediary possessing supernatural power' (Vendler, p. 118) but also struggling with cacophonous passions, straining for that other *music* which makes 'live not dead' (13, the central line), whereby the strange wonder of the fourth stanza can happen—'My alone only heart and breast, / My only music, striking me ev'n dead'. It is precisely in the process or act of dressing, in that defined and formal liturgical act, that the paradox of dying in order to live is fulfilled. This poem, with

> ... doctrine tuned by Christ (who is not dead
> But lives in me while I do rest),   (23–24)

manifests liturgy as the basis of theology, liturgy as the language of transaction which precedes and subsumes doctrine or theory or laws or cerebral control, the kind of cerebral control which the Dissenter and Wesley and other adapters, in the perfect spirit of eliminating all traces of Romish error, substituted for the enactment in the poem.

* * *

Liturgy and liturgical lyric of the kind I've been describing in Herbert are not so much a statement of paradox as they are the *enactment* of paradox, the embodiment of it in the continuum of the verse. According to an inventive and attractive theorist of liturgy, Aidan Kavanagh,[36] there is a sharp distinction to be made between *theologia prima*—that is, a theology which is 'aboriginally liturgical in context'—and '*theologia secunda*, that is, a "theology *of* the liturgy"' (Kavanagh, p. 75). In this view, *theologia prima* is the theology that arises from the experienced liturgy. The key distinction is between something like sets of doctrines on the one hand and acts of worship on the other. Kavanagh (p. 75) cites Massey Shepherd ('worship is the experiential foundation of theological reflection') and Alexander

Schmemann, who called liturgy 'the ontological condition of theology, of the proper understanding of *kerygma*, of the Word of God, because it is in the Church, of which the *leitourgia* is the expression and the life, [whereas] the sources of theology are functioning precisely as sources'. But there was a decisive shift from structure to interpretation, from *theologia prima* to *theologia secunda*, at the Reformation, particularly in England in the Act of Uniformity in 1549 and, in Rome, at the Council of Trent—that is, a shift from worship to doctrine, from liturgy to theological/political debate (Kavanagh, 81ff). Herbert intuitively evaded that shift.

In his simple but subtly elusive way, Herbert may well have been attempting to create a structure of liturgical worship in the lyrics of *The Church*.[37] I am not sure whether there is a discernible structure among these lyrics in the conventional sense of that term, and I have serious doubts about the claims for a tripartite structure for the whole so-called *Temple*. In the lyrics of *The Church*, Herbert strives for a unity or totality or integration of everything—stanza form, line form, line position, text position, rhythms, rhymes, images, metaphors, words, but all these are elements of a higher music rather than an architectural structure. The result is a form which is a kind of enactment, remarkably liberated and liberating, and is very far from the fixed forms of 'The Church-Porch' and 'The Church Militant', which are very limited and limiting.

The Church begins with a warning in 'Superliminare', at the entry to the *domus Dei*,[38] demanding worship, and follows with the injunction to 'taste / The church's mystical repast'. The one who is not yet 'holy, pure, and clear', but 'groaneth to be so, / May *at his peril* further go' (emphasis added). The emphasized phrase stresses the trembling and worry that must needs be present approaching the *mystical repast*. Herbert knew that, as Kavanagh puts it, the sacraments are 'unsettling encounters between living presences divine and human in the here and now' and not 'abstract ritual expression of a pattern set by Christ to give scope to the universal Kingdom' (Kavanagh, pp. 82–83).

'Love (3)' is that mystical repast; the whole collection of lyrics gathered together in *The Church* becomes a sustained act of worship, with this conclusion, that perfect love casteth out fear (and worship is essentially the striving for perfect love), of Aquinas's famous dictum, after so much palaver about knowledge and logic and reason and the supremacy of the intellect or judgement over the will: 'Love God that you may know Him'.

The kind of enactment that I emphasize in Herbert's poetry and that gives it something of a liturgical quality is best understood to reside in the provisional character of the poetry. Discussing 'Affliction (1)'[39], Ilona Bell argues that the poem demonstrates Herbert's 'Calvinistic ontology' (p.

92), showing him turning away from Hooker and the high Anglicans toward Calvin and the reformers. She points out that the poem appeals 'because Herbert's beliefs, like ours, are inherently provisional' (Bell, p. 75). This last statement is right on target, but not for the reasons offered. It is precisely in the liturgy as Herbert assimilated it to his poetry that the inherently provisional character of religious experience itself is best comprehended. This poem is, I think, about understanding the nature of liturgy and ceremony, rather than about rejecting it. The poem enacts contradiction in its rhythm, for in the end is the sudden surprising turn, the powerful acceptance beyond resignation, the achievement of a kind of poise that, like liturgical expression, is momentary, passing, full of prayer and hope, but inherently provisional, unstable, memorable, lasting, yet also elusive. It's interesting too that the five poems following 'Affliction (1)' move from 'Repentance' with its 'well-set song' (line 33), through testimony of faith, to the sublime 'Prayer (1)', 'something understood', and finally 'Holy Communion' and 'Antiphon'. Understood in the terms put forth here, these poems bristle with liturgical suggestiveness.

Every reader of Herbert has found his poetry both restless and certain, both groping and stable, both tormented and confident. I suggest that in the experience of liturgy these sharply contradictory elements are able to coexist, for liturgy itself is inherently both provisional and secure. Liturgy is the actual act of worship rather than the abstract structures or plans or schemata. In thinking about the act, begin with chant: the act of song, the very singing itself, especially of chant which does not take hold of you with an insistent beat, is transitory, contingent, in motion, unstable. The breathing, the notes, the sounds, the passing of the melodies in the air or in the listening—these leave us behind. (Kavanagh [p. 75] goes much further than this, descrying a kind of chaos in liturgy.) Yet there is also permanence—in the remembered melodies, in the words finally or provisionally achieved, in the object of the act, whether that object be the words of the song or the God being worshipped by the song. The same is true for many other elements of the liturgical act—the incense in some services, or the words recited by the celebrant, or the responsories.

The constant probing and the restlessness of Herbert's poetry are not resolved until the very end of *The Church*—until that act marking the end, at last, of recurring resistance ('So I did sit and eat'); that act going beyond resignation or submission or yielding or surrender, finally uncontrolled by the speaker, unwilled so to speak, truly an act of total acceptance and thus of total union, and so finally the consummation of liturgy; that act given without inner pressure, given as grace is given, and so one of pure worship, the justification of all acts of liturgy.

And yet the finality is not final. The fine wit of the early Church, developing the rite of the Mass, placed *Ite missa est* at the very end, and then following that statement—'Go, it is the dismissal; go it is the Mass'; or, in the common free rendering (which makes neither syntactical nor liturgical sense), 'Go, the Mass is ended'—come the first fourteen verses of the Gospel of John, beginning *In principio*, beyond the very beginning. In its profoundest sense, that ending also celebrates the mystery of the Real Presence, of the Eucharist as Roman Christianity understood it. No doubt this was why Cranmer's reformers felt it absolutely necessary to get rid of the final closing, to end any service (especially the communion service) with a solemn blessing and a definitive dismissal, without a hint of syntactical ambiguity. It was a logical, rational move; it cohered with reformed doctrine, taking a definite position on the question of Transubstantiation and Eucharist. But willy-nilly the decision lost something irreplaceable in this ritual. The earlier Church understood that each ending is a new beginning, that each feast-day's cycle, like any part of its office, its hour, its season, or of the whole 'year', is itself yet another beginning. We do not come to closure, to final resolution, in this life—and liturgy is, if anything is, of this life. When you 'sit and eat', you then have to rise up again and go on.

Notes

1   One problem is that the subject has been conspicuously neglected or ignored in the religious histories, the cultural histories, the literary histories, and the studies of individual poets. Another is the lack of documentary materials that would help clarify the subject. We are not dealing with the history of ideas; we are dealing rather with the ways a common but not well-defined activity pervaded the whole culture that Herbert lived in. I want to emphasize that these speculations are mainly limited to forms of chant, that is to rhythms which are not measured or fixed. Part-music, which would also have been part of Herbert's context, must also be investigated.

2   The few relevant studies in the critical scholarship on Elizabethan and seventeenth-century culture or poetry have focused more on devotion or piety broadly imagined than on liturgy specifically understood.

3   Reinhold Hammerstein, entry in P. Wiener, ed. *Dictionary of the History of Ideas*, 5 vols (New York: Scribner, 1973) discusses liturgy very briefly under 'music as divine art' (after the section 'music as demonic') (3: 269-270). He hasn't a lot to say but is suggestive, pointing out the extraordinary stability in liturgical forms and the almost invariable continuity and drawing attention to celestial liturgy as a major theme in medieval art—the illustration of liturgical books, cathedral sculpture, stained glass, frescoes, panel paintings, and so on. (In the Italian Renaissance, of course, music-making angels are ubiquitous.) He notes that the celestial liturgy

was thought of as very close to earthly liturgy and that the psalter meant an instrument as well as the scriptural book of psalms, but only mentions in passing the
concept of number and its relationship to liturgy and music.

4   *The Rule of St. Benedict . . .*, ed. and trans. by Abbot Justin McCann (New York:
Newman Press, 1952). Chapters 8–19 are entirely about the liturgy, and several
other chapters are largely or at least indirectly about liturgy: see for instance chapters 42, 45, 47, 52.

5   See Aidan Kavanagh, *On Liturgical Theology: The Hale Memorial Lectures of
Seabury-Western Theological Seminary, 1981* (Collegeville, MN: Liturgical Press,
1992), 93, a study that has helped stimluate this essay.

6   My main source is G.J. Cuming, *A History of Anglican Liturgy* (2nd ed., London:
Macmillan, 1982), 47. See especially his detailed and interesting description on pp.
47–69.

7   For Herbert's relationship, both liturgical and biblical, to the BCP, and its pres-
ence in various ways in his poetry, see the careful study by Rosemary Margaret
Van Wengen-Shute, *George Herbert and the Liturgy of the Church of England*
(Oegstgeest: De Kempenaer, 1981).

8   See Eamon Duffy, *The Stripping of the Altars: Traditional Religion in England c.
1400-c. 1580* (New Haven: Yale UP, 1992), 465, 469ff, 589-93. See also Francis
Proctor and W.H. Frere, *A New History of The Book of Common Prayer* (London:
Macmillan, 1907), 55ff and 65ff.

9   In *Western Plainchant: A Handbook* (Oxford: Clarendon, 1993), vii, David Hiley
points to the 'enormous expansion of plainchant studies in the last few decades'.
His own bibliography occupies 65 large pages (his book, in quarto size, is around
750 pages) and he cites a new bibliography of over 4,200 items by Thomas Kohl-
hase and Günther Michael Paucker, *Beiträge zur Gregorianik* 9–10 (1990). The
relevant articles in Stanley Sadie, ed., *The New Grove Dictionary of Music and
Musicians* (Washington: MacMillan Press Ltd., 1980) are also particularly rich and
informative. Willy Aspel's *Gregorian Chant* (Bloomington: Indiana UP, c. 1958)
is still a fundamental work for the study of plainchant.

10   There is a current revival of interest in plainchant, thanks largely to the phenomenal success of the recordings made by the Benedictine monks of Santo Domingo
de Silos, but its depth and breadth are impossible to gauge.

11   In a very early treatise, *De musica* by Johannes de Grocheio, edited by Christopher
Page in 'Johannes de Grocheio on secular music: a corrected text and a new translation', *Plainsong & Medieval Music* 2 (1993): 19f., Grocheio attempts to explain
that *cantus planus* is not arbitrary or unmeasured, but it simply is not *precisely*
measured: 'Si autem per immensurabilem non ita praecise mensuratam intellegant,
potest, ut videtur, ista divisio remanere.' ('If, however, by the term "immeasur-
able" is understood music that is not so precisely measured, then it is evident that
this division may be allowed to stand.')

12   Cf. the roughly similar view pervading the study by Van Wengen–Shute.

13   Though written not long after the event, Melville's poem was not published until
1620. Herbert's collection was mainly written in response to the publication but
was itself not published until 1652. The most useful and perceptive discussion of
Herbert's suite of poems is pp. 26–34 of W. Hilton Kelliher's 'The Latin Poetry of

George Herbert', in: J.W. Binns, ed., *The Latin Poetry of English Poets* (London: Routledge & Kegan Paul, 1974), 26–57.

14   James Milliken makes the important point that Herbert's is not merely a passive defence of ritual; he believes firmly that ritual should be maintained and argues that the Latin poems provide some substance for understanding Herbert's notion of 'ritual as an important instrument in bringing people to a religious truth'; he cites the poems in *Lucus* to show that, for Herbert, 'Ritual played a necessary and practical part in religious observance ... '. See Milliken, 'The Latin Poetry in an Evaluation of George Herbert', *Crosse-bias* 16 (1992), 4-9. Stanley Stewart, *George Herbert* (Boston: Twayne, 1986) notes that Herbert 'invariably condemned the arrogance of papal claims but seldom, if ever, mentioned the differences between the Roman and the Anglican rites or ceremonies' (32).

15   Quoted from the Scolar facsimile of the first edition, the unnumbered second page of 'The Printers to the Reader'. See also Hutchinson, 4.

16   It is unlikely that Ferrar knew *The Country Parson*, first published in 1652. Herbert instructed his parishioners on the finer points of the liturgy, so that they could take fuller part in the ritual and appreciate it more fully.

17   William Empson, *Seven Types of Ambiguity* (London: Chatto & Windus, 1930), 244, 284ff; Rosemond Tuve, *A Reading of George Herbert* (London: Faber & Faber, 1952).

18   Van Wengen-Shute, p. 22. Barbara Lewalski, *Protestant Poetics and the Seventeenth-Century Religious Lyric* (Princeton: Princeton UP, 1979), 11. The larger question of Herbert's theology raised by Lewalski would take us far afield. Though the question is implicated in some of the issues developed in this paper, the argument thus far, whether pursued by Lewalski or by Richard Strier, *Love Known: Theology and Experience in George Herbert's Poetry* (Chicago: U of Chicago P, 1983), the other leading proponent of Calvinism as Herbert's theology, relies entirely on documents, while this study prescinds from documents.

19   Tuve, p. 41; see Van Wengen-Shute, p. 24. In one of his 'Notes on the Temple and Synagogue', Coleridge wrote: 'G. Herbert is a true poet, but a poet sui generis ... [The reader must have] a constitutional Predisposition to Ceremoniousness [and find the Church's] Forms and Ordinances Aids of Religion, not sources of formality.' See George Whalley, ed., *Coleridge: Collected Works* (Princeton: Princeton UP, 1984), 12:2, Marginalia 2, p. 1034.

20   See, besides Van Wengen-Shute, C.A. Patrides, ed., *The English Poems of George Herbert* (London: Dent, 1974), 10, who notes that echoes of the Psalter 'reverberate across Herbert's poetry to an extent unmatched by any other poet in English literature'.

21   'In the poems whose titles refer to details within an actual church [from 'Church-Monuments' to 'The Windows'], Herbert uses the externals of the building as types that have their antitypes within man. After these meditations on the soul as a spiritual house, the poet sums up, in "Trinitie Sunday", his understanding of the means and purpose of his being ... ', according to John Mulder, *The Temple of the Mind: Education and Taste in Seventeenth-Century England* (New York: Pegasus, 1969), 140.

22   Helen Wilcox, whose '"Curious Frame": The Seventeenth-Century Religious Lyric
      as Genre', in *New Perspectives on the Seventeenth-Century English Religious
      Lyric*, John R. Roberts, ed., (Columbia: U of Missouri P, 1994), 9-27, is 'an
      inquiry into the possibility of a looser generic union between these very varied
      poets'.

23   There is a common trap here. Herbert's experiments have been noticed but rarely
      examined at length; it is only too easy to overemphasize the *occasional* form in his
      poetry.

24   Wilcox, 'Curious Frame', p. 15, points out that 'such attentiveness to poetic struc-
      ture was . . . an expression of a sense of proportion and an interest in what Marvell
      termed the proper or "sober frame". [from the opening of *Upon Appleton House*]
      The frame was ... both the actual poetic form and its larger significance; the poets
      were testing the multiple dimensions of the lyric as well as giving form to an ideal
      of expressiveness. Like Donne's God, these poetic structures were both "literall"
      and "figurative" [from 'Expostulation 19' of the *Devotions* in Anthony Raspa's
      1975 edition].

25   The word *grace* appeared twice in the Williams MS version of 'Whitsunday', the
      poem which immediately precedes 'Grace', but the Williams version was heavily
      revised; the word doesn't appear in the 1633 or Bodleian version. Though not an
      uncommon word in Herbert's poetry, *grace* appears in a fairly regular presentation
      throughout the poem whose title is eponymous: lines 3, 7, 15, and 19, in other
      words the third line of four of the six stanzas; in the third line of stanza 3, *grass*
      implicitly contrasts with *grace*; in the third line of stanza 6, no *grace* appears, for
      the plea is either *come* (line 21) or *Remove me* (line 23).

26   The *Liber Usualis*, with introdution and rubrics in English, edited by the Benedict-
      ines of Solesmes (Tournai: Desclée & Co., 1934), 1868. Originally published in
      1896 and revised 1903 and 1934, and reprinted many times, the *Liber* (the title
      means 'book for general use') combines the main contents of the four basic books,
      presenting them generally 'in their proper oder as they occur during the day and
      the year'. The four basic books are: the Graduale (chants for the Mass), the Anti-
      phonale (chants for the Office), and two corresponding liturgical texts, the Missale
      and the Breviarium. See Willi Aspel (n. 9 above), pp. 15ff.

27   *Veniet Dominus, et non tardabit ... et manifestabit se. ... Jerusalem gaude gaudio
      magno, quia veniet tibi Salvator. ... Dabo in Sion salutem. ... Montes et omnes
      colles humiliabuntur et erunt prava in directa. ... : veni Domine, et noli tardare. ...
      Juste et pie vivamus, exspectantes beatam spem, et adventum Domini.* See *Liber
      Usualis*, 338–39. On the fleece generally, see Judg. 6–8 (the story of Gideon), esp.
      6: 36–40; Heb. 11: 32; 2 Sam. 11: 21, and the body of interpretation, especially as
      synthesized by Cornelius à Lapide.

28   Helen Vendler, *The Poetry of George Herbert* (Cambridge, MA & London: Har-
      vard UP, 1975), 214.

29   Vendler describes Herbert's condition here as a 'primal level of deprivation'
      which 'surfaces in the poverty of the repeated prayer' (p. 218), and here too one
      notices the relevance of Advent liturgy, the way in which the *rorate* chant suffuses
      the poem. She also calls attention to the images of 'reciprocal strife in the world'
      (p. 218) or the 'strain of duality' (p. 219).

30 Note also the motif of *silence*, as in *silent ears* ('Denial', line 1) and the contrast between song and silence in the first line of the Christmas hymn, just following. The Christmas liturgy engages a profound *silentium* of its own: see for instance the Mass of the Sunday in the octave of Christmas.

31 Van Wengen-Shute, pp. 29ff. Establishing verbal links, Van Wengen-Shute does not always discriminate between commonplaces and clearly evocative echoes, particularly in her observations on 'Sighs and Groans' and on 'Grace', both of which she links (questionably in these instances, I think) to the Litany.

32 For interesting and quite diverse discussion of this poem, see the following items listed in John R. Roberts, *George Herbert: An Annotated Bibliography of Modern Criticism. Revised Edition 1905-1984* (Columbia: U of Missouri P, 1988), 215 and 978, musical adaptations; 295, an example of *over-logicality*; 446, tri-partite structure, out of Quintilian; 489, two conflicting emotions towards God built up and resolved; 602, similarities to Jonson's 'Hymne to God the Father'; 788, 'dialogue' mode; 1106, a pattern poem; 1206, God seen as Cupid.

33 *The Study of Liturgy*, edited by Cheslyn Jones *et al.*, revised edition (Oxford: Oxford UP, 1992), 544. The poem can be seen as a mimesis of much else; as Grierson noted long ago, each stanza 'suggests metrically the swelling and dying sound of a bell; and, like a bell, the rhymes reiterate the same sound' (pp. 231–232 in his edition of *Metaphysical Lyrics*; quoted from Hutchinson, 538).

34 See *Select Hymns Taken out of Mr. Herbert's Temple* (London, 1697), reprinted with introduction by William E. Stephenson, Augustan Reprint Society, 98 (Los Angeles: U of California, 1962); the Dissenter revised for congregational singing thirty-two of Herbert's poems. The best discussion of this and other adaptations is Helen Vendler's fourth chapter.

35 Helen Vendler, contrasting her own reading vigorously with typical nineteenth-century enlightened readings, defines the poem as a conversion poem: the poet is 'saying that there *is* a hell, there are the dead, sins threaten an eternity of no rest, the priest has the *super*natural power to raise the dead, and the priest should take care not to be himself one of the dead' (p. 117). Vendler's sharp analysis underscores the way in which the liturgical substance, expressed richly in the vesting prayers, contrasts sharply with the adapter's (and the nineteenth-century readers') hyperlogicality and pious rationalism.

36 Some of what follows is based on Aidan Kavanagh (see n. 5 above), particularly his fifth chapter.

37 I do *not* mean by this that the poems imitate or are influenced by the details of liturgical services, or that one can trace a systematic kind of organization which clearly, almost mechanically, reflects liturgical details.

38 *Terribilis est locus iste: hic domus Dei est et porta caeli: et vocabitur aula Dei. Liber*, p. 1250: the Introit for the Dedication of a Church; see Gen 28: 17.

39 Ilona Bell, 'Revision and Revelation in Herbert's "Affliction (I)"', *John Donne Journal* 3 (1984), 73–96.

2

SACRED SINGER / PROFANE POET:
HERBERT'S SPLIT POETIC PERSONA

ELIZABETH CLARKE

The Temple, so often approached with reverence by believers and non-believers alike, would seem to be one literary space in Renaissance literature free from intrusion by the profane. Most readers have found there only the image of Herbert as perfect Anglican priest. The textual construction of an idealized identity for Herbert is an ongoing practice, from the work of Herbert's early biographers to current accounts of his life by two modern poets, W.H. Auden and R.S. Thomas, who should perhaps know better.[1] Yet even Herbert's first biographer, Barnabas Oley, who had a political interest in recreating him as an Anglican saint, was aware of a discontinuity within Herbert's poetry. In composing the Latin poems, says Oley, 'he made his ink with water of Helicon': the poems of *The Temple*, however, 'these preparations propheticall', were 'distilled from above'. Oley underlines the perceived superiority of this divine inspiration in a direct comparison between the Latin poems and the lyrics of *The Temple*: 'In those are the weake motions of Nature, in these Raptures of Grace'.[2] Oley's judgement would seem to indicate the presence of both the sacred and the profane within Herbert's wider poetic activity, if not within *The Temple*. In this article I shall first consider Oley's opinion, and then pursue the search for the 'weake motions of Nature' into the very Temple itself.

In 'The Pearl' Herbert confesses to a proficiency in profane textual practice, yet critics of Herbert tend to ignore the most obvious examples of 'the quick returns of courtesie and wit': his Greek and Latin epigrams. The poems of the *Musae Responsoriae*, in particular, are rather more witty than courteous. The myth created by Izaak Walton, which posits a 'profane' phase in Herbert's career followed by the holy years at Bemerton, has the advantage of neatly explaining the split in Herbert's poetic persona.[3] However, detailed attempts at dating the poetry by Amy Charles and others suggest the foolishness of assigning the poems of *The Temple* to the very brief period in which Herbert came close to fulfilling the biographical requirements for the holy Christian poet.[4] It is clear that composition of the Latin epigrams went on alongside the composition of some of the most profound lyrics of *The Temple*. The *Memoriae Matris Sacrae*, Petrarchan in style and tone, must have been written at the same time or after the anti-Petrarchan poem 'Jordan (1)'. Similarly, Herbert's grossly flattering elegy for Sir Francis Bacon, who died in 1626, must have been written after the rejection of 'courtesie' in 'The Pearl'.

Barnabas Oley's reading of Herbert's poetry ignores chronology and highlights a different disjunction: the difference between Herbert's writing in the vernacular, and his classical compositions. Leaving aside Oley's judgement on the differing sources of inspiration for the classical and English poems, there are obvious differences in character between them. There is an abundance of classical reference in the Latin poetry, whereas the English lyrics eschew classical allusion altogether. The Latin poems are often concerned with contemporary politics and gossip: the English deal with the timeless issue of how an individual Christian may relate to his Creator. There is a great deal of metrical innovation in *The Temple*, whereas the Latin collections consist of imitations of classical forms. Oley was not alone in his judgement of the inspired status of *The Temple*. Lack of obvious precedent for *The Temple* fostered the assumption that the poems had sprung fully formed from some other creative power than Herbert's own.[5] The anonymous J.L., writing a poem for the second edition of Harvey's *The Synagogue, or The Shadow of The Temple*, seems to have a very clear view of what was special about Herbert's poetry, in both theological and literary terms:

> *Herbert!* whose every strain
> Twists holy Breast with happy Brain,
>   So that who strives to be
>   As elegant as he,
> Must climb Mount *Calvary* for *Parnassus* Hill
> And in his Saviours sides baptize his Quill;
>   A Jordan fit t'instill
> A Saint-like stile, backt with an Angels skill.[6]

Whilst taking seriously these claims for the baptism of profane poetry into holy lyric, it seems sensible to consider a more humble origin for Herbert's *Temple*, within English and European, classical and Christian, rhetorical and anti-rhetorical traditions.

The Protestant humanist devotional rhetoric developing in Europe is a good place to start in an attempt to trace the origin of the poems to Parnassus rather than Calvary. The Latin verse collections of such prominent European Reformers as Marcantonio Flaminio and Theodore Beza, displaying a remarkable virtuosity of form in treating both sacred and profane subject matter, testify to the validation of humanist poetic conventions by European Protestants.[7] Beza's *Poemata*, edited by the Scottish scholar

Buchanan and published in Paris in 1576, is a formidable feat of typography: it contains Greek and Hebrew poems as well as classical Latin forms such as elegy and epigram. Beza's collection also contains vernacular poetry: a French verse tragedy, *Sacrifice d'Abraham*, and a few poems, such as his sonnet on the death of Calvin.[8] Such a comprehensive mixture of classical and contemporary verse-forms, adapted for Reformed purposes, is very much in the spirit of Herbert's own experimentation with both English and Latin genres of poetry. In the context of European Protestant writing Herbert's entire poetic corpus is seen to be a typically humanist production, with its fondness for epigrams and anagrams, with which even *The Temple* is furnished. However, the self-conscious wit of the humanist epigrammatic style is not the favoured mode of *The Temple*, although it is absolutely characteristic of Herbert's Latin poetry.

Neither, I would argue, is the Counter-Reformation 'poetry of meditation' Herbert's preferred style for *The Temple*.[9] Again, it is enlightening to compare Herbert's Latin poems, especially the *Passio Discerpta*, with the *Théorèmes* of Jean de la Ceppède, a poetic text endorsed by the well-known exponent of Counter-Reformation devotion, St François de Sales.[10] There are many verbal parallels between Herbert's *Passio Discerpta* and La Ceppède's long series of sonnets on the events of the Passion, published in 1613. This may represent little more than the coincidence of subject matter, but the elaborately typological and often witty treatment of the Passion in La Ceppède's sonnets exactly matches the tone of Herbert's epigrams. The central conceit of one of the most anthologized of La Ceppède's poems, the so-called 'red' sonnet, is picked up by Herbert in his epigram on the 'red' robe of Christ, and also by Crashaw in 'Upon the Body of Our Blessed Lord, Naked and Bloody'.[11] However, I would argue that the very closeness of the imitation of Counter-Reformation rhetorical mode in *Passio Discerpta*, which was not published in Herbert's lifetime, indicates an experiment with this mode of Christian rhetoric that was ultimately rejected.

Standing out within the tortuous, self-conscious wit of Herbert's Latin epigrams is the Latin poem that most closely approaches the mode of *The Temple*. It is also the only poem in which Herbert appears to claim access to fluent and immediate divine inspiration. 'Ad Deum', positioned strategically at the end of *Musae Responsoriae*, perfectly illustrates the collusion of sacred and profane within Herbert's poetry.

> To God
> Once you, great God, bless
> With sweet dew him who writes,
> No futile labour makes it

A painful time for him: no aching
Fingers bother him for being bitten, no head
Aches, no quill is sad:
But in the pure body verse's
Ripe elan and vein are master,
Even as the Nile, unaware
Of dikes, overflows,
Lovely in its flooding. O sweetest
Spirit, you who fill up minds
With holy groans pouring
From you, the Dove, the writing
That I do, the pleasure that I give,
If I give it, is all from you.[12]

All the commonplaces of inspiration are represented here. No effort in composition is required, and metaphors of fluidity abound—the whole being of the poet is awash with what Oley called Raptures of Grace. The 'groans' of the Holy Spirit, which Paul and Augustine had represented as entirely non-verbal, are equated with poetry's 'elan', the intoxication with words so deprecated in 'Jordan (2)'. However, the implied spontaneity of the composition of this poem, which seems to signify its Spirit-inspired status, is undermined by the fact that some of the lines are a copy of an Horatian ode. Also, it is impossible to ignore the political capital to be gained out of a dedication to God of a set of polemic verses, let alone the audacious assertion that God Himself was the author of them. It is very difficult to take seriously Edmund Blunden's assumption that this is Herbert's 'theory of inspiration'.[13]

However, a poem that is so clearly intended to indicate its heavenly origins is a key to the features that Herbert (and perhaps more importantly, his audience) would expect from a divinely inspired poem. The personal, even intimate tone, the lack of classical reference, the lyrical form, are in fact very reminiscent of *The Temple*, and highlight the difference between Herbert's poetic modes in Latin and English. Yet many of the equally personal and devotional English lyrics of *The Temple* are similarly based on classical models. What is a pagan altar doing at the entrance to 'The Church', for example? Sacred parody of profane poems is a prominent feature in *The Temple*. The 'patterns' for both 'The Altar' and 'Easter-Wings' are straight out of the Greek Anthology, a standard European humanist textbook. Among Herbert's first poetic ventures at Westminster School would have been exercises in imitation of this pagan volume. The best known of Herbert's parodies is of course acknowledged as 'A Parody', but the opening of 'Joseph's Coat' must have reminded Renaissance readers of the violent shift of mood at the start of Petrarch's sonnet 230. And as many critics have noticed, some of the lyrics dealing most particularly with the appropriate style for religious poetry have unmistakeable echoes of Philip Sidney's sequence *Astrophil and Stella*.[14]

Among these, the two poems entitled 'Jordan' explicitly consider the baptism of profane poetry for sacred verse. The re-christening of the original title of 'Jordan (2)', 'Invention', mirrors the baptism of the rhetorical process of invention itself, as described in that poem. Whilst 'invention' in Sidney's sonnet is 'nature's child', there is evidence in this poem that Herbert found the concept problematic. One of Herbert's favourite devotional works, Savonarola's *De Simplicitate Christianae Vitae*, shows a similarly deep suspicion of human skill in rhetoric. Savonarola attacks artistic invention in no uncertain terms as anathema to truly inspired discourse: likewise, both 'Jordan' poems reject 'trim invention' for the God-breathed simplicity of their final thought.[15] Savonarola's *Apologeticus De Ratione Poeticae Artis*, a 'defence' of poetry that is more like an attack on it, goes even further in its suspicion of all rhetorical utterance, which has its origins in pagan classical rhetoric.[16] The activity described in 'Jordan (2)' involves enormous human effort, and results in the corrupt adulteration of 'sense' with 'self', as in *De Ratione Poeticae Artis*, where Savonarola finds poetic discourse inherently self-publicizing.

Despite Herbert's participation in a rhetorical humanist education at all levels, *The Temple* manifests a very strong suspicion of poetic discourse itself as essentially profane. This anxiety is characteristic of a Reformed England in which the works of Savonarola, who was adopted by Foxe as a Protestant martyr, were extremely popular. The apologetic tone of the preface to Giles Fletcher's *Christs Victorie and Triumph*, written at the same time as Herbert's first sonnets, testifies to a general association of poetry with paganism in Reformed England: 'some thinke it halfe sacrilege for prophane Poetrie to deale with divine and heavenly matters'.[17] It is not enough, as Beza had done, as Sidney had suggested, and as Herbert himself did in the Latin poems, to sanctify pagan verse forms by using sacred subject matter: in 'The Forerunners' Herbert expresses a personal imperative to baptize metaphor and poetic diction, those basic elements of poetic discourse. Herbert's sophisticated readership received the lyrics of *The Temple* as holy because they agreed with his own assessment: he had brought poetry to church, 'well-dressed and clad'.

'The Posy' demonstrates both the nature of Herbert's task in the attempt to purify poetry, and his method of proceeding. The competitive practice of composing 'posies', witty and personal mottoes, was a particularly suspect one for the Christian poet, whose responsibility was to write for the glory of God alone. Despite the fact that, on the evidence of his Latin poems, Herbert should have been particularly good at writing posies, he refuses to take part in the game, rejecting the internal effort of 'invention' and rhetoric:

>   Invention rest,
>   Comparisons go play, wit use thy will.[18]

His eventual choice of 'posy'—*Less than the least of all God's mercies*—is entirely derivative and needs no human invention at all in composition. It is also a post-baptismal utterance from Gen. 32. The story of Jacob's crossing of the brook Jabbok, a tributary of Jordan, the archetypal baptismal river, has been read by Roland Barthes as a narrative about the production of language.[19] For Herbert's Reformation spirituality, however, the significance of the story was as an epiphany of Christ, and the wrestle with the angel represented the kind of 'death' experience of which baptism is a symbol. The result of the struggle is that Jacob is deliberately disabled by the angel, and limps, in fact, for the rest of his life: his stick is a type of the Christian's dependence on the Holy Spirit, which the death of the pagan self in baptism necessitates. The self-effacing utterance of Gen. 32, 'I am not worthy of the least of all thy mercies', becomes the self-erasing 'Posy', *Less than the least of all God's mercies*, that ends Herbert's poem.

Barnabas Oley reports Herbert's sense of divine disablement in the composition of *The Temple*: 'God has broken into my Study and taken off my Chariot wheels, I have nothing worthy of God'.[20] *The Temple*, apparently, embodies an act of vandalism by God that disables Herbert's powers of composition. It is Herbert's perception of this act that, for Oley, marks these poems out as holy: 'And even this lowliness in his own eyes, doth more advance their worth.' What is not so clear is whether the perceived lowliness is virtual, in that all human effort by definition is unworthy of God, or actual: did Herbert really believe that the poems of *The Temple* were poor? However, in the dynamic of mortification, which is the first and fatal stage of baptism, all that matters is the correct spiritual attitude, the 'dying to' the poems. The Christian poet must not rely on his own rhetorical skills: if he refuses to 'mortify' them, God will destroy them. This destructive process is seen in Reformed theology as a necessary prelude to the second stage, the resurrection of the believer in the strength of the Holy Spirit. In Charles Wesley's poetic rewriting of Gen. 32 the disablement that is baptism is celebrated as a resurrection of divine strength:

> Lame as I am, I take the Prey
> Hell, Earth and Sin with Ease oercome
> I leap for Joy, pursue my Way,
> And as a bounding Hart fly home.[21]

Wesley's hyperbolic language may indicate success in the spiritual rather that the human realm, but Herbert's readership, on the whole, thought that he had succeeded in both. Christopher Harvey's eulogist described the death-dealing process of baptism as necessary for one who would be as 'elegant' as Herbert, an unlikely epithet for one whose poetic chariot has lost its wheels. Herbert's Protestant readers were well accustomed to the double-think involved in doctrines such as justification by faith, where holiness does not have to be actual and visible, as long as it is 'imputed' by God. The discrepancy between their enthusiastic reception of Herbert's poems, and the poet's apparent disregard of them, was not a problem, but an indication that *The Temple* was divinely inspired. Not for nothing was the story of Herbert's deathbed willingness to burn his poems so carefully reported by Izaak Walton in the biography that is essentially a hagiography.[22] The poet's stated awareness of his own inadequacy, and the gestures towards disablement that are built into the poems, are important to a Reformed ideal of holiness.

Herbert's extended sonnet 'Grief' is a good example of self-mutilation in action.[23] Louis Martz considered it as an example of the 'poetry of tears', the embodiment of Counter-Reformation spirituality and rhetorical practice, and it does begin in an almost exact imitation of a sonnet by Jacques de Billy. De Billy's sonnet, written both in French and Latin, is a perfect example of the poetry of tears, and the first lines of Herbert's 'Grief' are very similar.

> O who will give me tears? Come all ye springs,
> Dwell in my head and eyes: come clouds, and rain:
> My grief hath need of all the wat'ry things,
> That nature hath produced.[24]

The concentration on the outward and physical effects of emotion, without regard to the inward cause, is foreign to Herbert, and the heavy-handed use of the conventions of the poetry of tears should, I think, draw attention to the disjunction between the professed authenticity of the emotion and the artificiality of its supposed expression. The outrageous and elaborate puns on the 'feet', 'running' both in his verse and to his eyes, and the smooth-'running' line that supports the witticism, gives the lie to the sincerity of the 'rough sorrows' and alerts us to an irony, a double irony in that in this poem he is invoking a version of the sincerity *topos*. Only the final inarticulate gasp—the more powerful because of its contrast with the urbane poetry that precedes it—has any sense of authenticity.

> Verses, ye are too fine a thing, too wise
> For my rough sorrows: cease, be dumbe and mute,
> Give up your feet and running to mine eyes,
> And keep your measures for some lovers lute,
> Whose grief allows him musick and a ryme:
> For mine excludes both measure, tune, and time.
>   Alas, my God!

The 'ejaculation' of the last line, which derails the rhetoric of the poem and brings it to a crashing halt, is of more spiritual worth than the elaborate comparisons of the previous fourteen.

The subtitle of Herbert's 1633 volume was *Sacred poems and private ejaculations*, a paradoxical, and certainly neologistic, title that caught on: both Christopher Harvey and Henry Vaughan used exactly the same formulation for the titles of their collections of Christian verse. Herbert has hit on the perfect formula with which to validate a Christian poetry against the criticisms due to humanist rhetoric. It is the gesture towards 'ejaculation'—spontaneous, anti-rhetorical, limping, archetypally sincere, deeply spiritual—that confirms the poems as 'sacred', simply because it represents the ultimate threat to them: in order for the ejaculation to be heard, the poetry must 'cease, be dumbe and mute'. The rhetoric is sanctified by the poet's willingness to sacrifice it. Kenneth Burke has described sacrifice as the essence of religion, 'a kind of suicide ... simultaneously dying and non-dying'.[25] This is the double movement that is baptism, by which divine inspiration displaces human invention. Herbert describes this transfer, which is his ideal for poetic composition, in 'Love (2)':

>   then shall our brain
> All her invention on thine Altar lay,
> And there in hymnes send back thy fire again.

Like the pagan 'broken altar' at the entrance to *The Temple*, poetic discourse, which is essentially profane, is redeemed for a seventeenth-century readership by the absolute sacrifice that is at the heart of Reformation theology.

Notes

1   See David Novarr, *The Making of Walton's Lives* (Ithaca & London: Cornell UP, 1958), 333-339. See also the introductions to the selections of Herbert's poems by W.H. Auden in *George Herbert: Poems Selected by W.H. Auden* (London: Penguin, 1973) and R.S. Thomas, *George Herbert: A Choice of His Verse* (London: Faber, 1967).

2   *Herberts Remains, or, Sundry Pieces of that Sweet Singer of the Temple, Mr. G.H., sometime Orator of the University of Cambridge, Now exposed to Public Light*, edited by Barnabas Oley (London, 1652), sig. C6^r.

3   See Izaak Walton, *The Lives of Doctor John Donne, Sir Henry Wotton, Mr. Richard Hooker, Mr. George Herbert and Doctor Robert Sanderson* (London, 1895), especially pp. 201-202, where Walton strongly implies that the poems of *The Temple* reflect Herbert's post-ordination state of mind.

4   The authoritative biography by Amy Charles, *A Life of George Herbert* (Ithaca & London: Cornell UP, 1977) dates the latest Latin poem as no earlier than 1623, the earliest English poem no later than 1619, and the whole manuscript as finished around the mid 1620s.

5   See the judgement of Ralph Knevet, *A Gallery to the Temple*, written in the 1640s, not published until 1766, in *George Herbert: The Critical Heritage*, edited by C.A. Patrides (London &c: Routledge & Kegan Paul, 1983), 63, and of Henry Vaughan, *The Complete Poems*, edited by Alan Rudrum (London: Penguin, 1976), 142.

6   Christopher Harvey, *The Synagogue, or The Shadow of The Temple: Sacred Poems and Private Ejaculations in imitation of Mr. George Herbert*, 2nd ed. (London, 1647), sig. C8^r.

7   Thomas Heywood, for example, translated epigrams by Beza, Marcantonio Flaminio, and other French and Italian poets. See his *Pleasant Dialogues and Dramma's, selected out of Lucan, Erasmus, Textor, Ovid* (London, 1637), 272-279.

8   There are also Latin paraphrases of the Psalms, a paraphrase in both Greek and Latin of the Song of Songs, and Latin elegies on famous Protestant reformers such as Calvin, Luther, Peter Martyr and Melanchthon.

9   Louis L. Martz, in *The Poetry of Meditation: A Study in English Religious Literature* (New Haven and London: Yale UP, 1954) first posited the link between *The Temple* and writers of Counter-Reformation devotional treatises such as St François de Sales. Other writers such as Stanley Stewart in *George Herbert* (Boston: Twayne, 1986) have followed him in assuming the connection.

10 For the link between La Ceppède and St François de Sales see P.A. Chilton, *The Poetry of Jean de la Ceppède: A Study in Text and Context* (Oxford: Oxford UP, 1977), 50-51. A letter on the subject the *Théorèmes* from St François de Sales to Jean de la Ceppède emphasizes 'poetry as the infusion of piety into a primarily secular activity for concrete moral ends in society'. I hope to show that this is a very different poetic theory from that of George Herbert.

11 *Anthology of French Seventeenth-century Lyric Poetry*, edited by Odette de Mourgues (Oxford: Oxford UP, 1960). 70. Compare Herbert's epigram, 'In Arund. Spin. Genuflex. Purpur.', *The Works of George Herbert*, edited by F.E. Hutchinson (Oxford: Oxford UP, 1945$_2$), 405). The same conceit is used by Donne in

Hymn to God, my God, in my Sickness: 'So, in his purple wrapped receive me Lord'. *John Donne, The Complete English Poems*, edited by A.J. Smith (London: Penguin, 1971), 348.

12   *The Latin Poetry of George Herbert. A Bilingual Edition*, translated by Mark McCloskey and Paul R. Murphy (Athens, OH: Ohio UP, 1965), 61.

13   The ode in question is Horace, *Carmina* 4: 3; see Edmund Blunden's 'George Herbert's Latin poems', in *Essays and Studies by Members of the English Association*, 19 (1934). Quoted in Hutchinson, p. 590.

14   *Astrophil and Stella* Sonnets 1 and 3. Sir Philip Sidney, *Selected Poems*, edited by Katherine Duncan-Jones (Oxford: Oxford UP, 1973), 117-118.

15   See Savonarola, *De Simplicitate Christianae Vitae* (Strasbourg, 1615), 66.

16   Savonarola, *Apologeticus de ratione poeticae artis* (Venice, 1534), 17, 17^v.

17   Giles and Phineas Fletcher, *Poetical Works*, edited by Frederick S. Boas (Cambridge: Cambridge UP, 1908), 10.

18   George Herbert, *Complete English Poems*, edited by John Tobin (London: Penguin, 1991), 172.

19   Roland Barthes, *Image Music Text*, translated by Stephen Heath (New York & London: Fontana, 1977), 125-141.

20   Barnabas Oley, *Herberts Remains*, sig. C6^r; Biblical source, Exod. 14: 25.

21   Charles Wesley, *Wrestling Jacob*, in *Representative Verse of Charles Wesley*, edited by Frank Baker (London: Epworth, 1962), 39.

22   Walton, *Lives*, p. 223. The story reports Herbert's entrusting of the manuscript of *The Temple* to Nicholas Ferrar. 'If he can think it may turn to the advantage of any dejected poor soul, let it be made public; if not, let him burn it; for I and it are less than the least of God's mercies.' Walton concludes triumphantly, 'Thus meanly did this humble man think of this excellent book'.

23   Stanley Fish was the first to notice this 'self-consuming' tendency in Herbert's poetry in his chapter on Herbert in *Self-Consuming Artifacts: The Experience of Seventeenth-Century Literature* (Berkeley, Los Angeles & London: U of California P, 1972). He accurately perceived this movement in many of Herbert's poems, but failed to notice its proper significance within Reformed theology, emphasizing the destructive nature of the rhetorical process rather than its power to signify to a contemporary readership a constructive intervention by God.

24   Herbert, *Complete English Poems*, p. 154: compare Jacques de Billy, *Sonnets spirituels* (Paris, 1573), fol. 35^v, quoted in *Renaissance Latin Poetry*, edited by I.D. McFarlane (Manchester: Manchester UP, 1980), 99: 'Qui me donra de l'eau pour mon chef miserable / De larmes pour mes yeux un ruisseau tout entier?' De Billy was known in England: the Bodleian copy of his *Anthologia Sacra* was owned by another bilingual poet, the Englishman Richard Edes.

25   Kenneth Burke, *A Rhetoric of Motives* (Los Angeles & London: U of California P, 1969), 265.

3

'HOW ALL THY LIGHTS COMBINE':
HERBERT AND KING'S

DIANE KELSEY McCOLLEY

The King's of my title is King's College Chapel, Cambridge, along with the sacred and profane kings associated with it; and my purpose is to suggest how this configuration of secular history and sacred arts enters Herbert's poems and is transformed. But I'm going to begin profanely (*pro + fanum*, in front of or outside the temple) in the rooms of a student at Trinity College, named George Hanford.

Seven months after the sixteen-year-old George Herbert matriculated at Trinity in 1609, Hanford dated a manuscript of *Ayres to be sunge to the Lute and Base vyole*.[1] If, as seems likely, Hanford invited Herbert, as a musical member of a musical family, to a musick-meeting to air these ayres, he heard love laments urging a coy lady to 'Come away'. The Song of Solomon—that king who provided epithets for England's monarchs—invokes the beloved, 'Rise up, my love, my fair one, and come away'; this text as sacred allegory was set for liturgical use by, for example, Thomas Tomkins, who had also composed a coronation anthem for 'England's Solomon', James I. Songs and madrigals frequently reliteralize this sacred text by asking profane loves to 'come away' for explicitly unbiblical purposes; Dowlands's more famous 'Come away, come sweet love' asks the beloved to rise 'like to the naked morn' and fly to the grove 'To entertain the stealth of love ... Wing'd with sweet hopes and heav'nly fire'.[2] The betrothal of the soul to God attributed to the Song of Solomon is part of that from which the wooers in secular songs ask the beloved to come away.

Hanford's *Ayres* begin with a song about the fire of love as cruel mistress, or vice versa, which serves as general invocation:

> Come, come sweete fyre why stayest thou? alas,
>   Come quickly, quickly come,
> Consume me all at once and give me leave to try
> If lyfe be sweeter then a louers martyrdom ...
>
> Come come away o sweeter why doe you stay,
>   O come away sweete fyre,
> And let me prove yf rest to love my death can giue

Or yf my luke warme ashes haue not still desyre
To kind[e]³ heate of love wherein I dyeing live ...

One can see why the piously bred George Herbert sent home to his mother
the sonnet asking 'My God, where is that ancient heat towards thee, /
Wherewith whole shoals of Martyrs once did burn, / Besides their other
flames?' Another of Hanford's airs tells Venus that his beloved is her
temple, the 'Heavenly model of all bliss ... Whose lips your altars, where
would I, / In offering kisses, live and die'. And Herbert's sonnet continues,
'Doth poetry / Wear Venus' livery? only serve her turn? / Why are not sonnets made of thee? and lays / Upon thine Altar burnt?'

By contrast with Hanford, Thomas Tomkins (c. 1572-1656), prolific
composer of church music, resacralizes the refrain from the Song of Solomon in his setting of an anonymous text in which Christ is again the soul's
Bridegroom, but with the personal tone of a love song:

Above the stars my saviour dwells.
I love, I care for nothing else.

There, there he sits and fits a place
For the glorious heirs of grace.

Dear saviour raise my duller eine,
Let me but see thy beams divine.

Ravish my soul with wonder and desire,
Ere I enjoy, let me thy joys admire.

And wond'ring let me say,
Come Lord Jesu, come away.⁴

Entitled simply 'An hymne', the work was arranged both as a sacred madri-
gal for private use and as a verse anthem (combining passages for solo or
single-part voices and for full choir) for liturgical use, set for countertenor,
six-part choir, and organ. It is unusual among seventeenth-century anthems
in being what Herbert calls 'A True Hymn', written from the heart rather
than setting a prescribed text. By its desire for desire and the secular connotations of 'ravish', 'enjoy', and 'Come away', 'An hymne' becomes a
sacred parody of those profane parodies. Tomkins' setting uses modal modulations and occasional dissonance in the verse sections to express its personal quality as a love song, while affirmative tonal resolutions in the full-
choir responses suggest the stability of the eternal 'place' that the saviour
'sits and fills'. Word painting on 'raise' repeats in a rapturous instrumental

flight in response to the solo voice's 'ravish my soul', and the organ ac-
companiment engages in a rhapsody of its own to express the soul's 'wonder and desire' in the 'motions', or emotions, of harmonies, syncopations,
and runs. 'Come Lord Jesu, come away' takes a twelfth of the text but
nearly a third of the anthem; Tomkins illustrates the saviour's answer to the
soul's request to 'let me say' by letting the singers say these words (count-
ing by repetitions of the name 'Jesu') thirty-eight times in antiphonal polyphony which grows from one voice to six voice parts, both intensifying the
soul's plea and multiplying participants in it. Like many of Herbert's
poems, *An hymne* is both deeply personal and expansively choral.

Herbert's 'Doomsday',[5] by beginning each stanza with 'Come away',
is a sacred parody of profane parodies of a sacred text in an erotic genre.
But Herbert's choice of 'comings' is the most radical possible; he urges the
Bridegroom not only to renew his intimacy with the soul but to 'Come
away' from his dwelling above the stars and 'Help our decay' by his Second Coming. Unlike Tomkins' anthem, Herbert's poem presses the grim-
mer implications of the imperative, exploring the mortality and judgement
through which all flesh must pass as result of 'Flesh's stubbornness'. Its
description of the 'noisome vapours' of dead bodies gravely alters the expectations of a love song into a cure of profane love as well a cure of death:

> Come away,
> Make this the day.
> Dust, alas, no music feels,
> But thy trumpet: then it kneels,
> As peculiar notes and strains
> Cure Tarantula's raging pains.

But the prosodic *danse macabre* on 'Tarantula's' gives way to a prayer for
the logos-music that made and remakes all life:

> Come away,
> Help our decay.
> Man is out of order hurled,
> Parcelled out to all the world.
> Lord, thy broken consort raise,
> And the musick shall be praise.

A 'broken consort' is both a wounded Spouse and an ensemble of mixed
instruments. Although the primary meaning here may be an ensemble need-
ing repair, the plea to 'raise' it retains its meaning of diversity in unity, an

aggregate of mingled voices to be raised in the sense of assembling a following, of elevation, and of resurrection. The conventions of musical word-painting suggest that on 'raise' the reading voice should rise in pitch, as in Tomkins' anthem. The wish that Christ would 'come away' from his habitation beyond the stars illustrates the theme of divine kingship, contrasting the disorder of human beings who are 'parcelled out'—divided within and among themselves, packaged and sold as commodities—under the rule and misrule of secular kings with the music of God's kingdom laid open by a suffering servant who thus becomes their 'King of Glory'.

The *musica sacra* to which Herbert dedicated himself not only resacralizes *musica profana* but also incorporates the music he heard in the Chapels of Trinity and King's Colleges. It is to King's that I wish to accompany him, because the Chapel offers integrated visible, audible, intelligible, and expressive configurations such as Herbert achieved in his poems, strove for in his vocation as priest, and calls in 'The Windows' 'Doctrine and life, colours and light, in one'. The chapel's architecture is formally clear yet richly detailed, like the fabric of his poems, and the iconography of its windows appears in his typology.

Unlike more private college Chapels, King's gathered a liturgical community of both town and gown: clerical and secular, common, noble and sometimes royal, of commingled classes and sexes, as appears from the Jacobean edict, 'We do forbid that women of the town be permitted to repair to the chappell of any college ... unless it be in the case of an English sermon ad populum, for which the bells of such college is rung, or to the ordinary prayers in Kings College chapell'.[6] Given the Chapel's tradition of open services, it seems likely that much poetry was conceived beneath its storeyed windows and within the textures of its fabric and its music. Since the principal subjects of the windows are scenes of the Life of Christ and other events celebrated through the liturgical year, these scenes correspond with the music and poems written for those celebrations. Through the windows' depiction of this life runs a theme of just and unjust rulers, the types and parodies of the King of Kings; and this theme of Kingship appears also in the chapel's music and in Herbert's *Temple,* with Solomon, poet and Temple-builder as well as king, a figure common to all three.[7]

The Chapel's history and decorations associate it with secular royalty as well as with Christ the King, incorporating both parts of the epithet 'King of Kings'. Building was begun by Henry VI and continued with contributions from Edward IV, Richard III, Henry VII and his mother, Lady Margaret Beaufort, and Henry VIII. Although Henry VI required 'settyng a parte too gret curious workes of entaille and besy moldyng',[8] the Tudor rose and crown and the Beaufort greyhound and portcullis cover the antechapel walls, and other royal arms and cognizances appear in sculptures and window traceries. These symbols remind the viewer of the alliance of religion and the arts with royal power and patronage, for better and for worse, that was among the issues of the Reformation and the Civil Wars. Musicians, as well as visual artists, commented on this relation: Tomkins' coronation anthem, instructing James to 'observe the commandements of our God, to walk in his ways, and keep his ceremonies, testimonies and judgements', emphatically ornaments 'keep his ceremonies' with syncopations and ascending figures.[9]

The architecture, typology, and music of the chapel find analogues in Herbert's poems. These smaller temples are more circumspect and self-questioning employments of the sacred arts; yet as temples of the heart they are 'a court', as Richard Hooker calls 'the howse of prayer', in which 'the verie glorie of the place it self', even 'the outward forme thereof ... hath moment to help devotion'.[10]

As to the chapel's architecture, the directions of Henry VI required the Chapel to be 'in large fourme clene and substantial'.[11] Its Perpendicular structure, with strong horizontal as well as vertical lines, represents the intersection of heaven and earth and that crossing of flesh and spirit whom Herbert describes architecturally in 'Man': since a human being is 'a stately habitation' that, like the Chapel, is 'all symmetry, / Full of proportions', he asks God to 'dwell in it, / That it may dwell in thee'. In 'The Church-Floor' Herbert finds applicability to life even in a church's lowliest feature: 'Mark you the floor?' and notes the symbolic value of each part; at the end we discover that the temple whose floor he describes is within us: 'Blessed be the *Architect*, whose art / Could build so strong in a weak heart'.

The programme of the windows, as confirmed in the contract of 1526, depicts the two testaments, 'the olde lawe and the new lawe', providing one of the world's fullest typological cycles of what Milton in *Il Penseroso* calls 'Storied windows richly dight'. Late fifteenth-century blockbooks, the *Biblia Pauperum* and the *Speculum Humanae Salvationis*, and the work of late fifteenth- and early sixteenth-century engravers such as Albrecht Dürer, provide printed sources, though the programmes are not identical. Typology interprets persons and events of the Hebrew Bible as precursors or prefigurations of Christ and his Kingdom. Preaching on the Psalms, Herbert's contemporary Arthur Lake taught that:

[A]ll things came to the Iewes in types; therefore we may not think that King *David*, had an eye onely to the corporall places, his eye pierced farther, even to that which was *figured* therein, hee looked to the *Kingdome of Christ*.[12]

Most typological pairs are read as prophecies of Christ and their fulfil-
ments. As a secondary development, typology came to be applied to the
individual believer, as in the representation of Solomon as Henry VIII in the
King's College Chapel windows and in the spiritual experience related in
Herbert's typological poems.

The Chapel has twelve bays, or sections between the columns of the
vaults, containing twelve windows on each side, each having ten vertical
lights, and an East Window. Beginning at the northwest end and moving
east, the windows continue around the chapel and end near the southwest
corner. The lower sections of the side windows contain the stories of the
life of Christ, the Acts of the Apostles, the career of St Paul, and the Death,
Funeral, Assumption and Coronation of the Virgin Mary. Most of the upper
sections contain types or prefigurations of these events, usually from the
Hebrew Bible, read as prophetic of the Messiah. Each window has two of
these pairs. The East Window contains the story of Christ's trial and crucifixion.

In these windows, as Herbert says to Christ in 'The Windows', 'thou
dost anneal in glass thy story'. But in the poem, the window in which that
story needs to be annealed is the '[b]rittle crazy glass' of the preacher as
mere man, who becomes a window by grace, yet cannot win souls by
speech unless Christ makes his own life shine within his priest's. The story
annealed in glass at King's College Chapel is the story Herbert anneals in
his poems.

Although he was a student at Trinity, an orator at Great St Mary's, a
rector at Bemerton, and a worshipper at Salisbury Cathedral, none of these
had storied windows. The likeliest place for him to have seen Christ's story
annealed in glass is at King's. In 'The Holy Scriptures (2)' he exclaims,

> O that I knew how all thy lights combine,
>   And the configurations of their glory!
>   Seeing not only how each verse doth shine,
> But all the constellations of the story.

The sonnet addresses the Bible and the starry metaphor concerns the cosmos. But 'lights' is also a word for the sections of a window, and the lights
of Scripture's story are also constellated in the 'lights' of the typological
windows of the Chapel. Just as in the Bible 'each verse marks that', in the
Chapel the topics of the windows comment on each other. Herbert's sonnet
admires the inter-illumination of the parts of the Bible, and that is also the
point of the programme of the Chapel windows.

Herbert's poems address many of the events in the windows, often typologically. In 'The Bunch of Grapes', the story of 'the Jews of old ... pens and sets us down', so that God's 'ancient justice overflows our crimes'; and as in one of the windows' most striking images, 'Our Scripture-dew drops fast'. The type in the title, though, is missing in both the windows and the poem. In the *Biblia Pauperum*, which helped provide the programme for the windows, the bunch of grapes (Num. 13: 23) is a type of the Baptism of Christ, along with the Red Sea crossing; but it is not included in the windows, so that Herbert's question 'Where's the cluster?' might apply to them as well as to himself.

The typological scheme of the windows incorporates monarchs both sacred and profane: the Queen of Sheba bringing gifts to King Solomon as a type of the Three Kings; Queen Athalia as the type of King Herod in the Massacre of the Innocents; Solomon as the reverse type of Herod judging Christ; and the crowning of Solomon as the ironic type of Christ Crowned with Thorns. Solomon in these windows is represented as Henry VIII. This visual commentary on just and unjust uses of power culminates in the East window where, below the Crucifixion, a portly Pontius Pilate, the imperial governor, who has assented to the death penalty against his better judgement and turned Jesus over to the crowd to avoid 'a tumult', washes his hands to declare his innocence 'of the blood of this just person' (Matt. 27: 24). Francis Bacon, referring to the account in John 18, comments: '*What is Truth*; said jesting *Pilate; And would not stay for an Answer*'.[13] Christ stands before Pilate being tried and hangs above him on the cross inscribed 'King of the Jews',[14] the two thieves on either side making their respective choices. The window contrasts the ruler who does not search out truth to the mocked but true King who gave his life not only for his friends but even for his enemies.

The window nearest the East Window on the north side represents two pairs of scenes: first, the Scourging of Christ as antitype of the Torments of Job, who did stay for an answer: 'the cause which I knew not', he says, 'I searched out' (Job 20: 16); and second, Christ Crowned with Thorns as the ironic antitype of the Crowning of Solomon, who in his famous Judgement also stayed for an answer.

Herbert's epigrammatic Latin poems *Passio Discerpta* ('The events of the Passion') suggest familiarity with the iconography as well as the Scriptural narrative of these events, perhaps from studying such works as the *Biblia Pauperum*, one of the sources of the windows, which has a more complete programme. His English poem 'The Sacrifice' incorporates the events of the Passion while 'the Prince of peace' addresses its witnesses, 'Oh, *all ye*, who pass by, whose eyes and mind / To worldly things are sharp, but to me blind; / To me, who took eyes that I might you find: / Was ever grief like mine?'[15] Herbert's demanding rhyme scheme and the unusual roughness and grim drive of his diction hold the acute pain of musical settings of the Good Friday Reproaches in controlled intensity. As in the windows, in Herbert's poem 'Then from one ruler to another bound / They lead me; ... They bind, and lead me unto *Herod*: he / Sends me to *Pilate* ... Herod and all his bands do set me light ... *Herod* in judgement sits, while I do stand; ... *Pilate* a stranger holdeth off; but they, / Mine own dear people, cry, *Away away*' (lines 53-54, 73-74, 77, 81, 101-102): the most profane parody of all those comings away, to which Herbert replies, in 'The Call', 'Come, my Way'.

Along with its devotional uses, the window programme contains a political message that might serve as praise, warning, and education for the two princes known as 'England's Solomon', Henry VII and, preveniently, James I, the latter with particular reference to his peacemaking, as the name inscribes.[16] The Book of Common Prayer and many anthems have texts concerning the themes of kingship discernible in the Chapel decorations and windows, both honouring kings as God's vicars and praying for their justice in that vocation while declaring God's sovereignty. The BCP (I quote from the 1607 edition) contains numerous prayers for the sovereign, including two at Holy Communion, the first asking that God's 'chosen seruant James ... (knowing whose minister he is) may above all things seeke thy honour and glory, and that we his subjects (duely considering whose authority he hath) may faithfully serue, honour, and humbly obey him'; and the second that since 'we be taught by thy holy Word, that the hearts of kings are in thy rule and gouernance, and that thou doest dispose & turne them as it seemeth best to thy godly wisdome', God should so 'dispose & and gouerne the heart of James, thy seruant our King & gouernour, that in all his thoughts, words, and workes, he may euer seeke thy honour and glory, and studie to preserue the people committed to his charge, in wealth, peace, & godliness' (sig. C3). The prayer 'for the whole state of Christs Church militant here in earth' asks that under James 'we may be godly and quietly gouerned' (sig. C3ᵛ), and the litany asks the 'King of Kings' and 'onely ruler of Princes' to replenish the sovereign 'with the grace of thy holy Spirit, that he may always incline to thy will, and walke in thy way', granting strength that he may 'vanquish and ouercome all his enemies, and finally after this life, he may attaine euerlasting joy and felicity'. Whether these verses pray for continuance or amendment, and whether the enemies are without or within, would depend on the political viewpoint of each beseecher. James himself, as King of Scots, states simplistically in the verse 'argument' to *Basilikon Doron* (1599) that kings

sway God's sceptre, and so must 'Walk always so, as ever in his sight /
Who guards the godly, plaguing the profane'. All these prayers for reciprocal justice and obedience cut two ways, upholding authority while admon-
ishing the powerful of their responsibilities and, perhaps, implying that, in
John Donne's words, souls perish 'which more chuse mens unjust / Power
from God claym'd, then God himselfe to trust'.[17]

The *Magnificat*, said or sung daily at Evensong, also contains commentary on power that may be taken as a warning to the overweening, and these
verses were regularly set with expressive word painting, especially 'He hath
showed strength with his arm', often in strong homophony; '[The Lord]
hath scattered the proude in the imagination of their hearts', the voices
scattered in broken polyphonic phrases; and 'He hath put down the mighty
from their seats: and hath exalted the humble and meeke', the notes falling
and rising accordingly.[18]

The liturgy, art, and music constellated in King's Chapel are full of
such reminders of the magnificence and power for good of royalty and the
responsibility, fallibility, and mischief of rulers, subordinating the king's
power to God's and inviting '*all ye*, who pass by' to consider the relations
between human and divine kingship. These witnesses included youths pre-
paring for administrative offices and holy orders, confronting the life of the
Kings. Ideally, such meditations would affect the course of justice, though
the ethical offerings of the arts do not always penetrate the breasts of their
intended recipients.

Herbert's poems addressing kingship go considerably beyond these ca-
veats. In 'Praise (1)', 'Man is all weakness; there is no such thing / As
Prince or King'. In 'Peace' the speaker looks for 'Sweet Peace' in all the
wrong places, including the court:

> Then went I to a garden, and did spy
>   A gallant flower,
>   The Crown Imperial: Sure, said I,
>   Peace at the root must dwell.
> But when I digged, I saw a worm devour
>   What showed so well.

The 'Crowne Imperiall', according to John Gerard's *Herball*, is a lily of
great beauty, but 'The whole plants as well rootes as flowers do sauour or
smell verie loathsomly like the fox'. As if addressing a warning to would-
be courtiers seeking employment. Gerard adds, 'The vertues of this admir-

able plant is not yet knowne, neither his faculties or temperature in work-ing'.[19]

In 'Submission' Herbert renounces a disappointed quest for secular 'place and power' as a base for sacred praise; but perhaps it was not this denial, but his vocation as, and in, God's consort that turned him poet-priest, praising in 'Praise (2)' the 'King of Glory, King of Peace' who has heard and spared him:

> Wherefore with my utmost art
>   I will sing thee,
> And the cream of all my heart
>   I will bring thee.

Within the fabric and among the lights of the chapel Herbert found a better dwelling-place than the secular court: the music that also fills his poems. In 'Church-Music', after, perhaps, contemplating in the windows the life, trial, and death of the 'King of grief' and 'King of wounds' ('The Thanksgiv-ing') who became 'King of Glory, King of Peace', and after meanwhile being carried to heaven's door on music's wings by the chapel choir, Her-bert thanks this 'Sweetest of sweets' because 'when displeasure / Did through my body wound my mind, / You took me thence, and in your house of pleasure / A dainty lodging me assigned'. Rescuing him from bodily and political pain, music frees him to enter and soar: 'Now I in you without a body move, / Rising and falling with your wings'. The stanza's rhythms imitate the wings' motion, but come back to earth to pray for the peace of the rest of the world by praying for its rulers: Herbert and church music 'both together sweetly live and love, / Yet say sometimes, *God help poor Kings*'.[20]

What music did he hear there? Some of it is collected in the manuscript identified by Thurston Dart as belonging to Henry Loosemore,[21] organist at King's College Chapel from 1627, and in manuscripts from Ely Cathe-dral.[22] These include Loosemore's setting of Herbert's 'Antiphon (1)', 'Let all the world in ev'ry corner sing' and other works probably composed in the 1630s, as well as earlier works from a choral tradition going back to the mid-sixteenth century. Both manuscripts contain works by Tallis and Byrd, whose published works Herbert probably sang himself; Orlando Gibbons, organist at King's until 1606 and of the Chapel Royal until 1625; Edmund Hooper, organist of Westminster Abbey while Herbert was at Westminster School; Thomas Tomkins, Hooper's successor as organist of King James's Chapel; and local composers, notably John Amner, organist of Ely from 1610-1642. Several of these anthems honour royalty, including Byrd's and

Child's settings of prayers for the sovereign, Tomkins' 'Prince Henryes Funerall Anthem', Weelkes' 'O Lord Grant the King a long life', and Child's 'Give the King thy judgments';[23] others praise God as true King, such as Tomkins' and Childs' 'Thou art my king O God', and Amner's 'O God my king'.[24]

The King's, Ely, and Peterhouse manuscripts all contain Orlando Gibbons, 'Glorious and powerful God'[25], a verse anthem for countertenor and bass with five-part choir and organ. Like Tomkins' 'Hymne', the anthem uses not a Scriptural text but an anonymous poem that touches on the themes of the Chapel architecture and windows and of Herbert's *The Temple*, especially 'The Altar':

> Glorious and powerful God, we understand
> > Thy dwelling is on high,
> > Above the starry sky.
> Thou dwell'st not in stone temples made with hands,
> But in the flesh hearts of the sons of men
> > To dwell is thy delight,
> > Near hand though out of sight.
>
> We give of thine own hand, thy acceptation
> > Is very life and blood
> > To all actions good:
>
> Whenever here or hence our supplication
> From pure and unfeigned hearts to thee ascend,
> > Be present with thy grace,
> > Show us thy loving face.
> O down on us full showers of mercy send;
> > Let thy love's burning beams
> > Dry up all our sins' streams.
> Arise, O Lord, and come into thy rest.

The text seems, also, an Anglican answer to the controversy that led to the iconoclasms of the 1640's—'we understand ... Thou dwell'st not in stone temples made with hands'—as well as a response to the Apostles' dismay at the Ascension. In Gibbons' setting the solo voices sing through the words of each verse, producing intelligibility; then the choir repeats some or all of the text in polyphony. Expressive word-painting rises and falls like wings, with both notes and key rising on 'Above the starry sky', ascending organ runs on 'hearts', eighth-notes, or quavers, to enliven delight, descending phrases on 'O down on us fall showers' and upwards ones on 'Arise'. These are integrated in a clean and substantial form, carefully unified in a through-composed anthem that is 'all symmetry, / Full of proportions', suitable for God's stately habitations 'here or hence'.

Herbert is of course strongly conscious, like Gibbons, that God dwells 'not in stone temples made with hands', however fine, but in 'flesh hearts' on earth and 'Above the starry sky' in the 'endless habitation' of which Christ is 'Founder and foundation'. In Herbert's 'Sion', Solomon's Temple is the type of the temple of the heart, and the glory of outward edifices is of value only insofar as it may aid inward edification and regeneration. In Solomon's temple, as in the choir of King's, 'the wood was all embellished', and everything 'showed the builder's, craved the seer's care'. Words like 'flourished', 'brass', 'embellished', and 'pomp' fill this temple, C.A. Patrides suggests, with 'musical overtones'.[26] Demonstrating the proportions of harmony,[27] King's College Chapel resembles Solomon's Temple in several particulars specified in the First Book of Kings: made of stone 'brought hither', with 'windows of narrow lights', 'chambers round about, against the wall of the house', and 'without in the wall of the house ... narrowed rests ... that the beams should not be fastened in the walls' (1 Kings 6). But this temple of 'the olde lawe' with its 'pomp and state', Herbert says, 'sowed debate'—like the church-music controversies of the Reformation—and God found out a remedy: 'now thy Architecture meets with sin; / For all thy frame and fabric is within'. There, life is a struggle between God and a 'peevish heart', with the object of the battle to extract 'one good groan' more dear than 'All Solomon's sea of brass and world of stone'. And here Herbert generously dismisses artful fabrics and musics, including by implication his poems, as worthless by comparison with a contrite heart:

> And truly brass and stones are heavy things,
> Tombs for the dead, not temples fit for thee:
> > But groans are quick, and full of wings,
> > And all their motions upward be;
> And ever as they mount, like larks they sing;
> The note is sad, yet music for a king.

There is comfort for an afflicted conscience in the thought that groans of shame and sorrow mount like larks, singing as they rise, however heavy they may feel, and that repentance is the music that best pleases God's ears. God's music[28] is a consort into which all hearts, common, noble, even royal, of commingled classes and sexes, may join. Yet the poem, for all its dismissal of outward frames, is itself a temple, a carefully constructed fabric in rectangular form having the same number of lines as the chapel has bays, and is filled with verbal music that expresses and can extract from the hearer those groans that are far more precious than it—and so give it incalculable value. Similarly, not by itself, but as suitable binding for the gatherings of hearts that groan and rejoice together in it, King's College Chapel and its music participate in the calling that Herbert's poems proclaim and perform: 'Let all the world in ev'ry corner sing, / *My God and King*'. In those poems, all *his* lights combine to form portable—and sometimes self-iconoclastic—chapels of the architecture, story, and music of language.

Notes

1   Trinity College MS R. 16.29.

2   John Dowland, *The First Book of Songes or Ayers of fowre partes with tableture for the Lute* (1597, 1600, 1603, 1613). In *English Lute-Songs,* edited by Edmund H. Fellowes, rev. Thurston Dart, series I, vols 1-2 (London: Stainer & Bell, 1965), 22.

3   MS has 'kindly'. I have also supplied lineation and punctuation for the first verse.

4   *Thomas Tomkins: Musica Deo Sacra II*, edited by Bernard Rose, in *Early English Church Music*, gen. ed. Frank L. Harrison (London: Stainer & Bell, n.d.), 9: 24-33. Liturgical sources include the 'Batten' Organ Book (c. 1630), the Durham cathedral partbooks (c. 1620-70), and York Minster MS M. 29 (s), 1640. Its date of composition is unknown—the absence of a manuscript before 1620 proves nothing, however, since few earlier seventeenth-century church music manuscripts have been preserved—and I offer it only as an analogue.

5   # 73 in the Williams MS. C.A. Patrides points out the similarity to the anonymous text of 'Come away, come sweet love' in his edition of *The English Poems of George Herbert* (London: Dent, 1974), 212n.

6   James Heywood and Thomas Wright, *Cambridge University Transactions during the Puritan Controversies of the 16th and 17th Centuries* (London: Henry G. Bohn), 2: 276.

7   In addition to settings of the Song of Solomon, in *Hosanna to the Son of David*, set by Orlando Gibbons and by Thomas Weelkes, 'the Son of David' is, historically, King Solomon, typologically and genealogically Christ, and by application James I.

8   Hilary Wayment, *The Windows of King's College Chapel, Cambridge*, in *Corpus Vitrearum Medii Aevi, Great Britain,* supplementary volume 1.9.

9   Tomkins, 'Be strong, and of a good courage', in *Thomas Tomkins, Musica Deo Sacra VI*, edited by Bernard Rose, in *Early English Church Music* 39 (London: Stainer & Bell, 1992), 24-41.

10   Richard Hooker, *Of the Lawes of Ecclesiastical Polity* 5.24, edited by Georges Edelen, in *The Folger Library Edition of the Works of Richard Hooker*, gen ed. W.

Speed Hill (Cambridge, MA & London: The Belknap Press of Harvard UP, 1977), 2: 114.

11   Wayment, *King's College Chapel*, p. 9.

12   *Sermons with some religious and diuine meditations. By the Right reuerend Father in God, Arthur Lake, late Lord Bishop of Bath and Wells* (London, 1629), 224.

13   Frances Bacon, 'Of Truth', in *The Essayes or Counsels, civill and Moral*, edited with introduction and commentary by Michael Kiernan (Cambridge, MA: Harvard UP, 1985), 7.

14   *I[esus] N[azarenus] R[ex] I[udaeorum].*

15   The second Responsory for Holy Saturday in the Roman and Sarum rites, '*O vos omnes, qui transitis per viam, attendite et videte si est dolor similis sicut dolor meus*', is taken from Lam. 1: 12: '... all ye that pass by ... behold, and see if there be any sorrow like unto my sorrow'. The Good Friday Reproaches, derived from the Lamentations on which Herbert's poem meditates, were not included in the Book of Common Prayer, but portions or versions of the Holy Week Responsories were set by many English composers including Robert White, Tallis and Byrd in Latin, and Ferrabosco, Hooper, Amner, and John Milton the Elder in English.

16   Herbert's oration for Prince Charles (later Charles I) in 1623 commends what Amy M. Charles in *A Life of George Herbert* (Ithaca: Cornell UP, 1977), 100, calls 'a supposed desire of the Prince's for peace. In full knowledge that Charles and Buckingham has returned home [from Spain] determined on war, Herbert courageously extolled the blessing of peace'.

17   Donne, *Satyre III*, quoted from John T. Shawcross, ed., *The Complete Poetry of John Donne* (New York: Anchor Books, 1967), 26.

18   Claudio Monteverdi's *Magnificat a sei voce* (1609) puts a swagger and a bit of processional music into '*Deposuit potentes de sede*'.

19   Gerard, *The Herball or Generall historie of Plantes* (1597), 1: 53-54. My thanks to Jeremy Maule for calling my attention to this emblematic flower.

20   'The Thanksgiving' and 'Church-Music' are both in *W*.

21   New York, Drexel MS 5469. Part of this MS is missing, the dates of particular pieces uncertain, and the attribution based partly on the signature 'Edward Tuck Chorister of Kings Colledge 1729' in a later hand on pages 38 and 104; but its 227 pages give a fair idea of the kind of music sung at King's during Herbert's, Milton's, and Marvell's residences in Cambridge. See Thurston Dart, 'Henry Loosemore's Organ Book', in *Transactions of the Cambridge Bibliographical Society*, Vol. 3 #2 (1960).

22   Cambridge University Library, Ely MSS 1, 4, 28-29 (two organ books, tenor and bass part books), 'possibly containing fragments of pre-Restoration books' according to Peter le Huray, *Music and the Reformation in England, 1549-1660* (Cambridge: Cambridge UP, 1978), 95; these manuscripts record a long musical tradition at Ely.

23   Also set by Weelkes. The words are 'Give the king thy judgments, O God, and thy righteousness, and look upon the face of thine anointed. Let the words of his mouth and the meditations of his heart be always acceptable in thy sight, O Lord, our strength and our redeemer'.

24   From Ps. 145. Anthems for 5 November, commemorating the Gunpowder Plot, might also fall into the category of national anthems, such as Hooper's 'Harken yee nations' in the Drexel MS and Weelkes' 'O Lord how joyful is the king', with a vengeful text celebrating the defeat of the plot: *Weelkes: Collected Anthems*, Walter Collins and Peter le Huray, eds, in *Musica Britannica* 23 (London: Stainer & Bell, 1966).

25   *Orlando Gibbons I: Verse Anthems*, edited by David Wulstan, in *Early English Church Music* (London, Stainer & Bell, 1962), 3: 52-67.

26   Patrides, *The English Poems of George Herbert*, p. 129n.

27   E.g. Martin Mersenne, *Harmonie Universelle* (1636), Book 2.

28   A 'musick' was an ensemble of musicians.

4

FROM VENUS TO VIRTUE:
SACRED PARODY AND GEORGE HERBERT

JOHN OTTENHOFF

Sacred parody—the adaptation of secular verse to religious use—obviously has an important position in the 'interplay' of sacred and profane literature. Yet parody often seems to perplex us—especially as we approach George Herbert's art—for it resists clear definition, raises uncomfortable spectres of zealous religious activity, and threatens to plunge our high-minded discussions of devotional art into the realms of abysmal subliterature. Such prejudices have some grounds, but the problems of parody also offer rewards in thinking about the interplay of sacred and profane and in better understanding the importance of sixteenth-century forerunners to Herbert and Donne. And while other devotional forms—biblical paraphrases and Psalm translations in particular—were vastly more important to a developing English devotional tradition, the elusive phenomenon of sacred parody merits some attention.

Parody, of course, flourished throughout the sixteenth century, gaining impetus from the Protestant Reformation, especially Reformed hymnology.[1] The central position of the Word for Luther and Calvin presented a powerful argument for poetry with religious subjects, and injunctions for transforming the secular world naturally led the Reformers to appropriate popular tunes and ballads for religious use. *Transformation* is an important concept, for it suggests the need to be in the world actively engaging the products of the world. Transformation requires knowledge, understanding, even appreciation for what is to be transformed. Yet such practice has been easily dismissed. Joseph Ritson, an early editor of songs and ballads, speaks of this as 'a foolish practice ... introduced by the puritan reformers, of moralising, as they called it, popular songs; that is, parodying all but a few lines at the beginning of the song, to favour their particular superstition ...'.[2]

While Protestantism lies behind important collections of parodies in the *Gude and Godly Ballatis* (*GGB*) and John Hall's *The Court of Virtue* (*CV*) (opposing, of course, the *Court of Venus*), the phenomenon also appears well before the Reformation—in such English collections as the *Harley Lyrics* and interesting parodies such as 'The New Notbrowne Mayd upon the Passion of Cryste' (published c. 1502).[3] The phenomenon is also well used by Counter-Reformation poets such as Robert Southwell, as Louis

Martz has vigorously established.[4] Sacred parody, then, seems both nondenominational and widespread but also very timely and pointed, a particular manifestation of certain theological positions. And parody could go both ways: this vigorous intertextuality embraced movement from sacred originals to secular parodies as well as from secular to sacred.[5]

Clearly delineating sacred parody—any kind of Renaissance parody, really—is not easy, for 'the boundary lines between someone else's speech and one's own speech were flexible, ambiguous, often deliberately distorted and confused'.[6] Similarly, songs and ballads were freely and easily interchangeable; 'all kinds of permutations' occurred for many songs.[7] The sixteenth-century poet, borrowing freely, could closely imitate the style or appropriate the substance of another work without intending to ridicule or without suffering from the charge of lacking originality. Further, as several commentators have pointed out, the definition of *parody* presents many problems. William Keach, for instance, claims

> whether the Elizabethans had a developed theoretical concept of parody or not is questionable. The word is not recorded until 1607. ... In any case 'parody' is not taken up in Elizabethan theoretical treatments of imitation, a fact which may account for its absence from most modern discussion of Elizabethan literary imitation. Yet we all know that the Elizabethans were exuberant and accomplished masters of verbal parody, particularly in drama. When one thinks about it, in fact, no other form of imitation seems quite so well suited to the Elizabethan taste for verbal ingenuity.[8]

But despite the popularity and ubiquity of the sacred parody, our accounts of it remain rather sketchy. The two most influential positions are extremes. On the one hand, Lily Bess Campbell and others have assigned a crucial place to sacred parody in what they see as a concerted effort to *displace* love poetry. For Campbell, sacred parody was an important weapon in the campaign 'to substitute divine poetry for ... secular poetry' and to compete with the chronicles of love. Campbell describes a tradition that extends throughout the sixteenth century to Donne, Herbert, and Milton, consisting primarily of opposition to secular poetry.[9] Rosemond Tuve, on the other hand, in writing about George Herbert's 'A Parody', finds little reason to associate Herbert with parodic literature she characterizes as crude and fanatical and argues for 'a long history of formal imitation and exchange, unselfconscious and ordinary, provocative neither of ambiguities nor ironies'.[10] Similarly, Thomas Roche hopes to 'offset that hideous dichotomy of sacred versus secular that hounds our reading of Medieval and Renaissance literature'[11] and finds specifically in the religious sonnet tradition no tension or displacement; Roche describes a continuum that makes no essential distinction between secular and sacred love.

Surveying the full range of sixteenth-century sacred parodies obviously lies beyond the scope of this paper. Instead, I wish only to investigate two major threads concerning the interplay of sacred and secular. First, in considering sacred parodies, I argue that we can find considerably more than mere combat and, frankly, some mixed signals about the usefulness of the sacred/secular dichotomy. Even in works such as the *GGB* and *CV*, where zealous attacks on the secular do occur, we can find complexities in the relationship and *devotion*, rather than simply zealous arm twisting. But I also wish to question whether we can leave George Herbert so completely out of this 'mess' and carve out a special place for him, as Tuve does. Finally, I think, we must admit that whether we find 'neutral' parodies, obsessive religious combat, or something else, depends a whole lot on what we are looking for. Readers' responses, often left out of the discussion about sacred parody, might be seen as very close to the heart of the matter.

As I have already suggested, we must take more care in assessing the contexts and precedents of sacred parody that Herbert might have had before him. In looking at the variety of sixteenth-century parodies, we find much that does not fall into the stereotyped opposites of neutral or combative imitation. For instance, the parodic 'New Notbroune Mayd upon the Passion of Cryste' presents some interesting commentary upon the original poem without explicitly correcting its moral stance.

While the parodist of the 'Nutbrown Maid' used the original chiefly as a formal model for his devotional tribute to Christ, he also engages in some subtle commentary on the original poem, honoring Christ, the saviour 'banished' for mankind. Clearly, the 'New Notbroune Maide' achieves a certain devotional effectiveness as a parody. In its elaborate echoings of its original and in its complex relationships of meaning, the parody of the 'Nutbrown Maid' appears unusual in the sixteenth century. A much more common phenomenon among the sacred parodies is the taking over of popular songs, either by adaptation of part of the lyrics or by simple appropriation of the music. Poets easily disregarded a song's lyrics and substituted their own to create a 'moralization' or a courtly version (Stevens, p. 53). While much could be said about these adaptions, we shall simply note that in the songs lie further examples of parodies that are neither wholly neutral nor harshly correcting.

Many explicit statements can be found in the sixteenth century whereby poets vow to reform corrupt secular poetry and turn it to God's service. Among the more interesting of those efforts is the Scottish *GGB*, which also offer many examples of extreme, polemical parodies that set out Reformed doctrine. One of the more interesting parodies consciously corrects a love poem in the Scottish Bannatyne MS with a moralistic fervour quite indicative of combat with secular forces. Among the parodies is 'Ane Dissuasioun from Vaine Lust', which turns a good-natured appeal for license in the original, 'Was nocht Gud King Salamon', into a rather stern warning against the miseries brought on by women.

Was nocht gud king Salamon
Revisit in sindry wyiss,
With every lufely paragon,
Glistering befoir his eis?
Gif this be trew, trew as it wass,
    lady, lady,
Suld nocht I scherwe yow, allace,
    my fair lady?
            (*Bannatyne*, 1-6)

Was not Salomon, the King
    To miserie be wemen brocht?
Quhilk wisdome out of frame did bring,
Till he maist wickitly had wrought.
A thousand wemen he did keip,
    Allace, allace!
Quhilk drownit him in Sin sa deip,
As come to pas.
            (*GGB*, 1-8)

The parodist follows quite closely, stanza by stanza, the examples of the original poem, transforming them, of course, to tell of the misery incurred by Paris, Troilus, Ovid, Pyramus, Hercules and others. Following some 'Exemplis takin out of the Bybill', the final stanza, unparalleled in the original, seems an explicit attempt at turning from the poetry of Venus to a Christian example and aesthetic:

Of him lat us exempill tak,
And never think on Cupides dart:
Venus can nouther mar nor mak,
Gif unto God we joyne our hart;
And leif this art of langing lust,
    Allace, Allace!
And in the Lord baith hope and trust,
    Quhilk is and was.
        (*GGB*, 176-184)

Yet even *GGB* do not consist exclusively of this kind of zealous competition with secular literature. The preface to the volume, for example, applies some of that fervour and encouragement to Protestant hymn singing, but also registers a concern for more neutral religious literature. While *GGB* represent one of the clearest sources of tension between secular and sacred, they also demonstrate the possible complexity of that relationship.

A similar observation holds for what is perhaps the most sustained and strident English attack against secular poetry, John Hall's *CV* (1565).[12] Campbell terms *CV* the 'antibody' to the secular forerunner (*Divine Poetry* 47). But, as Fraser points out, *CV* 'is not based on *The Court of Venus* nor does it levy on that work specifically, beyond the redacting of a few poems' (Fraser, p. xviii).

Hall makes his complaint most pointedly in a section of the prefatory 'dream epistle':

> Suche as in carnall love rejoyce,
> Trim songes of love they wyll compile,
> And synfully with tune and voyce
> They syng their songes in pleasant stile,
> To Venus that same strompet vyle:
> And make of hir a goddes dere,
> In lecherie that had no pere.

> A booke also of songes they have,
> And Venus court they doe it name.
> No fylthy mynde a songe can crave,
> But therin he may finde the same:
> And in such songes is all their game.
> Wherof ryght dyvers bookes be made,
> To nuryshe that moste fylthy trade.

These lines from the prologue represent Hall in his most vociferous voice, yet the combat against the forces of secular verse in his collection remains limited. Like *GGB*, *CV* collects many different kinds of poems, including redactions of Psalms, verses on various books of the Bible, invectives against pride, envy, and other vices, complaints, jeremiads, and redactions of popular songs and poems. The parodies best known—three parodies of Thomas Wyatt—do not represent a major part of the collection, but they mark the clearest connection between the secular and sacred in Hall's verse.[13]

Hall's three parodies of Wyatt follow the same general pattern: they do not closely imitate the original or overtly comment upon it, but usually appropriate only a few lines. Hall generally turns to a different subject rather than to close imitation or travesty. His parodies contribute to a 'new Christian aesthetic', in Campbell's terms, only by combining an oblique commentary upon the original with parody of certain stylistic elements. The pattern is seen in Hall's parody of Wyatt's 'My pen, Take Payn a Lytyll

Space', retitled 'A Dittie of the Pen Inveiyng Against Usury and False
Dealyng' as well as his restyling of Wyatt's 'My Lute Awake' as 'A Song
of the Lute in the Prayse of God, and Disprayse of Idolatrie'. Although
these parodies are concerned with providing an alternative to the love
poetry of Wyatt and others who write in 'Venus' service', they do not constitute much of a problematic comment upon the original secular poem.
Wyatt provides a focus of attention but is quickly pushed aside.[14]

The most interesting of the Hall parodies, 'A Ditie Named Blame Not
My Lute, whiche under that title toucheth, replieth, and rebuketh, the
wycked state and enormities of most people, in these present miserable
dayes', largely follows the pattern evident in the other parodies. The most
pointed remark on Wyatt's poem comes in the first stanza:

BLAME not my lute for he must sownde	Blame not my lute though it do sounde
Of thes or that as liketh me;	The rebuke of your wicked sinne,
For lake of wytt the lutte is bownde	But rather seke as ye are bound to know
To gyve suche tunes as plesithe me:	What case that ye are in:
Tho my songes be sume what strange,	And though this song doe sinne
	confute,
And spekes suche wordes as toche thy	And sharply wyckednes rebuke:
change,	
Blame not my lutte.	Blame not my lute.
(Wyatt, 1-7)	(Hall, 1-7)

But Hall continues his comment on love poetry generally and Wyatt's poem
particularly in the second stanza, where he repeats Wyatt's rhyme of
'offende'/'intende' and amplifies Wyatt's tone of defensiveness. While
exhibiting a distinct lack of grace in his constrained word choice—showing
the obvious limitations of parody—Hall asks his reader to accept with
'grace' the 'truth' of his work:

My lutte, alas, doth not ofende,	My lute and I sythe truth we tell,
Tho that perforus he must agre	(Meanyng no good man to offende)
To sownde suche teunes as I entende	My thynke of ryght none should refell
To sing to them that hereth me;	The godlynes that we intend:
Then tho my songes be some what	But muche rather if they have grace,
plain,	
And tochethe some that vse to fayn,	They will our good counsell imbrace,
Blame not my lute.	Then blame my lute.
(Wyatt, 8-14)	(Hall, 8-14)

Hall does not continue this kind of close imitation throughout his sixteen-
stanza parody of Wyatt's six-stanza poem; he focuses instead on his own

preoccupation with replacing vice with 'truth'. Wyatt largely remains a
starting point for Hall's excursion into the poetry of Virtue.

John N. King dismisses Hall's 'unsophisticated literalism' which 'leads
him into serious misreading of Wyatt. The courtly habit of experimentation
with varied *personae* eludes him; ... the fine ironies of these poems and the
ideal of fidelity that they assume are closer to Hall's ideological position
than he could ever realize' (King, pp. 227-228). Indeed, little sophistication
emerges in Hall's work, and one must also acknowledge that he offers little
in the way of 'redeeming' love poetry that would be of much use to a poet
like Herbert. Hall's work, seemingly at the extreme edge of 'combative'
sacred parody, raises doubts about theories that place such literature in the
mainstream tradition that leads to the flowering of devotional lyrics in the
seventeenth century. But Hall also demonstrates at least a measure of interesting poetic sensibility, especially in his identity with Wyatt's speaker, and
suggests that *combat* may not be as central here as an interesting form of
dialogue between texts.

As I have noted, Rosemond Tuve has most strongly opposed the notion
that George Herbert's parody of secular lyrics necessarily introduced conflict between the secular and sacred. Tuve identifies a 'neutral' form of
parody in George Herbert's poem 'A Parody', adapted from a secular lyric
attributed to William Herbert, the third Earl of Pembroke. Herbert's poem
closely imitates Pembroke's original, particularly in the first twelve lines:

Soul's joy, now I am gone,	Soul's joy, when thou art gone,
And you alone,	And I alone,
(Which cannot be,	Which cannot be,
Since I must leave my selfe with thee,	Because thou dost abide with me,
And carry thee with me)	And I depend on thee;
Yet when unto our eyes	
Absence denies	Yet when thou dost suppress
Each other's sight,	The cheerfulness
And makes to us a constant night,	Of thy abode,
When others change to light;	And in my powers not stir abroad,
O give no way to grief,	But leave me to my load:
But let belief ...	
	O what a damp and shade
	Doth me invade!
(Pembroke, 1-12)	(Herbert, 1-12)

Tuve describes Herbert's parody as largely formal and rooted in musical
practice. She strives throughout her essay to prove that Herbert's parody
does not fix on the 'sense and intent of the original author upon which his

imitation constitutes a comment' and does not intend 'sidewise' derogatory comments on the ideas and themes of Pembroke's poem' (Tuve, p. 210). Her reading has been largely uncontested.[15] For example, Richard Strier, who offers perhaps the most extensive commentary on Herbert's 'A Parody', claims 'As Tuve has shown, Herbert's poem is intended to "parody" the earl's only in a specific musical sense'.[16] But Tuve's description of Herbert's parodic technique raises several questions about this phenomenon and runs into some serious problems, especially in light of changing critical assumptions.

Tuve in effect makes Herbert's parody *sui generis*. Unlike other poems described in the seventeenth century as 'parody', his intends no 'sidewise derogatory comments on the ideas and theme of Pembroke's poem' (Tuve, p. 210). And while it bears resemblance to the widespread practice of substituting sacred for secular lyrics, Tuve refuses to make the link:

> ... Herbert in turning secular arts to sacred purposes and specifically in
> writing 'parody' is doing something many generations of men had
> done before him, and yet ... this is not evidence for thinking either that
> he must share the intentions of the puritan reformers or must resemble
> in style the pious parodists (Tuve, p. 247).

Tuve clearly argues for her definition of parody to counter those who find a line from sixteenth-century religious parodies to Herbert in the 'turning' of the poetry of Venus to godly poetry. In roundly criticizing the search for 'baroque dubieties' in that transformation, she insists that Herbert's poem is a special case of neutral sacred parody. Perhaps because of her interest in linking Herbert to the medieval religious tradition, Tuve has no desire to associate him with the largely Reformation phenomenon of sacred parody —she presents his neutral religious parody as the alternative to fanatical and unpoetical reforming. As she puts the matter, 'Surely it somehow lessens Herbert as a poet to conceive of him as nervously and tensely anxious to convert whatever hinted at the power and interest of love between human beings to pious uses' (Tuve, p. 231). Tuve is no more willing to associate Herbert with the Counter Reformation and is especially critical of Louis Martz, who claims that Robert Southwell's 'campaign to convert the poetry of profane love into poetry of divine love' had a strong impact upon seventeenth-century poetry (Tuve, p. 184).[17]

Tuve's caution against eagerly finding 'ambiguities' and 'dubieties' in the Renaissance treatment of religion certainly merits attention. Secular and sacred surely could exist side by side without a great deal of tension. Moreover, Tuve properly corrects Martz's rather narrow view of the art of par-

ody as having its genesis in Southwell's aesthetic of the Counter Reformation. As she points out, the Reformation, rather than the Counter Reformation, accounts for most of the sacred parodies written in the sixteenth century. But Tuve's attempt to 'protect' Herbert from the 'cheapening' evangelical pitch of parodies depends upon a peculiar reading of the parodic
context preceding Herbert and of parody in general. It seems to preclude
recognition of possible *devotional* contributions—rather than reforming
impulses—in the religious parodies. Presumably, Herbert had a *religious*
purpose in altering Pembroke's lyric into the praise of God. For Herbert, as
for the other parodists, that purpose would not have to be as extreme as the
'nervous and tense' impulses that Tuve represents as the alternative to 'neu-
trality'. The alternative to parodies that make no comment on the original
poem need not be 'baroque dubieties' or 'ironic dissonances' or reforming
substitutes.

Thomas Merrill suggests one way of thinking about that relationship:
'Such a neutral definition (innocent of intended travesty) encourages a
popular notion that a profane love lyric can be rendered a "righte chanel" to
the Divine through a simple substitution of proper names: "God" or "lord"
for "Stella"'. But, claims Merrill, such a view assumes that 'devotional
utterances and expressions of human love share a common logic and a
common language' when in fact they do not. 'The point is that the sheer
presence of "God", implicitly or explicitly felt within a linguistic context,
radically changes the semantic terrain; it literally tyrannizes the structure of
the discourse into which it is introduced'.[18]

Such a view of language presents a challenge to Tuve's position that
'neutral' parody is possible and present. Similarly, recent views of parody
as a form of intertextuality raise significant issues. As Vincent Crapanzano,
quoting Linda Hutcheon, suggests, parody 'is a perfect postmodern form, in
some senses, for it paradoxically both incorporates and challenges that
which it parodies'.[19] In Bakhtin's terms, parody as 'double-voiced words'
always involves some act of appropriation: 'The words of one speaker are
appropriated by a second speaker as the words of the first speaker but used
for the second speaker's own purposes "by inserting a new semantic orientation into a word which already has—and retains—its own orientation"'
(Crapanzo, p. 437). Words are *recontextualized* in the parody, an act that
can perhaps be free of ridicule or correction but not free of significance.
'Parody is essentially hierarchical. It dominates its target' (Crapanzo, p.
437). No matter what Herbert's motives might have been, one might argue
that the parodic form itself offers commentary about the replacement of
secular language with sacred.

Tuve's confident assertions about Herbert's parody also reveal problematic assumptions about the poet's motives and reader's methods. Quite simply, Tuve wants to claim that Herbert just didn't go in for this kind of stuff. She dismisses the most frequently cited evidence for Herbert's interest in opposing secular love lyrics—his two early sonnets printed in Walton's *Lives*—youthful mistakes. She claims they are clearly out of character with Herbert's mature work. Yet perhaps the break is not so clear. *The Temple* frequently discomforts its close readers, who question whether the mature Herbert, who clearly has designs upon his readers, truly stands so far from the angry young man. Regarding 'A Parody', one must also express caution in assuming that we can know Herbert's motives. David Bennett's claim is useful here: 'Logically speaking, a parodic reading is either intentionalist or voluntarist: either it presupposes a complicity between the reader and the author in their critical apprehension of the way the parodied discourse misfigures reality, or it is motivated by interests extrinsic to the text for which the reader is accountable'.[20] Can we find such clear signals in the text or elsewhere that we are to find no incongruity in the turning of this lyric into Godly service?

Similarly, parody as 'double voicing' functions 'not simply as the interaction of two speech acts, but as *an interaction designed to be heard and interpreted by a third person ...* whose own process of active reception is anticipated and directed' (Crapanzano, p. 437). As is always the case with parody, one must assume familiarity with the 'target' work in order to assume some resonance. In the case of Herbert's 'A Parody', presumably, the reader recognizes the Pembroke original at the root of Herbert's poem and then comes to some conclusions: Perhaps, as Tuve argues, one essentially dismisses the echo; after all, it is merely a formal, musical echo. But we might also consider a fervent religious reader who welcomes the transformation of a trivial secular poem to God's service (whether or not Herbert intended such a welcoming). And, of course, we must consider a modern uninformed reader who remains unaware of the secular original and whatever interplay, intended or not, may be present.

In short, where Tuve finds an unusual formal, musical echo, I find a significantly more complex set of problems in Herbert's 'A Parody'. Strier suggests that 'the great advantage Herbert has over Pembroke in making use of the you or I "cannot be alone" conceit is that Herbert is able actually to mean what he says' (Strier, p. 241). Similarly, Merrill calls attention to the way Herbert sets up 'a situation in which two rival language games are deliberately brought into collision for the purpose of evoking religious insight' (Merrill, p. 202). Such comments suggest that parody here represents a complex case that includes appropriation, imitation, and correction—all in the service of devotion.

The sacred parodies of the sixteenth century represent to some degree the replacement of secular poetry with religious themes, the combating of 'pagan' ideas with religious ones. But to label most of the age's parodies—and, indeed, of its religious poetry in general—as necessarily in conflict with secular poetry is obviously misleading. Several of the parodies, Herbert's included, forge relationships with their originals that are neither combatively innocent nor neutral; many of them pursue devotional rather than corrective themes. Similarly, close examination of parody as a phenomenon suggests that Tuve's notion of a purely formal parody breaks down, considering the dialogic stance of these texts. The appropriation of secular texts for sacred purposes may not involve the extremes of tense, religious counter-reaction or cool, musical formalism but did involve an interesting and complicated *dialogue* of texts, languages, and sensibilities that ultimately seem as idiosyncratic as the writers creating them and the readers—and intended spiritual audiences—decoding them.

Notes

1   See, for instance, the Preface to Martin Luther's *Songbook* of 1524. See also John N. King, *English Reformation Literature: The Tudor Origins of the Protestant Tradition* (Princeton: Princeton UP, 1982), 45ff, who quotes Erasmus' argument for setting biblical texts to popular tunes: 'Would that ... the farmer sing some portion of them at the plow, the weaver hum some parts of them to the movement of his shuttle, the traveller lighten the weariness of the journey with stories of this kind!'

2   See Ritson, ed., *Ancient Songs from the Time of Henry III to the Revolution* (London: J. Johnson, 1790), lvi.

3   Editions consulted are: A.F. Mitchell, ed., *A Compendius Book of Godly and Spiritual Songs, Commonly Known as the 'Gude and Godly Ballitis'* (1897; rpt. New York: Johnson Reprints, 1966); George Bannatyne, ed., *The Bannatyne Manuscript* (1568), 4 vols (1896; rpt. New York: Johnson Reprints, 1966); W.C. Hazlitt, ed., 'The New Notbroune Mayd upon the Passion of Cryste', in *Remains of the Early Popular Poetry of England*, 4 vols (1866; rpt. New York: Johnson Reprints, 1966), 3: 1-22; and William A. Ringler Jr, ed., '"The Nutbrown Maid": A Reconstructed Text', *ELR* 1 (1971), 27-51. For a background to the later middle ages as a whole, see Rosemary Woolf, *The English Religious Lyric in the Middle Ages* (Oxford: Clarendon P, 1968). (1968).

4   See Louis L. Martz, *The Poetry of Meditation: A Study of English Religious Literature of the Seventeenth Century* (1954; New Haven: Yale UP, 1962).

5   The *Harley Lyrics* (1314-1325) nicely show the interaction of secular and sacred,
     towards the sacred in the companion poems 'The Way of Woman's Love' and
     'The Way of God's Love' but in the opposite direction in a number of bawdy
     appropriations of spiritual language. See G.L. Brook, ed., *The Harley Lyrics: The
     Middle English Lyrics of MS. Harley 2253* (1948; Manchester: Manchester UP,
     1964) and Daniel J. Ransom, *Poets at Play: Irony and Parody in the Harley Lyrics*
     (Norman, OK: Pilgrim Books, 1985). For a different background, see Terence C.
     Cave, *Devotional Poetry in France, c. 1570-1613* (Cambridge: Cambridge UP,
     1969).

6   M.M. Bakhtin, *The Dialogic Imagination: Four Essays*, edited by Michael Hol-
     quist, translated by Caryl Emerson and Michael Holquist (Austin: U of Texas P,
     1981), 69. On the theoretical context see also Margaret A. Rose, *Parody/Meta-
     Fiction* (London: Croom-Helm, 1979).

7   John Stevens, *Music and Poetry in the Early Tudor Court* (London: Methuen,
     1961), 53. For primary texts see, for instance, William Chappell, *Old English
     Popular Music* (London: Chappell & Co., 1893) and Henry Huth, *Ancient Ballads
     and Broadsides Published in England in the Sixteenth Century* (London: Whit-
     tingham & Wilkins, 1867). See further Bruce Wardropper, 'The Religious Conver-
     sion of Profane Poetry', edited by Dale B.J. Randall and George Walton Williams,
     (Durham, NC: Duke UP, 1977), 203-221.

8   William Keach, 'Verbal Borrowing in Elizabethan Poetry: Plagiarism or Parody?',
     Centrum 4 (1976), 22. Keach notes that 'The *OED* tells us incorrectly that Ben
     Jonson uses "parody" in the 1598 version of *Every Man in His Humour*. ... But in
     fact the passage cited by the *OED* does not appear until the revised version of Jon-
     son's play printed in the 1616 folio'. The 1607 citation is from Thomas Walking-
     ton's *The Optic Glasse of Humors*.

9   Lily Bess Campbell, *Divine Poetry and Drama in Sixteenth-Century England*
     (Cambridge: Cambridge UP, 1959), 5, and 'The Christian Muse', *Huntington
     Library Bulletin* 8 (1935), 29.

10   Rosemond Tuve, 'Sacred "Parody" of Love Poetry, and Herbert', rpt. *Essays by
     Rosemond Tuve*, edited by Thomas P. Roche Jr (Princeton: Princeton UP, 1970),
     230. See also Tuve's *A Reading of George Herbert* (Chicago: U of Chicago P &
     London: Faber, 1952).

11   Thomas P. Roche Jr, *Petrarch and the English Sonnet Sequences* (New York:
     AMS, 1989), 154.

12   Hall's *Court* apparently underwent an interesting and even ironic interaction with
     the secular work it attacked. Hall first published in 1550 *The Proverbs of Solomon,
     Three Chapters of Ecclesiasties, The Sixth Chapter of Sapientia, The Ninth Chap-
     ter of Ecclesiasticus, and Certain Psalms of David*. While the preface to this 1550
     edition violently faults the popular collection *The Court of Venus*, Hall's *Certain
     Chapters on Proverbs and Select Psalms* appeared again in *The Psalms of David*, a
     1551 collection which includes the work of Thomas Sternhold, William Hunnis,
     and Sir Thomas Wyatt, himself a contributor to the notorious *Court of Venus*. The
     1550 Preface laments that 'in our myrth it is manifest what our doynges are, for
     our songes are of the Court of Venus, yea, and rather worse'. Hall, too, contrasts
     the secular verses of the *Court of Venus*, 'the whych have bene a greate occasion
     to provoke men to the desyre of synne', with the holy translations of Scripture, in

which 'thou shalt learne to fle from evyl company, from dronckenes & dronkards, from covetousnes & slouthfulnes, from wrathe and envy, from whoredom & all the subtyle behaviours of whores, from pryde, yea & finallye from al wickednes and sinne'; see John Hall, *The Court of Virtue* (1565), edited by Russell A. Fraser (London: Routledge & Kegan Paul, 1961), xii.

13   Quotations are taken from Kenneth Muir, ed., *Collected Poems of Sir Thomas Wyatt* (Cambridge MA: Harvard UP, 1960).

14   For another context see Eugene R. Cunnar, '"Break not them then so wrongfully": Topical Readings of Sir Thomas Wyatt's Riddling and Bewitched Lute and the Feminine Other', *Cithara* 32 (1992), 3-30.

15   But see Anthony Martin's perceptive article 'George Herbert and Sacred "Parody"', forthcoming. Martin concludes that 'A Parody' is a 'tactful correction, a repetition or re-proof which sets something right.'

16   Richard Strier, *Love Known: Theology and Experience in George Herbert's Poetry* (Chicago: U. of Chicago P., 1983), 239.

17   Although the central subject of Martz's study, the adaptation of Counter Reformation meditative techniques in the poetry of Southwell, Donne and Herbert, concerns a form of parody, Martz appeals to Tuve's concept of 'neutral parody' in stating that 'sacred parody of love-poetry plays an essential part in much of Herbert's best work, and points the way to a fundamental relation' between Herbert and Southwell (Martz, pp. 184, 186). But, as Tuve points out, Martz uses 'parody' to refer rather broadly to the use of secular poetic techniques in religious poetry. He does not limit himself to her strict definition of sacred parody which excludes 'sidewise derogatory comments' on the secular original. Moreover, Martz fails to acknowledge the extensive background of parodies before Southwell. Instead he merely speaks of the 'poor estate of English religious poetry which hobbled about in wornout garb' prior to Southwell (Martz, p. 180). See also Rosemary Freeman, 'Parody as a Literary Form: George Herbert and Wilfred Owen', *EC* 13 (1963), 307-322.

18   Thomas F. Merrill, 'Sacred Parody and the Grammar of Devotion', *Criticism* 23 (1981), 197.

19   Vincent Crapanzano, 'The Postmodern Crisis: Discourse, Parody, Memory', *Cultural Anthropology* 6 (1991), 436.

20   David Bennett, 'Parody, Postmodernism, and the Politics of Reading, *CQ* 27 (1985), 30.

'SWEET PHRASES, LOVELY METAPHORS': HERBERT'S LANGUAGE

5

GEORGE HERBERT'S LANGUAGE OF CANAAN

ROBERT CUMMINGS

The expression I appeal to is ultimately Isaiah's (Isa. 19: 18), when he threatens that Egypt will come to speak the language of Canaan, of the 'low country' as an unlikely etymology has it. By this expression Isaiah means Hebrew, but we mean by it the language of heaven as against that of the world. It is the language we speak when we have crossed a metaphorical Jordan. The Dutch may be more comfortable with the expression that the English, no doubt because the Hebraic analogy runs deeper and wider in their culture.[1] The English cannot quite imagine their own language is a holy language, though exceptionally it may become so. Herbert himself did not confidently inhabit the further side of the Jordan:

> I did toward Canaan draw; but now I am
> Brought back to the Red Sea, the sea of shame.
>
> 'The Bunch of Grapes'

Canaanite English is something very different from plain English, and beyond merely human eloquence. The ideal language of the preacher has, as Herbert puts it, a 'Character, that Hermogenes never dream'd of' (Hutchinson, p. 233). He never calls it Canaanite, but some do. The language of preachers is ideally 'not only the language of Canaan, but also the masculous Schiboleth: their words have weight, and are as goads piercing the hearts of the hearers, and fastening them to God in the Sanctuarie'.[2] The 'masculous Schiboleth', because if we get it wrong, we die. And 'it is impossible for a man of an unsalted heart, so to counterfeit the language of Canaan'.[3] That it is not the language of everyday makes it in various ways an unavailable language. The language of Babel opposes the language of Canaan. 'Go to', says the Lord when those that dwelt in the land of Shinar had built their tower (Gen. 11: 7), 'let us go down and there confound their language, that they may not understand one another's speech.' We on the wrong side of this linguistic catastrophe may take the language of Canaan for babble. And indeed it is not from Isaiah but from Bunyan that this paper's title is immediately taken. When Christian and Faithful enter Vanity Fair, there is a great hubbub. For several reasons, says Bunyan—because their clothes were odd, or because they took no interest in what was for sale—but here relevantly because 'few could understand what they said; they naturally spoke the language of Canaan'.[4]

The darkness of Scripture is variously rated: it is where the lamb and the elephant can both swim.[5] It is at the same time to most eyes accessible and impenetrable.[6] But its rhetorical oddity is everywhere apparent, not just in prophetical writing (repetitious, oriental, opaque, 'stammering'), but even in evangelical writing (oblique, discontinuous, doubtfully grammatical).[7] When Jesus says, 'Before Abraham was, I am' (John 8: 58), he offers little enlightenment. 'It is an excellent observation which hath been made upon the answers of our Saviour Christ to many of the questions which were propounded to Him,' says Bacon, 'how they appear impertinent to the state of the question demanded'.[8] This general rhetorical oddity is actually exacerbated in the English of the AV. Partly against their declared ambitions the attention of the translators seems set to duplicate not the sense but the texture of their original. Selden commends this Hebraism in the resulting version, its apparently unpopular refusals of ordinary English. 'If I translate a *French* Book into *English*,' says Selden, 'I turn it into *English* Phrase, not into *French English*. I say 'tis cold, not, it makes cold, but the Bible is rather translated into *English* Words, than into *English* Phrase. The Hebraisms are kept, and the Phrase of that Language is kept'.[9] It is an idiom intelligible to those familiar with the language of Canaan in its strict and ordinary sense, those who know Hebrew; 'but when it comes among the Common People, Lord, what Gear do they make of it!'

Herbert's language is not conspicuously deformed, and the consensus is surely right that commends the purity of his diction. His poetic etiquette is predominantly Jonsonian. It is 'the perfect well-bred gentleman', says Coleridge, that supplies 'the expressions and the arrangement' of his poetry.[10] Yet Rosalie Colie seems to me right when she says that the experience of reading Herbert is like that if reading a language where one is familiar or half-familiar with the roots, and nothing else:

> One knows that the arrangement of words forms a poem, recognises just enough of the cognate words to suspect that the poem is good, but in the end one is forced to recognise the brute fact that one doesn't know the language.[11]

Colie says it's like reading Swedish. And Coleridge, who thinks rightly that Herbert is an English gentleman, gives nice testimony of this in his notes on the poet. Having announced that Herbert is unintelligible to all but devout and devotional sons of the Church (of England, he means), Coleridge decorates his margins with such commentary as 'I do not understand this stanza', 'I understand this but imperfectly', 'Some misprint'.[12] Modern commentary is full of less neat testimony.

Herbert is not a perspicuous poet. I suspect he is not a perspicuous poet even to those who are 'holy, pure, and clear'—the condition he explicitly requires of his proper readers (in 'Superliminare'). But perspicuity is evidently not what he valued in sacred discourse. The instructions to love God and our neighbour, to watch and pray, to do as we would be done by, are only ironically 'dark instructions' ('Divinity'), 'dark as day'. They are only ironically undoable Gordian knots. But the Gordian knot they offer is undone by a gesture as seemingly irrelevant—as impertinent—as Alexander's:

> But he doth bid us take us take his bloud for wine.
>   Bid what he please; yet I am sure,
> To take and taste what he doth there designe,
>   Is all that saves, and not obscure.

Even for sermons Herbert recommends the language not of disputation but devotion.[13] Scripture itself he poetically represents as a night-sky, or as 'dispersed herbs that watch a potion' ('The Holy Scriptures [2]')—this is the phrasing that Coleridge took for a misprint.

In the *Considerations* of Valdesso, Herbert meets the reflection that:

> The unlearned man, that hath the spirit, serveth himselfe of *Images* as of an Alphabet of Christian Pietie ... In like manner a learned man, that hath the spirit, serveth himself of *holy Scriptures*, as of an alphabet of Christian pietie, ... untill such time, as it penetrate into his mind (Hutchinson, p. 309).

This looks innocuous. But the alphabet is an obvious case of a cashable symbolism: we exchange the image of the word for the vocally realized word, itself only the image of a thought.[14] Its function is only mediatory, and then between our understanding and yet another symbol; its place is exterior and remote. This orthodoxy can be challenged. Thomas Fuller, meditating on the use of the alphabet, tells the story of a 'devout but ignorant' Spaniard who by way of prayer would simply repeat the alphabet and ask God to put the letters together to spell syllables and words 'to make such sense as may be most to thy glory'.[15] But this is not the use of the alphabet. Herbert himself writes with relish of writing; he is himself open to being surprised by the alphabet, and he knows, as he puts it in 'The Flower', that 'Thy word is all, if we could spell'. But this is not the use of the alphabet. So distrustful is Herbert of cashable symbolism that he writes a protesting note:

> I much mislike the Comparison of Images and H. Scripture, as if they were both but Alphabets and after a time to be left. The H. Scriptures ... have not only an Elementary use, but a use of perfection, neither can they ever be exhausted (as pictures may by a plenary circumspection) ...

I don't know why he should suppose that pictures are exhaustible. The point about the inexhaustibility of God's word can survive without it. He goes on:

> but still even to the most learned and perfect in them there is still something to be learned more: therefore David desireth God in the 119th Psalm, to open his eyes, that he might see the wondrous things of his laws, and that he would make them his study. Although by other words of the same Psalm it is evident that he was not meanly conversant in them (Hutchinson, p. 309).

He mislikes the notion that the value of scripture might be elementary or cashable: sacred language is not a medium of exchange, we do not parley with God, however fain we are to. The law, says the Psalmist, is delightful; it is 'better unto me than thousands of gold and silver' (Ps. 119: 72).

Herbert amplifies his point about inexhaustibility in the following note. Valdesso compares the consolations of scripture to those of the promissory note given by the master to the servant, intending presumably the consolations of anticipated benefit. Herbert takes up the image. But he has an odd way with its implications, for his promissory note is not to be cashed but enjoyed:

> For as the servant leaves not the letter when he hath read it, but keepes it by him, and reads it againe and againe, and the more the promise is delayed, the more he reads it, and fortifies himselfe with it; so are wee to doe with the Scriptures and this is the use of the promises of the Scriptures (Hutchinson, p. 310).

The recommended use of Scripture is not alphabetic and elementary (its primary figurative sense), nor trivial and set among 'the Catchismes and Alphabets / Of unconcerning things, matters of fact' (Donne's *Second Anni-*

versarie, pp. 284-285), nor is it performed with a view to benefits. It offers a promise, but to hear the promise affords immediate pleasure for itself.

'I have rejoiced,' says the Psalmist (Ps. 119: 14), 'in the way of thy testimonies, as much as in all riches.' The word given as 'testimonies' (*edwoth*) is from a root which means 'to repeat'. What the Psalmist repeats gives delight. What we repeat and read over is the source of our religion. So indeed according to the common, if mistaken etymology of the word. Cicero says that 'those who scrupulously observed and repeated all the ritual belonging to the worship of the gods were called 'religious' from the verb 'relegere'.[16] This fanciful etymology (the word more likely derives from 'religare') influentially contaminates subsequent understanding of what it is to be religious. It is not Calvin has to say 'often to reread and diligently weigh what was true', but simply to fix one's attention on it, to be incapable of distraction—perhaps, since his definition assumes Cicero's, a superfine discrimination.[17] But again, perhaps not, for Calvin would wish to press claims for Scripture's intelligibility. It may be however a sufficient sign of one's being religious that one rereads the holy text, though perhaps without understanding it. It is not clear that the 'roll' that Bunyan's Christian receives from the third of the Shining Ones is designed to be read at all: he is given 'a Roll with a Seal upon it, which he bid him look on as he ran, and that he should give it in at the Coelestial Gate'. A roll that is handed over sealed for delivery elsewhere is surely not for reading. True, the dreamer dreams Christian reading it for his private refreshment and by way of not talking to Formalist and Hypocrisy (but this is an unlikely situation for reading, at least in fiction), and he dreams him reading it for his comfort in the arbour on Hill Difficulty (but with the consequence that he falls asleep and loses it). When Christian recovers the lost roll, it gives him joy, not as reading matter, but as 'the assurance of his life and acceptance at the desired haven', and he never reads in it again.[18] It seems rather that it is simply to be possessed. And there is a piquancy in the reflection that the servant that Valdesso and Herbert imagine may actually have been only partially literate, a man to whom the promissory note would have been strictly illegible. For the ability to read manuscript (as opposed to print) was probably a privilege of the super-educated.[19] Even the super-educated might treat script with religious awe: Pascal kept sewn into his clothes his own 'Memorial', abrupt and formulaic, fragments gathered out of scripture or philosophy; Lancelot Andrewes kept a Greek letter from Herbert himself in his bosom 'near his heart, till the last day of his life'.[20]

When Calvin says that to be religious we should steel ourselves against distraction he means presumably that we should attend to the transmitted truth. Faced with scripture we should attend to what we understand of its transmitted truth. This is the orthodox mode of exegesis. It is not the only way. Augustine's objection to Jerome's glosses rests on his resistance to the notion that Scripture is translatable to the rhetorical mode of the gloss. 'Let us not think the gospel is in the words of Scripture, but in the sense,' says Jerome, 'not on the surface, but in the marrow, not in the leaves of speech, but in the root of reason'.[21] Jerome assumes indefinite possibilities for the retranslation of scripture: it was his *métier*. He is in any case indifferent to the merely phenomenal, to the issue of leaves on the tree. Augustine may sometimes seem to speak that way, for he makes culpable what he calls the 'bondage to signs', as if we should be able to master them. But that condemnation is variously qualified to suggest a view wholly other than Jerome's, the advocacy of a posture nervous but trusting and essentially childlike. 'Let us leave off worrying about what we have not managed to understand,' he says, 'and postpone our understanding of it: we can be confident about something's being good and true even is we do not understand what it is.' Or with a more desperate inflexion, but as irrelevantly to what we would think of as 'understanding': 'Rise up, seek, sigh, pant with desire, beat on the locked door.' The metaphors out of Roman elegy can be dispensed with. Even in the chapter where he castigates the bondage to signs, he promotes a value for them independent of their signification:

> He however who does not know what a sign signifies, but yet knows that it is a sign, is not in bondage. It is better to be in bondage to unknown but useful signs than, by interpreting them wrongly, to draw the neck from under the yoke of bondage, only to insert it in the coils of error.[22]

The servant in Herbert's note who takes the promissory letter and reads it again and again is in bondage to a scripture whose promises are always deferred, but his expectation of them is never frustrated.

The poet who wrote 'The Flower', delighted when his 'shrivelled heart' recovers greenness, when he buds again in age, cares more for leaves than roots. Causes and reasons do not take his imagination much. In *The Temple* Herbert offers a sequence of poems to be possessed rather than understood. Or indeed for the poems to possess us, or to be the agents of our possession. The ideal reading of a Herbert poem is Simone Weil's when she records that her repetition of 'Love (3)' eventually had the force of a prayer, and Jesus came down and took possession of her.[23]

Donne confidently speaks of Scripture being made current, as if there were a market where it might be exchanged for goods: 'the whole frame of the Poem is a beating out of a piece of gold, but the last clause is as the impression of the stamp, and that it is that makes it currant'.[24] Donne is looking to explain why David reserves the most important part of Ps. 6, his thanks to God, to the final verses; and he argues therefore that the final part of the poem is the place of honour. But we may suspect his monetary metaphor, just as Herbert suspected Valdesso's alphabetic one. Herbert would in any case have been incapable of it. The roses and lilies in the early sonnet given by Walton, that 'speak' God do not 'mean' by their perfume in the way a coin 'means' by its stamp. Herbert's poem are not cashable against something else, transmitting ideas which we can then take away. What his poems are about is not something else out there, but a property of our experience of them. When Donne, however nervously, calls his God's language figurative and metaphorical, he seems to assume we read by contriving systematic analogies, as if God had something to tell us and there were an alternative discourse for it.[25] Herbert's God, if not quite 'direct'—as Donne in the same place admits God may be, is 'literal'.

I've thrown out in an unargued fashion some prejudices about the possibility of writing not designed to be intelligible, or at least not translatable into a profane language—a language whose intelligibility is not at a premium. I want now to turn to how Herbert is sometimes in thrall to the accidents of his own writing, that he confronts his own writing as the servant confronts the promissory note, that he is himself in the position of the reader, innocently but painfully bonded to signs whose import he does not himself recognize, but longs to. Herbert's more obvious manipulations of language have about them the careful air of demonstrations, not of attempts to persuade us of anything, nor (as prophets might) to derange our feelings about things. He is mannerly, courteous, tentative and encourages the same style in his readers. Herbert's marvellous is presented as something casually discovered, as in 'Anagram': 'How well her name an *Army* doth present, / In whom the *Lord of Hosts* did pitch his tent.' Herbert seems to invite us to make of this what we will. He presents it in any case as something won by attention to the accidents of the merely literal: the discovery, in 'JESU', that the name of Jesus heals the broken heart follows from a pretended misreading of the name. He respects the literal, the facts of his own inventions, as if there might always be a reason, though he never has to make it explicit, for their being just the way they are. Peter Brown has it of Augustine that he does not ask what something means, but 'why this incident, this word and no other, occur at just this moment in the interminable monologue of God'.[26] Herbert's reading of his own language is rather like that, and contagiously, his readers' reading of it. The failure of satisfactory answers anticipates conclusions like those of Rosalie Colie, that Herbert, for all his mannerliness, is not writing English at all.

The writing that Herbert confronts as he sits at his desk, the linguistic accidents he relies on, are (he says) in an important sense not the accidents of his own writing. '*Yet not mine neither: for from thee they came.*' So in 'The Dedication'. The parts of the broken altar that he rears in 'The Altar' are 'as thy hand did frame'. And the evidences of alternative authorship in *The Temple* are everywhere strewn around in italicized quotation and half-quotation. So in 'A True Hymn':

> My joy, my life, my crown!
> My heart was meaning all the day,
> Somewhat it fain would say:
> And still it runneth mutt'ring up and down
> With only this, *My joy, my life, my crown.*

The meaning and the saying are activities distinguished from one another. What the poet means, what he wants to say, is registered in the words of another, in reassembled fragments of scripture. 'Lord, I will mean and speak thy name', he says in 'Praise (3)'. Intention here seems to precede utterance, for 'meaning' comes before 'mutt'ring; but all we can be sure of is that the one is independent of the other. We might indeed insist that the name ('Lord') is what is spoken before it is meant. Beyond that, it's not clear that the intention to praise is ever fulfilled: 'Praise (3)' may remain rather a poem about wanting to praise. The desire to speak may follow on the desire to mean, but the suggestion seems to be that we can't actually mean anything until we've said it. The whole apparatus of praise in any case 'antedates' Herbert's attempts to mean it. 'A True Hymn' represents a thought—the unitalicized 'My joy, my life, my crown'—which is incoherent. The italicized *My joy, my life, my crown* speaks the thought but cannot re-articulate it into sense. It is presumably taken from Ps. 21: 'The king shall rejoice ... Thou ... hast set a crown of pure gold upon his head. He asked life of thee, and thou gavest him a long life'; and something very close to Herbert's formula is laboriously derived in Andrewes's sermon on its these first verses: 'in the *safety both of His crowne, and His life*; is all ... this *joy* ... of the Text'.[27]

Once uttered and identified however, it may become possible to coax the formerly incoherent desire into sense. Before Herbert identified his thought with a fragment of borrowed speech, that is, we may assume Herbert was in a kind of ignorance of what it was. The hymn is true because it refuses to submit to the explanatory protocols of unholy language, where people try to say what they mean. In the language of Canaan, the words represent what with an effort we can persuade ourselves we must have meant: 'The fineness which a hymn or psalm affords, / Is, when the soul unto the lines accords'. The soul works itself to agreement with the lines, and not the other way about. It is the words 'My Master' into which Herbert, in 'The Odour', 'thrusts' his mind, not his intention to serve. 'A True Hymn' is a poem which God actually completes for the poet, where God, in defiance of grammar (but acknowledging the accident of rhyme), 'doth supply the want': 'As when th' heart says (sighing to be approved) / *O could I love*! and stops: God writeth, *Loved*.'

We could say that Herbert's poetry is all God's doing; and indeed Herbert himself did. But, in a rather obvious way, the secondariness of his own intentions comes about because of the kind of versifying that Herbert commits himself to. Speaking before he means, his intentions are unrealized except as what enters his speech by way of something beyond the intentional. The mechanically elaborate versification, the predominance of figured speech (rather than figured sense), the very self-conscious reliance on rhyme (as in 'Denial'), actually enforce this unintentionality. Words take their place where or how they do in Herbert's lines because they look or sound as if they belong together rather than because they represent somehow what he wants to say. It is the ground of Daniel's praise of it that rhyme contradicts intention. that it gives a poet wings to mount and carries him beyond what he could otherwise have thought of saying.[28]

All merely schematic figuration is similarly mindless. I offer with scant commentary a few observations on a few cases of word play covered by the term *allusio*—which involves adding or taking away or changing letters in a word, and is sometimes synonymous with paronomasia.[29] 'Fasting into feasting' is one of the examples given by John Hoskins—one played on in Herbert's 'Lent'. *Allusio* is commonly used, says Henry Peacham (the father of the more famous emblematist), to 'illude'—to deceive, to jest at the expense of. It abuses the language. Peacham means it 'illudes' the reader, or perhaps that the words 'illude' each other.[30] It seems to mis-write a primary intention and then correct it. But it is not necessarily more than play with the alphabetic in the most obvious and literal way. What it need not do is encash the symbolical value of the letters as Peacham's gloss suggests it should.

Herbert's motives are less deliberate than Peacham's gloss on the figure suggests they might regularly be. He is full of recognizable doublets—alliterating doublets like 'drought or dew' ('The World'), 'work or woo' ('Constancy'), or rhyming doublets like 'sadness/gladness' ('An Offering'), or assonating like 'cross to thy decrees' ('The Sinner'), or contrived by shuffling affixes 'serve/deserve' ('Love [3]'). The relationships between these words is not clear. They feel sometimes like slips of the tongue. Sometimes they are almost explicitly so presented. In 'Good Friday', we get 'And be my sun. / Or rather let / My severall sins their sorrows get'; in 'Giddiness' we get 'Lord, mend or rather make us'; in 'An Offering', 'There is a balsam, or indeed a blood'; in 'The Pilgrimage', 'the wild of Passion, which / Some call the wold'; in 'Love Unknown', 'I found that some had stuff'd the bed with thoughts, / I would say *thorns*'; in 'The Rose', 'Or if such deceits there be / Such delights I meant to say'. What he meant to say in the last example or the one before, conforming with allegorical or sentimental fictions, was the less enlightened thing. The slip of the tongue can reveal a lot. What some call the 'wild of Passion' is only the more conventional thing, what people say. The mistake is the more truthful thing. And the radical corrections of 'mend' to 'make' or 'balsam' to 'blood' rely schematically on what is perceived as an inadequate formulation only after the completion of the scheme. Without the mistake, the true word would never have occurred to the speaker.

Herbert values therefore what his schematic way of proceeding throws up. He values the accidents of his own wording even when he wants to disown the sense it must originally have implied. I take two cases, not obviously related to any argument about word-play, which I hope make the point clearly. A remarkable but possibly trivial instance comes in 'Employment (2)'. Herbert identifies himself in the draft of the poem with 'laden bees' that can can 'mount up instantly' and drop blessings on the rest of us. He rejects it favour of identifying himself with the 'Orange-tree' that can 'ever laden be'. A multitude of motives might inform this change and some are rehearsed by commentary on the poem.[31] All I want to point out is that the 'laden be' is still there. The phrase precedes the thought of what it might come to mean.

The same sort of consideration applies in 'The Elixir', a poem I take it derived from Ps. 143 ('Teach me to do thy will ... Quicken me O Lord for thy name's sake'), and thematically engaged with the character of perfect action. There is no consensus on the meaning of this poem nor on the motives of its successive revisions, and I don't intend to speculate here on either matter. But what is probably uncontentious is that Herbert discovered only once a version of the poem was in front of him what might be its true direction. This I suggest he discovered in the opposition of 'perfections' and 'actions' thrown up in the final stanza of his first version of the poem, reused in the revision with a rather less spectacular shift of the sense than in his reuse of 'laden bees', but nonetheless radical. He discovered the sense he wanted in that opposition and in a rethinking of what seems to have been a watering metaphor, reached in the first version by way of a little and perfectly conventional allegory of man as a fruiting tree. 'Tincture' in the first Williams MS draft is what enables general growth heavenward: it probably carries baptismal connotations (as in Herbert's own *De Signaculo Crucis*). In the first revision and thereafter, it is identified with the alchemical *rubedo* as the agent of transmutation, and so with blood—in the first instance by virtue of its colour, and confirmatorily by virtue of its properties: 'How much more shall the blood of Christ ... purge your conscience to serve the living God' (Heb. 9: 14), 'Now the God of peace ... through the blood of the everlasting covenant ... Make you perfect in every good work to do his will' (Heb. 13: 20-21). The baptism of water (shadowed in the poems which immediately precedes this in the Williams MS, later re-titled 'Jordan') is replaced by the baptism of blood. As in 'Divinity', 'To take and taste what he doth there designe, / Is all that saves'. The poem which immediately followed this in the Williams MS, 'The Knell', which invokes the converting and colouring blood of Christ as relief from 'the great combat of our flesh and reason' is cancelled as redundant. But it is not usual that redirections of the sense can be identified.

In a chapter on metaphorical equivocation Emmanuele Tesauro exemplifies various ways of scrambling letters to witty effect. And this is, he reassures his readers, less tasking than may seem. Slips of the tongue daily produce the possibility of stylish punning; and so it comes about even the stupidest people, simply by virtue of speaking badly, are capable of puns that the rarest wits would envy. For those looking round for such possibilities, he recommends the reading of printers' errata pages at the end of books, or of wordlists and dictionaries, all of which are a source of wonderful equivocations simply by virtue of alphabetical accident. In the dictionary we discover that since 'plaga' means both 'wound' and 'net', we can turn the Saviour's wounds and love's snare; or that, since 'pernix' and 'perniciosus' are neighbours on the page we can contrive a moral about haste and ruin.[32] It *may* always be true that words accidentally misprinted, or neighbours by an accident of the alphabet, are truly related.

Of money Herbert writes in 'Avarice', 'Man found thee poor and dirty in a mine'; of God's 'dreadful look' in 'Judgement' that it is 'Able a heart of iron to appal'; of the ingratitude of man in 'Home' that he would not at a feast 'Leave one poor apple for thy love'. The end of the line plays with the beginning. Donne is keen on beginning and ending lines with the same word, by an ordinary kind of epanalepsis. But the distorted repetition makes us interrogate also the word—to rehearse, probably despairingly, the plausibility of a connexion between 'able' and 'appal', or 'leave' and 'love'—in the same way as witty rhyme is reckoned to. And sometimes this quasi-

anagrammatizing has obvious and calculated epigrammatic point, as at the
end of 'The Size' when we read *'These seas are tears, and heav'n the
haven'*. In 'The Banquet' 'Wine becomes a wing at last' because the
Eucharistic wine lifts us heavenward. In 'The Flower', 'growing and groaning' are identified as ways to heaven, as activities to the same effect. So in
'Life': 'Farewell dear flowers, sweetly your time ye spent', there is a poignant hint that 'flowers' is an anagram of 'farewell': the idea of 'farewell'
is realized especially in flowers, for whom withering away is a vocation—
in this poem, since Time 'beckons' them, literally so. In 'Submission'
'raising' God and 'praising' God are the same thing; in 'Mortification',
'mirth and 'breath' are simultaneously 'exchanged'. In these places we see
the plausible connexion as much as when we read 'Anagram' or 'JESU'.

In the belief that accidents may be in some quiet way providential,
Herbert surrenders himself to the schematic possibilities of the language he
uses; and sometimes can take advantage of what is revealed. Sometimes
not. 'My prayers mean thee, yet my prayers stray'—says Herbert in 'Justice
(1)'. The case earlier quoted from 'Good Friday', where Herbert picks up
from the word 'sun' the correction 'Or rather let / My severall sins their
sorrows get' may, as Richard Strier complains, actually damage the larger
rhetorical consistency of the poem.[33] And sometimes not, because some
beautiful effects seem to me quite without point, or points so elusive as to
be unarguable for. The principle of these effects seems precisely to be that
their import should be uncertain. Puttenham, who treats this sort of thing I
mean under the figure 'Traductio, or the Translacer', confusingly classes
this as 'sententious', a figure that combines auricular with 'sensable effects'
—at once scheme and trope. But he gives prominence to the notion of play
in it: 'ye turne and translace a word into many sundry shapes as the Tailor
doth his garment, and after that sort do play with him in your dittie'.[34]
There are parts of 'Affliction (1)' where the syllable can disconcertingly
acquire its own life:

> Thus argued into hopes, my thoughts reserved
>   No place *for* grie*f or fear*.
> There*fore* my sudden soul caught at the place,
> And made her youth and *fier*ceness seek thy face.
>
> At *first* thou gav'st me milk ...

That is, where it can acquire sense, as from 'fear' or 'fierceness', it does so;
and then carries this truckle of association into quite innocuous contexts, so
that the word 'therefore' comes to echo the notion of 'fear', or the word

'first' the notion of 'fierceness'. Words as significant entities are rendered of little account: the disintegration of 'grief' into a nonsense grunt and an echo of a preposition is made up again into something new and sinister when the repeated preposition transforms itself to 'fear'. And the effect may be a good deal less specific. The poem goes on:

My days *were* st*raw*'d with flo*w'rs* and happiness;
    The*re w*as no month but May.
But with my years so*rrow* did twist and *grow*,
And made a party una*war*es fo*r woe*.

Some of the echoes here are no doubt more finely or more deliberately calculated than others. And if the ear (or the eye) is tuned exclusively to the repetitions, as it may come to be, the lines dissolve into nonsense. The anagrammatized *rw* root is allowed everywhere to 'burnish, sprout, and swell' in untrained ramifications, in 'the leaves of speech', detaching itself from where it belongs and attaching itself where it doesn't. Asserted against the babble is the measure of the verse, and indeed of the printed words, which are part of a system of significant divisions. But the contradiction between what is significant and what is not is suspended in 'Affliction (1)'—that is, the contradiction is not focused to a point, at least until the final full echo line, 'Let me not love thee, if I love thee not'. Even here however the formal conclusion concludes nothing.

Poems which do reach conclusions are apt to seem overmanaged. So perhaps is 'Paradise', in which Herbert—or as he would have it, God—has pruned sets of words to their common significant letters:

I bless thee, Lord, because I GROW
Among thy trees, which in a ROW
To thee both fruit and order OW.

The mechanical, schematic, auricular or typographical trick acquires the force of a conceit. 'Owing' is an implication of 'growing', formally in the dispensation of the poem, but also in that of Providence. The art of the poem confirms the argument: as pruning is a triumph of art over disorder, so measured or divided speech is a triumph over incoherence or mere prose, so grace is a triumph over nature. In 'Affliction (1)' that 'ow' would have represented only a sigh.

There was a Rabbi who argued that the division of the Torah into words and sentences was only one possible division of a text that truly consisted entirely of the names of God.[35] This was wishful thinking, as wishful as that of Fuller's ignorant and devout Spaniard. But it's the kind of wishful thinking that would I think have gratified Herbert. What I have tried to suggest is that Herbert writes at a distance from the sense his own language might be expected to carry, that the division of stretches of verse into units of sense is something only provisional, and that if we are lucky God 'will supply the want'.

Notes

1   Simon Schama, *The Embarrassment of Riches: An Interpretation of Dutch Culture in the Golden Age* (Collins, 1987), 93-125). Compare the entries in the *OED* under 'Canaan' with those under 'Kanaän' in the *Woordenboek der Nederlandsche Taal*.
2   William Struther, *True Happines, or King David's Choice*, (Edinburgh, 1633), 101. For 'Shibboleth' see Judg. 12: 6, and for the heart-piercing 'goads' Eccles. 12: 11.
3   Samuel Hieron, *Workes* (?1620), 2: 489.
4   *The Pilgrim's Progress*, edited by James Blanton Wharey, 2nd ed. (corrected reprint) edited by Roger Sharrock (Oxford: Clarendon Press, 1975), 89-90.
5   Gregory, *Moralia in Job*, prefatory epistle, cap. 4 (*PL* 75: 515).
6   Augustine, Epistle 137 (*PL* 33: 524).
7   Herbert Marks, 'On Prophetic Stammering', *Yale Journal of Criticism* 1 (1987), rpt. in Regina M. Schwartz, *The Book and Text* (Oxford: Clarendon, 1990). But the observation is not novel. Calvin on Ps. 5: 6 says: 'The language is indeed abrupt, as the saints in prayer often stammer; but his stammering is more accept-able to God than all the figures of rhetoric.' Thomas F. Merrill, 'George Herbert's "Significant Stuttering"', *GHJ* 11/2 (1988), 1-18. (1988) argues for the ultimate availability of Herbert's language.
8   *Philosophical Works*, edited by John M. Robertson (1905), 635.
9   John Selden, *Table-Talk* (1689), in English Reprints, edited by Edward Arber (1868), 20.
10   Roberta Florence Brinkley, ed., *Coleridge on the Seventeenth Century* (Durham NC: Duke UP, 1955), 538.
11   Rosalie L. Colie, *Paradoxia Epidemica: The Renaissance Tradition of Paradox* (Princeton: Princeton UP, 1966), 191.
12   Brinkley, *Coleridge on the Seventeenth Century*, p. 535.
13   *A Priest to the Temple*, Chapter 7, in Hutchinson, pp. 232-235.
14   Aristotle, *De Interpretatione* 1: 1, and quoted e.g. in Bacon, *The Advancement of Learning* 16: 2 (in *Philosophical Works*, p. 121), *De Augmentis*, 6: 1 (*Philosophical Works*, p. 521).
15   'Meditations on the Times', 11, in *Good Thoughts in Worse Times* (1647); *Fuller's Thoughts*, edited by A.R. Waller (1902), 115.
16   *De Natura Deorum*, 2: 28:72.
17   *Institutes of the Christian Religion*, edited by John T. Mitchell, and translated by Ford Lewis Battles, 2 vols (Philadelphia: Westminster Press, 1960), 1: 117.

18 *Pilgrim's Progress*, pp. 38-45.

19 See Keith Thomas, 'The Meaning of Literacy in Early Modern England', in *The Written Word: Literacy in Transition*, edited by Gerd Baumann (Oxford: Clarendon, 1986), 97-131, especially p. 100.

20 For Pascal's 'Memorial see *Œuvres Complètes*, edited by Louis Lafuma (Paris: Editions du Seuil, 1963), 618; and for Lancelot Andrewes, see Izaak Walton's 'Life of Mr. George Herbert', in *The Lives* (London: Oxford UP, 1927) [World's Classics], 273.

21 On Gal. 1 (*PL* 26: 347), quoted in William Whitaker, *A Disputation on Holy Scripture* (Cambridge: Cambridge UP, 1849) [Parker Society], 402.

22 *The Tractates on John's Gospel* 18.1 and 7 (*PL* 35: 1536 and 1540); *De Doctrina Christiana* 3: 9 (*PL* 34: 70-71). A letter to Jerome (1: 28; *PL* 33: 111) betrays Augustine's worries about Jerome's departures from texts to which Augustine had committed himself.

23 Quoted in *Simone Weil: An Anthology*, edited by Sián Miles (London: Virago, 1986), 35, from *L'Attente de Dieu* (Paris: La Colombe, 1950).

24 *The Sermons of John Donne*, edited by George R. Potter and Evelyn Simpson, 10 vols (Berkeley & Los Angeles: U of California P (no. 55 in *LXXX Sermons*).

25 'Expostulation 19', *The Devotions* (Ann Arbor: U of Michigan P, 1959), 124.

26 Peter Brown, *Augustine of Hippo* (London: Faber, 1967), 253.

27 *Sermons preached upon the V. of August*, Sermon 5 (1615) on Psalm 21: 1-4, in *XCVI Sermons*, 3rd edition (1635), especially pp. 829-831.

28 Samuel Daniel, *A Defence of Ryme*, in Arthur Colby Sprague (Chicago & London: Chicago UP, 1965), 137-138.

29 See Judith Dundas' essay elsewhere in this volume.

30 Lee Sonnino, *A Handbook to Sixteenth-Century Rhetoric* (London: Routledge & Kegan Paul, 1968), 26-27.

31 The rewritings of 'Employment (2)' and 'The Elixir' are discussed by Janis Lull, *The Poem in Time: Reading George Herbert's Revisions of The Church* (Newark: U. of Delaware P., 1990), 39-40 and 94-100.

32 Emmanuele Tesauro, *Il Cannocchiale Aristotelico* (Venice, 1688), 235-236. Fuller is unimpressed by the misprints in 1653 Bible in his 'Mixt Contemplations on these Times', 2nd ser. 8 'Fie for shame', in *Mixt Contemplations in Better Times* (1660) in *Fuller's Thoughts*, edited by A.R. Waller (1902), 212.

33 Richard Strier, *Love Known: Theology and Experience in George Herbert's Poetry* (Chicago & London: Chicago UP, 1983), 54 (n. 59).

34 George Puttenham, *The Arte of English Poesie*, edited by Gladys D. Willcock and Alice Walker (Cambridge: Cambridge UP, 1936), 203-204.

35 Nahmanides, in the preface to his Pentateuch commentary, quoted by James L. Kugel, *The Idea of Biblical Poetry: Parallelism and its History* (New Haven & London: Yale UP, 1981), 304.

6

GEORGE HERBERT AND DIVINE 'PARONOMASIA'

JUDITH DUNDAS

Rhetorical technique is one thing; revelation through rhetorical technique is another. But God Himself is a rhetorician and has chosen to reveal by means of the incarnate Word.[1] Human words are also divinely ordained, at least according to the ancient faith in etymology, their true meaning being wrapped in their roots.[2] It is as a variation of this faith that George Herbert, following the example of ancient poetry, the Psalms, the Church Fathers, and medieval hymns, makes his puns.

The particular form of the pun that I want to consider is *paronomasia*, whereby two words or syllables similar in sound but different in meaning are juxtaposed to provide a double perspective. Rhetoricians had identified this type of pun as having a musical quality, like assonance.[3] Among the possible variations are the adding of letters, the omitting of letters, the transposing of letters, or the changing of letters. What is crucial is that 'similar words express dissimilar things'.[4] As if God had ordained these similarities of sound, Herbert uses them as an auditory structure to represent the structure of experience—specifically the religious experience, as in the pair 'heaven' / 'haven', one common in poetry at least as far back as Sir Thomas More and as far forward as Wallace Stevens.[5] In such echoes, the hovering of like sounds is pleasingly ambiguous; we cannot be quite sure what is being defined. Nevertheless, in the words of Donne, 'To make men sharpe and industrious in the inquisition of truth, God withdraws it from present apprehension and obviousness'.[6] In Herbert's poetry, it is the use of everyday language that paradoxically withdraws the reader from obviousness, and in this withdrawal, *paronomasia* plays a part.

It is no wonder that George Puttenham in his *Arte of English Poesie* calls attention to the teaching function of this figure when he classifies *paronomasia* among the 'Figures sententious, otherwise called Rhetoricall'. This is a category of verbal schemes that reaches the mind through the ear: 'the eare is no lesse ravished with their currant tune, than the mind is with their sententiousnes'.[7] This dual aspect, ornament and efficacy, made the figure particularly attractive to Herbert; his rhyming words themselves are often related by way of *paronomasia*. In the repetition of sounds, a criticism, an irony, even an act of conversion, may be implied. At the same time, the pleasures of pattern were not lost upon him; he knows its value for winning the soul: 'A verse may finde him, who a sermon *flies*, / And turn delight into a sacri*fice*.'[8] The rhyme 'flies' / 'sacrifice' underlines the transformation from escape to submission that is at the centre of so much of Herbert's poetry.

Like other Renaissance poets, such as Sidney, Herbert has the whole classical and medieval tradition behind him in the attention he gives to syllables as meaningful units. Such an emphasis may lead to abuse: Augustine, for example, has been criticized for his excessive fondness for the reiterated syllable, such as 'oris', 'cordis'; 'veritate', 'severitate'; 'aversio', 'conversio'.[9] Indeed, Thomas Wilson in his *Art of Rhetoric* (1560), analyzing the precedents for the wordplay so fashionable in his own time, says of Augustine, 'he forgot measure and used overmuch' such rhetorical figures as *paronomasia* with its near rhyming effect.[10] Bede, however, can point to the Psalms for an example of *paronomasia*: 'They *confided* in thee and were not *confounded*'—'In te *confisi* sunt et non sunt *confusi*'.[11] Sidney, in his metrical version of the Psalms, which Herbert almost certainly knew, frequently uses *paronomasia* to point up such contrasts; for example, in Psalm 4: 'And when your chamber you do *close*, / Yourselves yet to yourselves *disclose*.'[12] Adding a syllable to 'close' is opening a door into the mind, but, paradoxically, this is accomplished only by 'closing' off other things. Elsewhere, in Psalm 19, speaking of the book of nature, Sidney gives this rendering:

> There be no *eyn* but reade the *line*
>   From so fair book proceeding,
> Their Words be set in letters great
>   For everybody's reading.   (13-16)[13]

The addition of the letter 'l' to the word 'eyn' to make the word 'line' has the force of mastery: the 'eyn' are simply overwhelmed by the line of God's book.

The seriousness with which Renaissance poets took Plato's theory of language in the *Cratylus* begins to impress itself on our consciousness. According to Socrates, 'the name-maker grasps with his letters and syllables the reality of the things named and imitates their essential nature'.[14] Herbert's own Latin poetry revels in this playful kind of wit that has just such a serious basis. His anagram on the name 'Rome' uses all possible permutations, such as 'oram', 'Maro', 'ramo', 'armo', 'mora', and, finally, 'amor'.[15] Herbert's English poem on the name of the Virgin Mary similarly finds significance in the anagram '*Army*': 'How well her name an *Army* doth present, / In whom the *Lord of Hosts* did pitch his tent' (1-2; emphases Herbert's).

His writing of poems in Latin surely contributed to Herbert's habit of paying close attention to syllables. His epigram on the stoning of Stephen links 'silicem' (rock) with 'elicit' and 'elicuit' (draws forth and drew forth):

In Stephanum lapidatum

Qui silicem tundit, (mirum tamen) elicit ignem:
    At Caelum è saxis elicuit Stephanus.

Losing the verbal echoes, the English translation also loses some of the point:

How marvellous! Who
Pounds rocks gets fire.
But Stephen from
Stones got heaven.   (McCloskey and Murphy, pp. 82-83)

Another of Herbert's Latin poems, in an extremely ingenious way, takes the 'textor' (weaver) of the first line and repeats the last syllable 'tor' as the first syllable of the first word of the last line in 'torquet' (twists), followed by the first syllable, 'text', in 'textu' (here, scripture), so that the weaver (conventionally a Puritan), in twisting the Scriptures, misreads the gospel concerning Christ's calling of the fishermen:

De Textore Catharo

Cum piscatores Textor legit esse vocatos,
    Vt sanctum Domini persequerentur opus;
Ille quoque inuadit Diuinam taminis artem,
    Subtegmen reti dignius esse putans,
Et nunc perlongas Scripturae stamine telas
    Torquet, & in Textu Doctor vtroque cluet.

When the weaver reads that fishermen
Were called to fructify the bold work
Of the Lord, he too invades
, The priesthood's godly skill, thinking
The woof better than the net; and now
He twists endless threads throughout
The warp of Scripture, and in
Both weaves is famed a learned man.

            (McCloskey and Murphy, pp. 28-29)

Again, the English translation misses something of the analogy, here between weaving and ingenious biblical exegesis, through losing the echoes of 'textor' in 'torquet' and 'textu'. But Herbert liked the metaphor well enough to use it in 'Jordan (2)', when he rebuked himself for verbal elaboration on the theme of heavenly joys: 'So did I weave my self into the sense' (14).

What we might call a conceit typifies Herbert's use of sounds. They display his wit but they also convey his convictions. By pretending that syllabic resemblance between two words reveals a hidden connection of meaning, he, as it were, takes seriously the implications of echo poetry. His poem 'Heaven' gives Echo the function of answering questions truthfully, which was in fact her allegorical function as interpreted by various commentators, including the author of the *Ovide Moralisé*:[16]

> O who will show me those delights on high?
>   *Echo.   I.*
> Thou Echo, thou art mortall, all men know.
>   *Echo.   No.*
> Wert thou not born among the trees and leaves?
>   *Echo.   Leaves.*
> And are there any leaves, that still abide?
>   *Echo.   Bide.*
> What leaves are they? impart the matter wholly.
>   *Echo.   Holy.*
> Are holy leaves the Echo then of bliss?
>   *Echo.   Yes.*
>
>   (1-12)
>   (emphases Herbert's)

From the perishable leaves on trees to the imperishable leaves of the Scriptures, a structure of meaning is developed through syllabic repetition.

If we understand that such syllabic resemblance becomes in Herbert's poems representative of truth, we are in a better position to read his lines in 'The Flower': 'We say *amiss*, / This or that *is*: / Thy word is *all*, if we could *spell*' (19-21; emphases added). The making of false distinctions is jeered at by the repetition in 'amiss', / 'this', / 'is', finally giving way to the consonance of 'all' and 'spell'. Just how important 'spelling' is, becomes apparent as time after time Herbert demonstrates in his poems that words themselves may contain vital clues to understanding our place in the universe.

Another poem that has an echo effect without overtly using the figure of Echo is 'The Family'. What is generally discussed only in terms of contrapuntal effect, because shorter lines are rhymed with longer lines,[17] may also be viewed as a concealed echo poem:

> What doth this noise of thoughts within my heart
>   As if they had a part?
> What do these loud complaints and puling fears,
>   As if there were no rule or ears?   (1-4)

The rhymes 'heart' / 'part'; 'fears' / 'ears', and even 'puling' and 'rule', contrast the complaints of the long lines with the answers of the shorter echo lines. The House of the Lord, the ordered soul, gradually becomes less noisy: 'Joys oft are there, and griefs as oft as joys; / But griefs without a noise.' Echo continues to interpret for the unruly heart, and it is all done through slight alterations of words, keeping the main syllables the same.

For any of Herbert's imaginary debates with God or with himself, he finds a use for *paronomasia*. He draws our attention to the contrast between human efforts and their failure in the last stanza of 'Sepulchre' through the words 'persist' and 'perish', which provide a perspective on, or seeing through, the human heart:

> Yet do we still *persist* as we began,
> And so should *perish*, but that nothing can,
> Though it be cold, hard, foul, from loving man
>   Withhold thee.   (21-24)
>   (emphases added)

In the Christian and Platonic context, a false etymology is as good as a true one: 'persist' and 'perish' belong together not only through the preposition 'per', but also through the fact that in 'perish', an 's' is lost from 'persist' and the final 'st' becomes converted to 'sh', as though to represent the silence of the grave. Another false etymology links '*Cordial*' and '*Corrosive*' (emphases Herbert's) in the poem 'Sighs and Groans';

> But O reprieve me!
> For thou hast *life* and *death* at thy command;
> Thou art both *Judge* and *Saviour, feast* and *rod*,
> **Cordial** and **Corrosive**: put not thy hand
> Into the bitter box; but O my God,
>   My God, relieve me!   (25-30)
>   (bold emphases added)

No matter that '*Cordial*' and '*Corrosive*' have different roots; each contains
the syllable 'cor' (Latin *cor*), which in Herbert's mind reaches to the heart
of the matter.

Such linked words create a meta-metaphor, one beyond the separate
metaphorical significance of the individual words. Our attention is forcibly
drawn to what they have in common as represented by their similarity of
sound. In a number, if not all, of Herbert's uses of *paronomasia*, the effect
is sharply satirical. His poem 'Avarice', for example, exposes the love of
money to be a reversal of right relationships: 'Man calleth thee his wealth,
who made thee rich; / And while he digs out thee, falls in the ditch' (13-
14). The words 'dig' and 'ditch' illustrate what rhetoricians meant when
they called *paronomasia* 'a light and illuding [or mocking] form',[18] one
better suited to 'epigrams, satires, comedy' than to weightier, more serious
poetry.[19] But as we see this figure of words turning to trope before our
very eyes, we cannot but be reminded that Aristotle in his *Rhetoric* brings
together puns and metaphor. In both, the element of riddle delights, but 'the
solution is an act of learning'.[20] We may also recall Donne's words,
quoted earlier in this essay, to the effect that God withdraws truth from
obviousness.

For Herbert, mockery is the only way to clear away the mists of obviousness that cloud our vision. His poem 'Death' uses *paronomasia* in the
words 'shells' and 'shed' to awaken our sense of a great mystery:

> We looked on this side of thee, shooting sh*ort*;
> > Where we did find
> > The shells of fledge souls left behind,
> Dry dust which sheds no tears, but may ext*ort*.   (9-12)
> > > > > > > > > (emphases added)

The shells, or bodies, are shed—in a Platonic metaphor—but are themselves incapable of shedding tears, though they may 'extort', or wrench,
them from the living. The rhyme 'short' / 'extort' emphasizes the insuffi-
ciency of mortal vision by a combination of words that makes one word
comment on the other to arrive at a more comprehensive metaphor than is
offered by either word alone.

Similarly, a transforming vision, this time based in what one could call
the aesthetics of virtue, is pointed up by the juxtaposition of the two words
'foil' and 'foul' in Herbert's poem 'The Foil'. It begins innocently enough
with the conventional symbol of stars to stand for virtue:

> If we could see below
> The sphere of virtue, and each shining grace
> As plainly as that above doth show;
> This were the better sky, the brighter place.   (1-4)

The second stanza makes the transition to sin, which is given its own foil:

> God hath made stars the *foil*
> To set off virtues; griefs to set off sinning:
> Yet in this wretched world we toil,
> As if grief were not *foul*, nor virtue winning.   (5-8)
>   (emphases added)

It is the echo of 'foil' in 'foul' that adds another metaphoric dimension to the artistic implications of 'foil' as the metal that sets off a jewel. By the last word, 'winning', we have a sense of something besides an artistic metaphor: if grief is 'foul', it is like a 'foul ball' in sports, a misdirected ball; virtue, on the other hand, is wining the game, or battle, in which foils have turned to weapons. Even so, the adjective 'winning' combines the idea of attractiveness with the idea of victory. In the end, beauty, in its ancient identification with virtue, wins out.

Connections in Herbert's poems are made not so much on a level of logic as on a more primitive, if you will, level of sound, as if the sounds of words constituted an invisible network of meaning, to which he need only allude. His criticism of the divided heart takes full advantage of *paronomasia*, the variety in the same, as it may be called, in his poem 'An Offering'. The heart that is offered to God may have many 'holes':

> But all I fear is lest thy heart displease,
> As neither good, nor one: so oft divisions
> Thy lusts have made, and not thy lusts alone;
> Thy *passions* also have their set *partitions*.
> These *parcel* out thy heart: recover these,
> And thou mayst offer many gifts in one.   (13-18)
>   (emphases added)

The divisiveness of passions is not merely stated but demonstrated, so to speak, by the sound echo: 'passions' / 'partitions' / 'parcel'. The last in this group may have a secondary meaning of 'cover', a nautical metaphor.[21] If so, then it contrasts directly with the word 'recover' in the same line: 'These parcel out thy heart: recover these.' In any case, the three words linked by syllabic repetition have the effect of turning the word 'passions' into a metaphor for divisions.

The half echoes of these words, like the half echoes of 'foil' and 'foul', give us pause: there is a connection to be sought. It is so with the associated words 'grass', 'grace', 'grave' of 'Grace', which reverberate with half-grasped (perhaps an inevitable *paronomasia*) meanings. Insistent as the repetitions are, they are also so unobtrusive that we might well overlook Hutchinson's note that in lines 11-12 of this poem, '*grass* replaces *grace*, which is found in the third line of every other verse except the last' (Hutchinson, p. 497). But this substitution makes perfect sense, for the stanza draws an analogy from nature, and at the same time, indicates where it breaks down. Although 'all flesh is as the grass', grass itself passively receives the dew that inevitably falls. The contrast between the realm of nature and the realm of grace is pointed up by the alliteration of 'dew' / 'dove':

> The dew doth ev'ry morning fall;
> And shall the dew out-strip thy Dove?
> The dew, for which grass cannot call,
>   Drop from above.   (13-16)

The balance Herbert strikes between the insistent and the unobtrusive is a measure of his art.

It is also a measure of the relationship between words and realities that constitutes the fabric of his poems. If there is one poem of Herbert's that seems explicitly to draw our attention to *paronomasia* as a principle of understanding, it is 'Assurance'. Here Herbert refers to syllables and letters as the stuff of his poetry; he also indicates how they include the promise of salvation:

>   But I will to my Father
> Who heard thee say it. O most gracious *Lord*,
> If all the hope and com*fort* that I gather,
> Were from my self, I had not half a *word*,
>   Not half a letter to op*pose*
>   What is objected by my *foes*.   (19-24)
>   (emphasis added)

The words 'Lord', 'comfort', 'word' all contain the syllable 'or'. They are thus related on the level of similarity of sound but also of meaning, for they make up a constellation of ideas. Especially is this true if we take into account Herbert's description of Christ in his poem 'Sepulchre' as 'the letter of the word'. In 'Assurance', the speaker, by himself, would, he says, have 'not half a word, / Not half a letter to oppose / What is objected by my foes.' Losing Christ, he would lose not only the Word, but the letter, the One who releases the written word from the Old Testament tablets.[22]

The combative language of foes and opposition is, of course, reminiscent of the Psalms, but it is exactly the kind of rhetorical context in which *paronomasia* is most at home.[23] Like echo poems, it makes one word answer another, and it serves Herbert well when he answers back to himself in his debate with a 'spiteful bitter thought', the doubts about his faith. Continuing the writing metaphor, in the next stanza he refers to the time when the league was made, the compact of faith, expressed through the Incarnation: 'Thou didst at once thy self *indite*, / And held my hand, while *I* did *write*' (29-30; emphases added). Christ wrote himself into the world, just as the poet mirrors the Incarnation as an artist, incarnating himself in the words he chooses. These are stated as parallel activities, and they share the 'I' between them: 'indite', 'I', 'write'.

If it is a fiction that words imitate reality, this fiction as it relates to the Christian theology of the Word could have a particular symbolic value. In Herbert's poem 'Paradise', each tercet successively shortens a word to represent the pruning hand of God:

> Such sharpness shows the sweetest FREND:
> Such cuttings rather heal than REND:
> And such beginnings touch their END. (13-15)
>
> (emphases, but not capitals, added)

The word 'FREND', joined to 'REND' and 'END', encompasses a theology and an attitude. There are words within words that constitute a revelation. To read thus is to read primitively but also metaphorically.

The musical effect of *paronomasia*, as of all echoing sounds, contributes to a sense of inevitability in the choice of words. Shakespeare must have felt this when he wrote the line in his 64th sonnet: 'Ruin hath taught me thus to ruminate.' Even outside the context of religious poetry, the fiction of relationships inherent in the syllables and letters of words had a force that today may not be apparent. Perhaps it can flourish only in cultures with some sense of a transcendent world order. The modern poet who uses *paronomasia* such as Wallace Stevens,[24] is more intent on constructing his own reality through art than in alluding to one pre-existing and all-pervasive.

On the function of echo, John Donne has something to say that can act as a gloss on Herbert's predilection for *paronomasia* in his poetry:

> The Scriptures are God's voyce; the Church is his Echo; a redoubling, a repeating of some particular syllables, and accents of the same voice. And as we harken with some earnestnesse, and some admiration at an Eccho, when perchance we doe not understand the voice that occasioned that Eccho; so doe the obedient children of God apply themselves to the Eccho of his Church, when perchance otherwise, they would lesse understand the voice of God.[25]

Donne here gives Echo her mystical role as a speaker of truth. But let us take note of the word 'admiration'. Our first response to Echo is wonder, and, as Donne implies, there is a certain ambiguity in her repetitive speech that compels our attention, our 'earnestnesse'. This myth, I would suggest, is related to the fiction that in the sounds and syllables of words their meaning is embodied, that there is a wisdom in sound that transcends discursive reason. By respecting the myth of Echo as, in the words of Henry Reynolds, 'the daughter of the divine voice',[26] Herbert effectively transforms *paronomasia* as a figure of words that mock one another, into an expression of faith.

Notes

1   For a collection of texts from Donne's sermons on God's rhetoric, see P.G. Stanwood and Heather Ross Asals, eds, *John Donne and the Theology of Language* (Columbia: U of Missouri P, 1986).

2   For classical poetry, see Frederick Ahl, *Metaformations: Soundplay and Wordplay in Ovid and Other Classical Poets* (Ithaca & London: Cornell UP, 1985). On etymology in classical and medieval literature, see also E.R. Curtius, *European Literature and the Middle Ages*, translated by Willard R. Trask (London: Routledge & Kegan Paul, 1953).

3   See Cicero, *De Oratore*, translated by E.W. Sutton, introduction by H. Rackham, vol. 1 (London: Heinemann, 1942), 2: 63:256.

4   *Rhetorica ad Herennium*, translated by Harry Caplan (London: Heinemann, 1954), 4: 31:29-31.

5   The last line of Herbert's 'The Size' reads: '*These seas are tears, and heav'n the haven*'. For More's use of the pair, see 'Lewis, the lost lover': 'Trust shall I God, to enter in a while / His haven of heaven, sure and uniform'. For Wallace Stevens, see Eleanor Cook, *Poetry, Word-Play, and Word War in Wallace Stevens*, Princeton: Princeton UP, 1988), 270. She attributes Stevens' use of 'heaven' / 'haven' to Gerard Manley Hopkins.

6   *Essays in Divinity*, edited by Evelyn M. Simpson (Oxford: Clarendon, 1952), 56.

7   George Puttenham, *The Arte of English Poesie*, edited by Gladys D. Willcock and Alice Walker (Cambridge: Cambridge UP, 1936), 197.

8   'The Church-Porch', 5-6 (emphases added). On the relationship between rhymes and puns, see Debra Fried, 'Rhyme Puns', in Jonathan Culler, ed., *On Puns: The Foundation of Letters* (Oxford: Blackwell, 1988), 83-89.

9   For further examples and discussion, see Sr Wilfrid Parsons, *A Study of the Vocabulary and Rhetoric of the Letters of Saint Augustine* (Washington, DC: Catholic University of America, 1923), 245-248.

10   *Thomas Wilson: The Art of Rhetoric* (1560), edited by Peter E. Medine (University Park: Pennsylvania State UP, 1994), 227. For commentary on the relationship of this passage to the euphuistic style, see M.E. Croll's introduction to John Lyly, *Euphues: The Anatomy of Wit* and *Euphues & His England*, edited by M.W. Croll and Harry Clemons (London: George Routledge, 1916), xli-xlii.

11   Gussie Hecht Tannenhaus, 'Bede's *De Schematibus et Tropis*—A Translation', *The Quarterly Journal of Speech* 48 (1962), 242.

12   Quotations from Sidney's translations of the Psalms are taken from *The Poems of Sir Philip Sidney*, edited by William A. Ringler Jr (Oxford: Clarendon, 1962), 273 (Ps. 4: 19-20). For the relationship of Herbert's poetry to the metrical psalms, see Coburn Freer, *Music for a King: George Herbert's Style and the Metrical Psalms* (Baltimore: Johns Hopkins, 1972).

13   Ringler, p. 294.

14   Plato, *Cratylus* 424, translated by H.N. Fowler (London: Heinemann, 1939), 137.

15   'Roma, Anagr.' See McCloskey and Murphy, pp. 102-103. The *Roma/amor* pun is described by Sidonius Apollinaris as already ancient in fifth century Gaul. See *Epist.* 9: 14:1.

16   *Ovide Moralisé* (Modern Language Association of America Photographic Facsimile 326), 33. See Mary Ellen Rickey, *Utmost Art: Complexity in the Verse of George Herbert* (Lexington: U of Kentucky P, 1966), 36. For a full discussion of echo poetry and the significance of Echo herself, see John Hollander, *The Figure of Echo* (Berkeley & Los Angeles: U of California P, 1981). See also Ben Jonson, *Cynthia's Revels*, 1: 2:36-37: 'But selfe-love never yet could looke on truth, / But with bleared beames ... '. Cited in the discussion of Narcissus and Echo in DeWitt T. Starnes and Ernest W. Talbert, *Classical Myth and Legend in Renaissance Dictionaries* (Chapel Hill: U of North Carolina P, 1955), 200.

17   On counterpoint, see Albert McHarg Hayes, 'Counterpoint in Herbert', in John R. Roberts, ed., *Essential Articles for the Study of George Herbert's Poetry* (Hamden, CT: Archon Books, 1979), 283-297.

18   Henry Peacham, *The Garden of Eloquence* (1593) (Gainesville, FL: Scholars' Facsmilies & Reprints, 1954), 56.

19   Julius Caesar Scaliger, *Poetices* 4: 4:32, cited in Lee Ann Sonnino, *A Handbook to Sixteenth-Century Rhetoric* (London: Routledge & Kegan Paul, 1968), 26).

20   *The Rhetoric of Aristotle* 3: 11, translated by Lane Cooper (New York: Appleton-Century-Crofts, 1932), 213.

21   *Parcel*: 'To cover (a caulked seam, etc.) with canvas strips and daub with pitch' (*OED*).

22 My colleague John Kevin Newman suggests that *lutēr*, a poetic word in Greek for 'releaser', may be relevant here.

23 On the place of *paronomasia* in retorts see Judith Dundas, '*Paronomasia* in the Quip Modest: From Sidney to Herbert', *Connotations* 2 (1992), 223-233. See also Debra Fried's response in *Connotations* 3 (1993-94), 115-117.

24 See Eleanor Cook, 'From Etymology to Paronomasia: Wallace Stevens, Elizabeth Bishop, and Others', *Connotations* 2 (1992), 34-51.

25 From Donne's 1625 sermon on the text 'And he said unto him, why callest thou me good? There is none good but one; that is God'. Cited in Stanwood and Ross Asals, pp. 287-288.

26 Henry Reynolds, *Mythomystes* (1632). Cited in Hollander, p. 16.

7

HERBERT AND ANALOGY

R.V. YOUNG, Jr

Recent years have witnessed increased interest in the historical interpreta-tion of seventeenth-century poetry, and George Herbert has received more than his share of such attention. Much of this scholarship has concentrated on analyzing the import of the poetry of *The Temple* by determining the author's social, political, and religious orientation. By placing his poems in a particular milieu or ideological context, scholars seek to define Herbert as Calvinist or Arminian; and they speculate whether, had he lived to see the Civil War, he would have favoured Parliament and the Puritans or the Stuart court and Laudian church. Critics of new historicist inclination try to explain devotional and doctrinal motifs in *The Temple* in terms of the socio-political imperatives of Jacobean and Caroline culture. Now it is self-evident that knowledge of the historical background will furnish valuable insights for the interpretation of Herbert's poetry; however, unless the poetry is, at some point, considered in its own right as poetry, then there is, finally, no point in studying it at all. A look at what might be called the logic of Herbert's figurative language provides a general perspective on *The Temple* as discourse and still links it to the intellectual developments of the poet's era. Herbert's deployment of analogy, in particular, discloses an affinity with the Scholastic vision of reality that is not ordinarily attributed to him and suggests that he was resistant to the dominant intellectual ten-dencies of the seventeenth-century.

By considering the analogical properties of Herbert's poetry, one can avoid the reductive tendencies of historicisms, old and new, which gener-ally result in delivering the poet into the camp of his Puritan enemies. This is effected by splitting apart the tenors and vehicles of metaphors—the con-temporary equivalent of Puritan iconoclasm. One scholar, for example, concedes that, '*The Temple* as a whole is permeated with ecclesiastical and liturgical language. However,' he continues, 'these ecclesiastical references are, from the beginning, clearly metaphorical or otherwise internalized, representing spiritual realities that come to exist fundamentally *within* the believer'.[1] Another scholar sets out 'to foreground the social and political presuppositions of theological doctrine' in *The Temple*[2] and virtually reduces Herbert's devotional poetry to a calculating ploy for heavenly pre-ferment. Apart from the specific issues involved in such judgments, the methodical dismembering of metaphors seems a heavy-handed way of dealing with poetry as witty as Herbert's. He was not a literalist, and he was not bound to any of the narrow party platforms current in his day: such was the essential meaning, I think, of his withdrawal from the court to a rural parsonage at Bemerton. One of his strengths as a poet is the capacity to see simultaneously converging planes of reality, as manifest in the density, the resonance, the wit of his language. It is just this poetic vitality that is threatened by efforts to tie the meaning of Herbert's poetry to an *a priori* historical construct. The effect is to strip the interior of *The Temple* as bare as the interior of a Puritan meeting hall.

Heather Asals strives to defend the wholeness of Herbert's vision by establishing its philosophical basis through a consideration of his work in terms of predication. She covers the same ground as M.M. Ross in his chapter on 'The Anglican Dilemma' in *Poetry and Dogma*; that is, the crisis faced by those members of the Church of England who wished to reconcile Reformation doctrine with some aspects of Catholic liturgical and devotional practice. Asals attempts to refute Ross in order to preserve a distinctive and substantial 'Anglican' way by arguing that Herbert deliberately substitutes an equivocal predication of God for Thomist analogical predication. 'Ross is wrong,' she maintains, 'in his assumption that analogy alone can create ontological relevance: this is not what Herbert's contemporaries, or Herbert, assumed'.[3] Although neither Ross nor Asals devotes any significant discussion to the meaning of 'analogy' or ever actually defines the term, both appear to accept implicitly the view formulated at the beginning of the sixteenth century by Thomas de Vio Cardinal Cajetan that, for St Thomas, analogy is a metaphysical category referring to the nature of being itself. If this interpretation is accepted, then Asals must be arguing that Herbert is substituting a logical mode of predication for a metaphysical doctrine—a procedure in itself problematic. Ralph McInerny argues, however, that St Thomas, contrary to Cajetan's explanation, regards analogy not as a metaphysical reality, but as a logical intention, indeed as a special kind of equivocation.[4] If either understanding of the term is accepted, then Asals' dichotomy between analogy and equivocation is put in question, and the dichotomy breaks down altogether upon consideration of the close resemblance between what she calls 'equivocation' in Herbert's poems and what St Thomas calls 'analogy'.

It is certainly true that a theology of equivocation was available during Herbert's era, but such a theology could not sustain the sacramental view of reality that pervades *The Temple*, and that affirms the creation's capacity to bespeak its Creator. The theology that confines itself to a purely equivocal predication of God finds its most unblushing statement in the words of Thomas Hobbes:

And therefore, men that by their own meditation,arrive to the acknowl-
edgement of one Infinite, Omnipotent, and Eternall God, choose rather
to confesse he is Incomprehensible, and above their understanding;
than to define his Nature by *Spirit Incorporeall*, and then confesse their
definition to be unintelligible: or if they give him such a title, it is not
Dogmatically, with intention to make the Divine Nature understood;but
Piously, to honour him with attributes, of significations, as remote as
they can from the grossnesse of Bodies Visibile.[5]

Hobbes was of course a scandal to the English clergy of the later seventeenth century, but his formulation is the genuine logical consequence of
insisting that only an equivocal predication of God is possible. 'Things are
equivocally named, when they have the name only in common, the definition (or statement of essence) corresponding with the name being different,'
writes Aristotle.[6] Hence Hobbes maintains that what we say of God is
purely arbitrary with regard to the actual nature of godhead and merely
reflects our piety. Hobbes's specific theological view grows naturally out of
his rejection of metaphysics in general. For him philosophy is the knowledge of 'bodies' and their relations only; there can be no knowledge of
'separated essences', much less of Being itself (*Leviathan* 4: 46, pp. 682-
695). Given a strict interpretation of 'equivocation' that excludes the Thomist analogical variant, it is difficult to agree with Asals that equivocal
predication can 'create ontological relevance'.

St Thomas Aquinas was not unaware of the problem of metaphysical
predication: 'It is impossible,' he writes, 'for anything to be predicated
univocally of a creature and God; for in all univocals, the rationale of the
name is common to both things of which the name is predicated.' But
things that share the reason or rationale of a name (*ratio nominis*—its intelligible meaning) are to that extent equals in terms of rational essence, and a
creature cannot share God's essence. 'Whatever there is in God,' Thomas
further observes, 'this is his own proper existence; for just as essence in
him is the same as existence, so his knowledge is the same in him as actual
knowing. Hence, since the existence proper to one thing cannot be trans-
ferred to another, it is impossible for a creature to attain the same rational
essence in possessing what God possesses, just as it is impossible for it to
reach the same existence.' St Thomas introduces analogy to explain how it
is possible for man to know anything at all about God and hence to say
anything about Him with a certain propriety:

And yet it cannot be said that whatever is predicated of God and creature is altogether equivocal, since if there were no real likeness of crea-

tures to God, then his essence would not be a resemblance of creatures, and he would then not know the creatures in knowing his own essence. Likewise we would be unable to arrive at any knowledge of God from created things; and of the names befitting creatures, one could no more be said of him than another, since among equivocal names it does not matter whichever one is applied, because there is no likeness to the thing.[7]

Thomas' remark that 'whatever is predicated of God and creatures is not altogether equivocal' (*omnino aequivoce*) suggests a degree of equivocity in analogy. Hence although Asals proposes Herbert's 'The Son' as a paradigm case of the poetics of equivocation, neither the poem nor her commentary seems to violate St Thomas' explanation of analogy:

> How neatly do we give one only name
> To parents' issue and the sun's bright star!
> A son is light and fruit; a fruitful flame
> Chasing the father's dimness, carried far
> From the first man in th'East, to fresh and new
> Western discov'ries of posterity.
> So in one word our Lord's humility
> We turn upon him in a sense most true:
>   For what Christ once in humbleness began,
>   We him in glory call, *The Son of Man*.   (5-14)

'This,' Asals writes, 'is what I consider to be Herbert's formal "apology" for equivocation; homonymous language turns to a "sense most true"' (*Equivocal Predication*, p. 9). However, if a pun is to have a 'sense most true', it cannot be, as St Thomas would say, 'altogether equivocal'. The entire point of this sonnet in praise of the English language is to disclose how its hidden network of correspondences mirrors the hidden correspondences of reality. The poet is at pains to show that the homophone *sun/son* (in modern spelling) is not a mere equivocation but conceals a 'real likeness'. If the poem is equivocal, it is equivocal in St Thomas' 'large sense' that 'includes in itself analogy', and that acknowledges varying degrees of likeness within the structure of reality.[8] The literary significance of these degrees of likeness is intimated by C.S. Lewis' shrewd observation that 'the *Romance of the Rose* could not, without loss, be rewritten as the *Romance of the Onion*'.[9] To see how far Herbert's poem is from pure equivocation, one need only consider a literary application of sheer equivocity (also employing religious language) in an exchange between James Joyce's washerwomen: 'Lord help you, Maria, full of grease, the load is with me! Your prayers'.[10] The *Lord/load* and *grace/grease* puns (probably far more homophonic in the speech of Joyce's working-class Irish women than in that of most scholars) are not intended to enhance our sense of the providential design of creation; Joyce's love of the English language was based on different considerations.

Asals rightly maintains that Herbert 'shared many assumptions about the nature of God with St Thomas (his predicates), and [that] he shared with Thomas a belief in the *need* to predicate God' (emphasis in original); but still to argue that Herbert 'substituted equivocal predication for analogy in his own ontological system' (*Equivocal Predication*, p. 15), is to place him, philosophically and ecclesiastically, in an untenable position. Purely equivocal predication allows one to make no assumptions about God at all; in fact, it would undermine the sacramental theology and liturgical practice toward which Herbert was plainly inclined. Purely equivocal predication can only serve the anti-metaphysical urge of the radical Reformation, with its hidden God, and lead ultimately to the oft-repeated agnosticism of Hobbes:

> But for Spirits, they call them Incorporeall; which is a name of more honour, and may therefore with more piety bee attributed to God him-selfe; in whom wee consider not what Attribute expresseth best his Nature, which is Incomprehensible; but what best expresseth our desire to honour Him (*Leviathan* 4: 46, pp. 689-690).

If Herbert believed that all predication of God was purely equivocal, then there is no way he could 'share assumptions' (or 'predicates') about the nature of God with St Thomas; equivocal predication is not about the nature of God since it is based on no real likeness between Him and the creation. Equivocal predication of God would not reflect His nature but rather, as Hobbes maintains, merely our feelings about Him.

In contemporary terms, equivocation is the language of ideology, the hermeneutic of suspicion. An effectively 'equivocal' reading of Herbert's poems with ecclesiastical and liturgical titles, would suggest that the governing images and figures are significant only as indices to 'the speaker's inner state'. Hence when Christopher Hodgkins insists that '"The Windows" (*W*, 67), one of Herbert's most affecting architectural poems, is not about how stained-glass windows inspire devotion, but how a preacher is a window' (*Authority, Church, and Society*, pp. 169, 172), he simply dismisses Herbert's metaphor by a didactic, critical procedure that casts aside the vehicle like a spent cartridge once the bullet of instruction is speeding on its way. An analogical reading would interpret 'The Windows' as a poem about the mutually enhancing effect of 'Doctrine and life, colours and light in one' (11). Analogy is thus inclusive of meaning, opening *windows* on the multi-layered density of reality.

What Asals offers as an equivocal use of language generally turns out to rest upon an analogical foundation. 'Anthropopathia,' she writes, 'is a metaphor of projection which allows the poet to discover within the "accommodated" actions of God the spiritual condition of self. "And should Gods eare / Which needs not man, be ty'd to those / Who heare not him, but quickly heare / his utter foes"? the speaker asks in "The Method"' (*Equivocal Predication*, p. 41). If these lines from 'The Method' exemplify equivocation, it is only that particular, qualified sort that St Thomas calls analogy: the lines (25-28) assume a real likeness—a responsiveness in God that corresponds to the human faculty of hearing. Although God has no 'eare' in a sense of the term univocally predicable of God and man, the trope is not purely arbitrary; it is not merely the subjective attribution of human wishes to Luther's utterly unknown God. To be sure, 'Gods eare' is not a properly proportional analogy, but a metaphor; however, the poet's confidence in the metaphor rests upon the possibility of predicating analogically of God such transcendental terms as wisdom, goodness, and justice as they are understood in human experience. Hence the metaphor signifies a genuine awareness of something truly in God's nature about which man can reason with *method*:

>   Then once more pray:
>   Down with thy knees, up with thy voice.
>   Seek pardon first, and God will say,
>   *Glad heart rejoice.*   (29-32)

If 'Gods eare' were purely equivocal, the speaker of this poem could have no such assurance of being *heard*.

'The Method', like 'The Son', thus establishes an analogical style of discourse that is not merely equivocal: the poet likes 'our language' because its rifts are loaded with providential ore. 'An Offering', with its eucharistic overtones, is still more significant in this respect: although the *language* may seem equivocal, its ultimate import—its *predication*—is not. 'Come, bring thy gift', the poem begins, with a hint of approaching to receive communion by way of an allusion to Matt. 5: 23-24: 'Therefore if thou bring thy gift to the altar, and there remembrest that thy brother hath ought against thee; leave thy gift before the altar, and go thy way; first be

reconciled to thy brother, and then come and offer thy gift.' In the fourth
stanza the eucharistic reference becomes explicit:

> There is a balsam, or indeed a blood,
> Dropping from heav'n, which doth both cleanse and close
> All sorts of wounds; of such strange force it is.   (19-21)

There is certainly a play of language here: a blood that is a balsam that
cleanses and closes wounds—an 'All-heal' (22). But underlying the paradoxical figures is the complex reality of the wine/blood of the eucharistic
species: this 'balsam' is '*indeed* a blood'. It operates in the realm of human
sin and suffering, but its origin is divine ('Dropping from heav'n'). 'Blood'
is not in Herbert's poem an 'altogether equivocal' predication; it is an analogical predication because it signifies the dual reality that is the marrow of
the sacrament. Although as an English Protestant Herbert stops short of
articulating the doctrine of transubstantiation, in this context it is worth
recalling that the relation between substance and accident is analogical.[11]
If Herbert's doctrine is vague, his devotion is intense. The 'blood' in his
poem has a genuinely restorative and transforming effect; it actually con-
veys sanctifying grace—a 'favour' that changes the 'offering':

> Yet thy favour
> May give savour
> To this poor oblation;
> And it raise
> To be thy praise,
> And be my salvation.   (37-42)

Herbert is in fact relentless in seeking out analogical likeness within apparent equivocation. His 'Anagram' goes beyond coincidence of sound in a
homonym and finds a correspondence of meaning in an apparently fortu-
itous rearrangement of letters:

> MARY
> *Ana*-{   }*gram*
> ARMY

> How well her name an *Army* doth present,
> In whom the *Lord of Hosts* did pitch his tent!

That these four letters are patient of such reordering would seem to be pure equivocation—the result of sheer, irrational chance; and the word 'army' would not, at first glance, seem to offer much opportunity for pious reflection in relation to 'Mary'. (One need only consider what James Joyce might do with it.) But again the point—the *wit*—of Herbert's poem is to insist that the anagram is not merely coincidence, not purely equivocal: it is the effect of God's providential ordering of the realm of contingent being in harmony with divine purposes. Herbert's 'Anagram' thus manifests the same kind of wit that Baltasar Gracián attributes to St Augustine:

> Augustine made the centre of his wit that Lady who was the centre of the infinite wisdom, and he said: the Eternal Word deigned to exchange the bosom of the Father for the sacred virginal womb of his Mother, and this Lady went from being the wife of a poor carpenter to being the wife of the Architect of Heaven.[12]

There is of course more at stake here than merely determining to call Herbert's poetry 'analogical' rather than 'equivocal'. The similarity between Herbert's mode of perceiving reality and Gracián's suggests that the English Protestant clergyman shared the Spanish Jesuit's sense of analogical correspondence as part of the nature of things. The poems of *The Temple* must therefore be read as representing more than one level of reality at the same time. Herbert maintains a remarkable poise between the Catholic traditions of the past and the doctrinal demands of the Reformation. His aim is to capture a sense of God's sacramental presence in forms of worship, whether private devotion or liturgical ritual. Only an analogical conception of the relationship between the eternal realm of God and the temporal created world provides the terms for an adequate metaphysical foundation.

There is no more effective illustration of this principle than the culminating poem of 'The Church', 'Love (3)'. An analogical consideration gives more resonance to the sexual images and implications in the poem, so assiduously exhibited by Michael Schoenfeldt. The sexuality is certainly there, as it is in many other poems in *The Temple* and in Christian devotional poetry in general. But it is misleading to suggest that 'Love (3)' is permeated by scarcely concealed erotic preoccupations under a surface of conventional piety. Nothing is more conventional than for Christian devotion to be expressed in unmistakably erotic figures that point beyond themselves to what—from a Christian perspective—is the most ecstatic fulfilment of the most intense desire. Hence Schoenfeldt rightly objects to Janis Lull's assertion that 'Love (3)' rejects the sexual analogy 'altogether'; like all analogies it is not rejected but subsumed in something greater.[13] Sexual desire is not the same as the love of God, but God loves and is loved by creatures who are subject to the desire of the flesh. When a man says to a woman, 'I love you', the usage of 'love' is not, as St Thomas would say, 'altogether equivocal' with respect to the statement, 'God is love' (1 John 4: 8, 16). Hence the erotic metaphors in 'Love (3)' are not mere figures of speech to be dispensed with once the spiritual meaning is determined, and much less are they furtive indications that the poet's devotion to God is some kind of displaced or repressed sexuality waiting to be exposed by the daring candour of postmodern criticism. In Herbert's vision of reality, sacred and profane love are analogous. Therefore, metaphors and images based on this analogy reveal the mutually illuminating and enhancing character of what, in our usually limited human perspective, appear to be discrete phases of the experience of love. To sum up, in Herbert's analogical vision, nothing is ever *merely* what it is; it is always something more.

Notes

1   Christopher Hodgkins, *Authority, Church, and Society in George Herbert: Return to the Middle Way* (Columbia: U of Missouri P, 1991), 169.

2   Michael C. Schoenfeldt, *Prayer and Power: George Herbert and Renaissance Courtship* (Chicago: U of Chicago P, 1991), 12.

3   Malcolm Mackenzie Ross, *Equivocal Predication: George Herbert's Way to God* (New Brunswick: Rutgers UP, 1954), 55-87; Heather A.R. Asals, *Equivocal Predication: George Herbert's Way to God* (Toronto: U of Toronto P, 1981), 6.

4   Thomas De Vio Cajetan (1468-1534), *De nominum analogia* (1498). For a thorough modern exposition of Cajetan's view, see James F. Anderson, *The Bond of Being: An Essay on Analogy and Existence* (1949; rpt. New York: Greenwood Press, 1969). For the view that analogy is an indispensable mode of understanding reality, but not in itself a metaphysical reality, see Ralph M. McInerny, *The Logic of Analogy: An Interpretation of St Thomas* (The Hague: Martinus Nijhoff, 1961); and McInerny, *Studies in Analogy* (The Hague: Martinus Nijhoff, 1968).

5   *Leviathan* 1: 12, edited by C.B. MacPherson (Harmondsworth: Penguin Books, 1968), 171.

6   *Categories* I (1a), translated by Harold P. Cooke (Cambridge, MA: Harvard UP, 1938), 171.

7   *De Veritate* 3: 11, *Quaestiones Disputatae* 11, 5th ed. (Turin: Marietti, 1927), 3: 58-59: 'Impossibile est aliquid univoce praedicari de creatura et Deo; in omnibus enim univocis communis est ratio nominis utrique eorum de quibus nomen univoce praedicatur; et sic quantum ad illius nominis rationem univoca in aliquo aequalia sunt, quamvis secundum esse unum altero possit esse prius vel posterius, sicut in ratione numeri omnes numeri sunt aequales, quamvis secundum nomen rei unus altero prior sit. Creatura autem quantumcumque imitetur Deum, non potest

pertingere ad hoc ut eadem ratione sunt in diversis, sunt eis communia secundum rationem substantiae sive quidditatis, sed sunt distincta secundum esse. Quidquid autem est in Deo, hoc est suum proprium esse; sicut enim essentia in eo est idem quod esse, ita scientia idem est quod scientem esse in eo; unde cum esse quod est proprium unius rei non possit alteri communicari, impossibile est quod creatura pertingat ad eamdem rationem habendi aliquid quod habet Deus, sicut impossibile est quod ad idem esse perveniat. Similiter etiam in nobis esset: si enim in Petro non differret homo et hominum esse, impossibile esset quod homo univoce diceretur de Petro et Paulo, quibus est esse diversum; nec tamen potest dici quod omnino aequivoce praedicetur quidquid de Deo et creatura dicitur, quia si non esset aliqua convenientia creaturae ad Deum secundum rem, sua essentia non esset creaturarum similitudo; et ita cognoscendo essentiam suam non cognosceret creaturas. Similiter etiam nec nos ex rebus creatis in cognitionem Dei pervenire possemus; nec nominum quae creaturis aptantur, unum magis de eo dicendum esset quam aliud; quia ex aequivocis non differret quodcumque nomen imponatur, ex quo nulla rei convenientia attenditur.'

8   *Summa Theologiae* 1: 13:10 ad 4: 'Philosophus largo modo accipit aequivoca, secundum quod includunt in se analoga.' For the sense of degrees of likeness, see the body of the article as well as the passage from *De Veritate* quoted above and in note 7.

9   C.S. Lewis and E.M.W. Tillyard, *The Personal Heresy* (London: Oxford UP, 1939), 97. See also McInerny, 'Metaphor and Analogy', in *Studies in Analogy*, pp. 81-83; and 'Metaphor and Fundamental Ontology', *Studies*, pp. 92, 93-94.

10   *Finnegans Wake* (1939; rpt. New York: Viking, 1959), 214.

11   See Cajetan, *In de Ente et Essentia D. Thomae Aquinitatis* 2: 21, edited by P.M.-H. Laurent (Turin: Marietti, 1934), 37: 'Substantia et accidens sunt analogata primo modo sub ente.'

12   *Agudeza y arte de ingenio* 4, edited by Arturo del Hoyo (Madrid: Aquilar, 1967), 248: 'Hizo Augustino centro de su agudeza a aquella Señora, que lo fue de la sabiduría infinito, y dijo: Dignose el Verbo Eterno de trocar el seno del Padre por el sagrado virginal vientre de su Madre, y pasó esta Señora, de esposa de un pobre carpintero, a serlo de Arquitecto del Cielo.' Gracián quotes Augustine from a Nativity sermon of questionable authenticity, *PL* (Appendix) 38-39: col. 1987: 'Exsultemus in fide et ad partum Virginis, quae dum desponsaretur fabro, coeli nupsit Architecto.'

13   *Prayer and Power*, p. 256. Janis Lull, *The Poem in Time: Reading George Herbert's Revisions of the Church* (Newark: U of Delaware P, 1990), 49. See also Chana Bloch, *Spelling the Word: George Herbert and the Bible* (Berkeley: U of California P, 1985), 339.

8

'A TITLE STRANGE, YET TRUE':
TOWARD AN EXPLANATION OF HERBERT'S TITLES

MATTHIAS BAUER

George Herbert's contemporary readers, who, 360 years ago, first looked into the little duodecimo volume of *The Temple*, may well have been surprised by a fact we tend to take for granted in collections of poetry. Every poem of this collection has a title, and, what must have been even more surprising, nearly every title consists of a single noun with or without an article.

Glancing through Elizabethan or Jacobean anthologies, we come to realize that individual short pieces of poetry, as a rule, did not have titles like those Herbert gave to his poems. In the Renaissance, the majority of shorter poems (of sonnets, for example) were not headed by titles, especially when they were part of a cycle. In most cases, titles were labels for mainly practical purposes. They could help to identify individual poems, as well as indicate the genre, addressee, or occasion ('An Ode. To Himselfe') or the dramatic situation of the speaker ('The lover complayneth the unkindness of his love'). Titles, of course, have a long tradition,[1] but the conspicuous absence of this subject from poetological treatises of the English Renaissance shows that the title was not regarded as an essential part of a poem. Puttenham, for instance, who deals with nearly every aspect of the poet's craft, has nothing to say about titles. As regards poetic practice, Donne may be listed as an exception (and before him, for instance, Southwell), but then the titles of his poems mostly seem to be later additions by others.[2] In each of Herbert's poems, however, the title is an essential part of the poetic message, and in many cases it is, to put it metaphorically, the germ as well as the quintessence of the poem.

The enigmatic or hieroglyphic nature of Herbert's titles has been pointed out, for example, by Joseph H. Summers, Mary Ellen Rickey and John Hollander,[3] who has stressed that 'it is only in the early seventeenth century in England that the ... "essential" title form appears at all' (pp. 217-218). Hollander recognizes that 'Herbert's titles, like his forms, are amazingly radical, in that their expressive character is in each case part of the poem's fiction' (p. 223).[4] But while the extraordinary nature of Herbert's titles has repeatedly been noticed, only a few of them have been analysed closely and we are only just beginning to understand their function and relationship to literary tradition. One of the first to have done so is Anne

Ferry, who has recently compared Herbert's titles with those of preceding or contemporary English poets, especially with collections of religious verse.[5] The closest model she finds, however, does not belong to sacred poetry but to a predominantly secular or humanistic genre. The characteristic one-word titles of *The Temple* are remarkably similar to the headings of Renaissance commonplace books, the *topics* under which related entries were grouped together by their compilers.[6]

Since the formal and functional differences between his titles and the group-headings of contemporary anthologies is not to be overlooked, however, it is more than likely that Herbert used and transformed other models as well. One of the differences is Herbert's frequent use of the definite article, as in 'The Sinner', 'The Collar', or 'The Glimpse'.[7] These titles are not quite the same as typical commonplace-book headings like 'Of God', 'Of Hope'[8], or 'Hearbes', 'Of Trees', 'Rivers'.[9] The common title 'Of ...', which is conspicuously absent from *The Temple*, follows the Latin convention of calling a work 'De ...' (as a short form of 'Liber de ...', 'Tractatus de ...'). Herbert was more than aware of the Latin roots of the English language, but he also recognized the opportunity offered by the article as a 'new' part of speech[10] for giving his titles a function quite different from the Latinate 'Of ...' convention and the collective plural headings of contemporary anthologies.

Beginning with the title of the whole book, *The Temple*, followed by 'The Dedication', 'The Church-porch' and (after the Latin title 'Super-liminare') 'The Church', 'The Altar', and 'The Sacrifice', Herbert draws special attention to the definite article, making his readers aware of *the* as a word, i.e. a sequence of letters. The reference to architecture, as well as the definiteness of the titles (there are only five titles with an indefinite article), suggests the lemmata or *topoi* of the house of memory.[11] Places of memory may also be indicated by those titles which consist of abstract nouns without article, such as 'Miserie' or 'Obedience'. In whichever case, Herbert's titles do not announce thoughts, reflections or witty phrases *on* or *about* something, nor do they group together a number of examples or related instances. They rather point out the thing or matter itself, calling it by its *nomen appellativum*.[12] The difference is quite similar to the distinction made by Quintilian (8: 6:47) and other rhetoricians between *permixta allegoria* and *tota allegoria*; Herbert's titles, like *tota allegoria*, present matters and things without explanatory additions. 'Miserie' and 'Obedience' can be read as personifications as well as announcements of poems on particular themes. When he uses the definite article, Herbert makes the objects of his titles appear as if they could be individually identified (such as 'The Altar' in the imaginative space of 'The Church') or—even at the same time—as if they were the type or quintessence of all things or matters of their kind.[13] This property of Herbert's titles points to another literary genre flourishing in his time which may have influenced his method of giving titles to his poems: the scientific inventory naming parts of the body, animals, plants, or stones, such as the 'Anatomy' and the 'Herball' that Herbert recommended every country parson to consult.[14] Seen in this light, Herbert's titles indicate that each poem has a particular place to fill in the poetic cosmos of *The Temple*.

When one tries to understand the function of Herbert's titles it seems helpful to remember that his own usage of the word 'title' testifies to his being quite aware of its origin and multiplicity of meaning. In 'The Sacrifice', Christ on the cross refers to himself as a text or image over which a title has been placed:

> A king my title is, prefixt on high;
> Yet by my subjects am condemn'd to die
> A servile death in servile companie: (233-235)

The meaning of 'title' as an appellation of honour is indicated by 'king' as well as the complementary 'subjects'. But the very word *subject* also points to the realm of language or composition, where title and subject are closely related. This connection makes the preposterousness of the event all the more conspicuous: a person's subject, so to speak, turns against his title; the *logos* is confronted with dumb illogicality. The reference to language is emphasized by the grammatical term *prefix* in 'prefixt', which also draws attention to the original meaning of *title* ('inscription placed on or over a subject, giving its name or describing it', *OED* 1.†a.). *Title* in its earliest use represented Latin *titulus*, the inscription on the cross.[15]

Herbert thus refers to the letters INRI forming a title in the sense of a superscription as well as a personal appellation or name. Similarly, when Herbert in the first line of 'The Thanksgiving' speaks of 'a title strange, yet true', he alludes to this inscription at the head of the cross, which stands in marked contrast to the tormented body of Christ. The truth made visible by this contrast finds expression in the oxymoronic address with which the poem begins: 'Oh King of grief!'

The *titulus* can thus be seen as a model or type of Herbert's own poetic titles, with which it has several characteristic features in common: it is a mystical abbreviation which secretly, and yet most plainly, points out truth; only at first sight may it appear inappropriate to the text or body to which it is 'prefixt'. *Titulus* as an abbreviation mark corresponds to English *tittle* (formerly also spelled *title*)[16] which may be well implied in Herbert's use of the word since it refers to the small stroke or dot that 'shall in no wise pass from the law' (Matt. 5: 18). In the context of 'the law', the spelling of the English Bible, *title*[17], has juridic connotations, for *title* (as well as titulus) has of course a legal meaning as well.[18] This, in the sense of 'An assertion of right, a claim' (*OED* †7c) is also suggested in 'A King my title is'. How subtly Herbert sometimes alludes to the legal sense of *titulus* and *title* can be seen in 'Obedience', a poem whose title is never directly referred to in the text. The speaker of the poem comes to realize that the paper which he first draws up as his 'speciall Deed' (p. 10) does not in fact document his own 'gift or donation' (p. 34) but Christ's purchase; accordingly, the only legal title he may claim his own can be gathered from looking at the title of the poem.

A further use of *titulus* is its reference to a proper name, of which the title the cross is a case in point.[19] As the example of 'The Odour' will show, this individual signification is an essential feature of Herbert's titles. *Tituli* were also used for purposes of memorizing, since they were regarded as the starting-point to which everything else in a text is linked.[20]

Last but not least, the *titulus* confirms a connection which has repeatedly been pointed out but—as far as I can see—has not been regarded in the light of the relation between title and text:[21] the *titulus* at the head of the cross is a special form of the text-image combination which also characterizes the *impresa* and the emblem.[22] In Herbert's time, the connection is verified, for instance, by Johann Heinrich Alsted, who calls the motto of an emblem *titulus*.[23] Common to both the 'title strange, yet true' of the cross and the emblem or impresa is the tension between *inscriptio* and *pictura*: the inscription endows the picture with a particular meaning which is often unexpected; or rather, the meaning is the result of an unexpected or even strange connection of verbal and visual elements.[24] In the case of the emblem the *subscriptio* or epigrammatic poem may be part of the reciprocal process of illustration, mystification, and explanation. Samuel Daniel, in his translation of Paolo Giovio's treatise on *imprese*, stresses that 'the figure without the mot, or the mot without the figure, signifie nothing, in respect of the intent of the author'.[25] This mutual dependence is also characteristic of the relation between title and poem in Herbert, while of course the analogy concerns the nature of the relationship rather than the parts themselves. In *The Temple*, the 'mot' or word of the title may indicate an object that is to be imagined by the reader and is therefore closer related to the *res picta* of the emblem than to its motto. This is the case, for example, with the title 'The Cross', while the poem itself is neither a description of nor a meditation on Christ's cross (as might be expected from the tradition of meditative poems on the signs of the crucifixion)[26] but an account of 'crosse actions' experienced by the speaker. On the other hand, the title may be an abstract term resembling a *topos* or lemma, such as 'Obedience', whereas the poem is concerned with a specific action made manifest in 'this poore paper' (line 5; cf. 10: 'And here present it as my speciall Deed'). In both cases, there is a tension between title and text which may be compared to the meaningful tension that characterizes the baroque conceit. Herbert's titles, as distinct from the traditional headings of prose or poetry or the topics of common-place books, do not just indicate the subject in question, but are stumbling blocks intended to set off a process of signification.

The 'new' quality of Herbert's titles is perhaps most easily perceived in cases which refer to the established convention of the formal or generic title. Titles like 'Song' or 'A Sonnet' were quite common, but, as a rule, they just meant that the ensuing poem was a song or a sonnet.[27] Herbert's titles of this kind, however, do not confine themselves to indicating the genre or form. In his 'Prayer' poems, for example, most obviously 'Prayer (II)', the text is a prayer and, at the same time, a poem about prayer. 'Prayer (I)' is an extended definition of the word that forms its title. The poem, so to speak, gives an answer to the question 'What is a prayer?' by means of paraphrase and synonymy. There is a traditional type of poetry beginning with 'What is ... ?'[28] but then Herbert never explicitly asks this question. Instead, the one word of the title unfolds itself and is transformed in the poem. We are told by the text itself why this poetic method is so appropriate to its subject. In one of the paraphrases of 'prayer', 'The soul in paraphrase' (3), the act of personal prayer is described as an exercise in giving definitions of—or coming to terms with—one's soul. Accordingly, 'Prayer (I)' with its rapid sequence of definitions is a mimetic representation of an ejaculatory prayer, as well as an attempt at finding words for the essence of what prayer is.[29] For our present purposes, it is of particular interest that the rhetorical device of *synonymia* (or *interpretatio*)[30] plays an important part in the relationship between title and text.[31]

Few cases, however, are as obvious as 'Prayer (I)'. In other poems, the definition of a poetic form may be the subject of a hidden game going on between the title and the text. One of the most intriguing examples is 'The Quidditie'. The poem presents a series of negative definitions of a verse, finally turning to a positive, sacred one. All this takes place in the spirit of *serio ludere* reflected by the title, which ambiguously refers to the essence of all definitions, the *quidditas* of a thing, and to a sophistical play upon words, a quibble. But this is just stating the obvious. As every schoolboy used to know, questions concerning definitions begin with 'quid'.[32] Accordingly, keeping in mind that 'verse' is just a another word for 'dittie', we come to realize that our title is identical with the very question answered directly in the first line the poem: 'What is a verse?' 'MY God, a verse is not a crown ...'.[33] Herbert here combines synonymy with paronomasia, another rhetorical device characteristic of the subtle interplay between his poems and their titles. In addition, 'The Quidditie' shows that Herbert's use of synonyms is not confined to the English language. The allusion to Latin synonyms or homophones of English words, in particular, is typical of Herbert's titles.

Objections might be raised to this on the basis of 'The Sonne', where the speaker declares (pp. 3-4): 'I like our language, as our men and coast: / Who cannot dresse it well, want wit, not words.' Still, I am not convinced that the great neo-Latin poet and Orator at Cambridge set aside his knowledge of Latin when he came to write the poems of *The Temple*. Moreover, Latin did not belong to 'foreign nations' but was the *lingua franca* of all learned people[34] (besides being one of the roots of the English language itself). Even in 'The Sonne' Herbert's wordplay is not entirely home-made. The pun on 'sun' and 'son' was far too common in his time to be a special sign of wit. Herbert succeeds in extending it, making it refer to his own art, the transformation of secular poetic forms to sacred purposes. The form of this poem is actually announced by its title, to which one only has to add the sign of the son, the cruciform letter T, in order to spell out the (Italian, and ultimately Latin) word 'sonnet'.[35] Thus 'The Sonne' is an example of yet another way of referring both to the form and the subject of a poem by means of its title.[36]

The use of Latin again provides the key to the mysterious title 'The Pulley'. At first sight, it has little to do with the imagery of the poem, which centres around the pouring of blessings from a glass vessel.[37] 'Rest' is the only blessing which is kept back. This last gift will not be bestowed upon God's creature before 'wearinesse' will 'tosse' man to God's breast. Then, however, it will be the lifeline or rope by which he is saved, the pulley by which he is lifted up to heaven.[38] In language, the connection is established through the fact that the Latin word for the *rope* that makes a pulley work is *restis*. Thus, the Latin near-synonym of the title turns out to be a homonym of the central word of the text. This is confirmed by the validity of the reciprocal process since a homonym of the title is the synonym of the central image of the poem. 'Pulley' echoes Latin *ampulla*, which is a synonym of the 'glass' or vessel from which the blessings are poured.[39] A tacit synonymic link between 'rest' and the title of the poem is also established by the verb *to tire*, which not only denotes weariness and the need for rest but is also an obsolete synonym of *to pull*.[40]

Another characteristic example of the fine-spun threads with which Herbert connects the titles of his poems to the poems themselves is pro-

vided by 'Life'. In the title and first line of this poem, there is a shift from
life to its synonym *quickness* (*OED* 1) in the sense of 'speed, fastness'
(*OED* 4): 'I Made a posie, while the day ran by ...' What time itself, the
speaker's life, and the flowers he has gathered have in common is the rap-
idity with which they 'steal away' (5). The imagery of the poem thus
expatiates on lexical properties of its title word. But this is only one thread
in an intricate pattern of verbal connections. The personification of the
flowers, for instance, which are transformed into sentient beings and follow
time's beckoning, is based upon a pun: 'wither'd' implies both their drying
up and taking leave, albeit the place *whither* they go is not mentioned.

The background to this image, needless to say, is the eternal metaphor
of the course of life. The affinity of *way* and *life* is mysteriously revealed in
the Latin paronomasia of *via* and *vita*.[41] In Herbert's poem 'Life', *via* is
etymologically present in 'a-way', while the image of the journey is also
referred to in 'ran by', 'becken to', 'steal away', 'convey', 'Farewell', and
'follow straight'. A relation similar to that between *via* and *vita* exists between the animated flowers and their becoming *follower*s of time (which, of
course, *flow*s).[42] This implicit anagrammatic wordplay in lines 4 and 5 is
made explicit in the last stanza, where the speaker's 'Farewell deare flowers' goes together with 'I follow straight'. In addition, the elements *ol* and
flow refer to the oil of the rose that is won 'after death for cures' (p. 15).

The sense of smell, which is referred to in all three stanzas of the
poem, is tied up with the image of decay and the passing of time. It is also
connected with the concept of mental perception, the speaker's mind smelling the figurative or emblematic meaning of the posy in his hand. The paradox of the smelling mind is an invention in the literal sense of the word, for
it is to be found in the words themselves. 'Whither' contains a remote echo
of Latin *vita* and a nearer one of the obsolete English word *witter*, 'knowing, cunning' (*OED* a.¹).[43] Moreover, the meaning of the posy is understood because it is conveyed 'sweetly', a word which carries conviction, so
to speak, since it contains 'weet'. 'To weet', however, as well as its parallel
'to wit', is not only another paronomasia of *vita* but the English equivalent
of Latin *sentire*. *Sentire*, in turn, is the root of the English *to scent*, used as
a noun in line 17 of the poem ('Since if my sent be good ...').

Thus, by means of paronomasia and etymology, the identity of knowledge and the sense of smell is pointed out twice, in 'sweet' and in 'sent'.
But the s(c)ent also leads us back to the image of the course of life. 'Sent'
is also the past participle of *send*, which fits logically (if not syntactical-
ly)[44] for it is the counterpart of 'follow' in line 16: the speaker follows
because he is being sent (or has a mission).[45] This verbal link is reinforced
by French *sentier* or *sente* 'path', derived from Latin *semita* (which also

denotes a track or trail, a scent followed by a hound, for example). Another reference to the *semita vitae* is implied in the allusion to 2 Cor. 2 in line 17. The 'good scent' is a literal translation of the 'bonus odor' (2 Cor. 2: 15) of the Vulgate, the 'sweet savour of Christ' (AV), which is the distinctive mark of the Christian's mission (or sending): 'God ... maketh manifest the savour of his knowledge by us in every place' (p. 14).

All this points to a central principle of composition: Herbert develops his poems not only along the lines of certain themes or conceits, but, first of all, he makes use of the inherent creative energy of language, which manifests itself in paronomasia, synonymy or etymology. In this process, the title is both the starting point or centre and the circumference or band which holds everything together. With respect to 'Life', this is most literally true. In lines 2-3, 'this band' within which the speaker's life is tied is identified with the 'posie' and thus, implicitly, with life itself. And again, language proves him right, since Latin *vitta* is just another word for *band*.

The numerous 'vertical' connections between the title of our poem and the text itself go together with a multitude of 'horizontal' ones between 'Life' and other texts and their titles. The band of life is woven through a number of poems in *The Temple*. As we have seen, the image of the *quick* passage of time at the beginning of the poem, which unfolds the semantic potential of *life*, goes together with the speaker's wish to 'tie' his 'life within this band'. Herbert here again works with implicit synonyms: the action of tying up life is—in accordance with the paradoxical logic of language— an attempt to make it *fast*. The same verbal complex is to be found in the poem 'Lent', where the speaker reminds us that obedience to the scriptures, which 'bid us *fast*' (p. 4), will result in 'Quick thoughts and motions at a small expense' (p. 20). The title of the poem is clearly another case of paradox or of *lucus a non lucendo* for *lent* promoting quickness and life is anything but *lento* (or *lentus*). This apparent contradiction goes together with the oxymoron of the 'feast of Lent' in line 1, which in turn draws attention to the paronomasia of *feast* and *fast*.[46]

Another line of connection exists between 'Life' and 'The Invitation', which is an offer to share the love which 'After death can never die' (p. 30). This invitation to a feast of eternal life, is, of course, the only kind of invitation true to its name. The feast of life is thus contrasted with the feasts of those 'whom wine/Doth define' (pp. 7-8) a relationship which is again 'found' in language: the similarity of *vita* and *vitis* (vine) also points to the true vine from which comes the juice 'Which before ye drink is bloud' (p. 12). In the next poem, 'The Banquet', the relationship is again referred to when 'Wine becomes a wing at last' (p. 42), indicating an upward movement which goes together with the speaker's prayer that God may 'take up my lines and life' (p. 51).[47]

As a final example, I have chosen the title of a poem which is, in several respects, a counterpart of 'Life': in 'The Odour, 2 Cor. 2', the speaker seeks lifelong employment (p. 30) in 'the breathing of the sweet' (p. 25) that comes from and returns to the Lord, just as in 'Life' his wish is directed towards a 'good' scent. 'The Odour, 2 Cor. 2' is one of the few titles in which the noun has a supplement, in this case an abbreviated biblical reference. This addition, however, is also a stumbling block, for in the relevant passage from 2 Corinthians 2, verses 14-16, the word 'odour' does not occur. Tyndale, the Bishops' Bible, the Geneva Bible and the AV all have 'savour' instead, as quoted above: 'God ... maketh manifest the savour of his knowledge by us in every place.' Herbert's term, *odour*, once more shows that he quotes or translates from the Latin, for it refers to the 'bonus odor' of the Vulgate to which he also alludes in 'Life'.

In order to become fully aware of the verbal radiance of its title, it is useful to keep in mind that language itself is a subject of the poem, or, to be exact, a dimension of language which goes beyond the merely denotative meaning of words. Two word-pairs, *My Master* and *My servant* are shown to have an aura as if they were not just groups of letters but live beings, 'flesh' (p. 13) that 'might creep & grow' (p. 14) or persons who are engaged upon paying a visit ('*My Master* ... Shall call and meet ... *My servant*', pp. 21-24; with an obvious pun on *meat*[48]). Language is personified; it is not so much a medium as an individual and has to be experienced like a human being. The little scene in which the word becomes flesh is, of course, a literal representation of John 1: 14, a reference to the mystery of the incarnation and the sacrament. *My Master*, and, as the speaker hopes, *My servant* are formulas which will have a wondrous effect upon the 'minde' (pp. 6, 10) of the speaker and upon the person addressed. This effect is not just compared to the 'rich sent' of 'Amber-greese' (p. 2). The wonder does not just consist in the fact that the words work upon the senses but that the sensual phenomenon, the 'Pomander' of the magic formula, may speak ('A speaking sweet ... / And tell me more', pp. 17-18). The meaningful phrase will be aesthetically pleasing but what is more, the beautiful sound is also 'rich', full of 'content' (p. 4) and meaning. The synaesthetic imagery of the poem thus reminds us to 'scent' its sentences, to regard the two formulae as a case in point of mystical linguistics. We are not only called upon to admire the sweet sound of linguistic signs but to discover significance in the body of the word itself.

In accordance with this implied poetological statement, the meaning of the title and its relation to the magic phrases with which the poem is concerned will unfold when we begin 'to hear with eyes'. The speaker hopes that the 'orientall fragrancy' of the words '*My Master*' may be complemented by '*My servant*' so that the '*cor*dials' (p. 9, emphasis added) of the first two words will be enriched by the other two in mutual exchange. One cannot but recognize in this an allusion to the abbreviated '2 Cor. 2' of the title, for the poem with its imagery of exchange echoes or parodies the topos of the *permutatio cordis*. The two formulae, '*My Master*' and '*My servant*', themselves teach us to discover such hidden meaning upon the material surface of the words, as they both contain the elements that make up a mystery, the letters M-Y-S-T-E-R. And they are mysterious indeed. *My ser*vant, by himself, is just a (rather miserable) miser who will not experience the growth of a 'new commerce'. What *My servant* needs is the 'cordial' which consists in his master's 'pardon of [his] imperfection', in other words, his *misericordia*. He has already prayed for it in the 'speaking sweet' of 'Pomander', which anagrammatically says 'pardon me'. And when the breathing of '*servant*' does 'Return to thee' (p. 28), it will of course have become an *answer*.

As we may by now expect, synonyms go together with homonyms. The servant, in this devotional poem, is a *minis*ter of the Lord. As such, how could he be otherwise than 'little' (p. 12) and in need of growth and of being told 'more' (p. 18)?[49] One of the synonyms of *odour* is *scent*, as it is used in the second line of the poem. Now, both the forms *scent* and *sent* used to be variant spellings of the word *saint* (cf. *OED*). In the light of 2 Cor. 2, this link is not out of place, since the Christians, whose distinctive mark is the *bonus odor* (the savour of the Saviour) are the 'saints' (2 Cor. 1: 1), to whom the epistle is addressed. Also, in the *Golden Legend*, there are several stories of saints who are expressly characterized by a sweet savour. The most prominent is, of course, St Ambrose, whose very name is derived from 'a stone named ambra, which is much sweet, odorant and precious'.[50] Accordingly, the sweet sound of '*My Master*', which is like 'Amber-greese', may be understood as an echo or counterpart of the Ambrosian *Te Deum*.[51]

But there is yet another saint in the *Golden Legend* who is alluded to in this poem. He was a martyr to whom the Lord appeared in prison, calling him 'my servant', and whose flesh was finally burnt by fire (cf. line 13 of Herbert's poem), 'in which fire he gave up his spirit ... . And all the people were replenished with right sweet odour ...'.[52] The saint's name is the title of our poem, Theodore, and even though this etymology is not expressly mentioned in the *Golden Legend*, it is to be assumed that the Latin word *odor* being part of his name gave rise to the story of the sweet odour at Theodore's death.[53] This onomastic interpretation of Herbert's title is supported by the fact that certain clusters of titles are characteristic of *The Temple*. In the neighbourhood of 'Mattens' we find 'Even-song' and 'Church-musick', which in turn is accompanied by 'Church-monuments', 'Church-lock and key', and 'The Church-floore'. In *The Temple*, there are (apart from 'JESU') only two poems who are explicitly headed by proper names, 'Marie Magdalene' and 'Aaron', and these two poems are immediately followed by 'The Odour'.

The case of 'The Odour' suggests that the nouns or *nomina* of Herbert's titles are to be understood not only as appellative but even as 'proper' names. A title is the name by which a poem is called,[54] identifying it as an individual rather than a member of a species or class. This is in keeping with a view of 'The Church' as representing not only a house of God but also a living congregation of saints (and sinners).[55] Each member of this chain of poems has a name which is a true *omen* and which, like many significant names in drama or fiction, helps to explain the text while it is itself explained by it. 'The Odour' shows that even the article as a part of speech that seems to carry little semantic weight may become expressive of a deeper meaning, to the extent that God himself, *theos*, is reflected in it. Thus we come to see once more that the names of Herbert's poems resemble the *titulus*, the 'title strange, yet true' of the 'King of grief'. 'Will not a verse run smooth that bears thy name?', Herbert asks in one of his early sonnets.[56] In this perspective, all his titles are but variations; they serve to define and re-define this one name (the name of all names) in whose honour his posies are made.

Notes

1   For a survey of the development of the poetic title since antiquity, see Hans-Jürgen Wilke's unpublished dissertation, 'Die Gedicht-Überschrift: Versuch einer historisch-systematischen Entwicklung' (Frankfurt am Main, 1955).

2   Helen Gardner does 'not [even] believe that more than a few of the titles are Donne's own'; see Gardner, ed., John Donne, *The Elegies and The Songs and Sonnets* (1965; Oxford: Clarendon, 1970), xciii (Textual Introduction).

3   Joseph H. Summers, *George Herbert: His Religion and Art* (London: Chatto & Windus, 1954), 128-129; Mary Ellen Rickey, *Utmost Art* (U of Kentucky P, 1966), 92-102; John Hollander, '"Haddock's Eyes": A Note on the Theory of Titles', in his *Vision and Resonance: Two Senses of Poetic Form* (New York: Oxford UP, 1975), 212-226. See also Rosemund Tuve, *A Reading of George Herbert* (Chicago: U of Chicago P, 1952), 130 and 145), and Dale B.J. Randall on the title of 'The Collar' in 'The Ironing of Herbert's "Collar"', SP 81 (1984), 473-495.

4   Hollander's assertion, however, that critical theory has confined itself more or less to 'Borgesian joking about how by a mad affirmation of synedoche, a list of titles might constitute the ultimate library' (p. 212), has to be taken with a grain of salt.

5   Anne Ferry, 'Titles in George Herbert's "little Book"', *ELR* 23 (1993), 314-344, especially 321.

6   For a more detailed discussion of Ferry's article see my forthcoming note in *Connotations* 4.3 (1994/95).

7   I am following F.E. Hutchinson's original-spelling edition of *The Works of George Herbert* (1941; Oxford: Clarendon, 1945). In accordance with common practice, however, I do not include the full stop after each title.

8   Examples from *Belvedére or The Garden of the Muses* (1600; rpt. New York: Burt Franklin, 1967).

9   Examples from *England's Parnassus* (1600; rpt. Menston: The Scolar Press, 1970).

10 See Ben Jonson's *The English Grammar* (1640), in C.H. Herford, Percy and Evelyn Simpson, eds, *The Complete Works of Ben Jonson*, vol. 8 (Oxford: Clarendon, 1965), 505-506): 'IN our *English* speech, we number the same parts with the *Latines*. ... Only, we adde a ninth, which is the *Article* ...'

11 On *The Temple* as a house of memory, see Inge Leimberg, 'George Herbert "The Sinner": Der Tempel als Memoria-Gebäude', *Archiv* 206 (1970), 241-250.

12 Cf. Jonson, p. 506.

13 It is quite remarkable that the emphatic use of *the*, 'in the sense of "the pre-eminent", "the typical", or "the only ... worth mentioning"' (*OED* 11) is first documented in 1824.

14 *The Countrey Parson*, chapter 23 (Hutchinson, p. 261).

15 *OED ibid.*; cf. John 19: 19: 'And Pilate wrote a title, and put it on the cross. And the writing was, JESUS OF NAZARETH THE KING OF THE JEWS.' *Titulus* also refers to the *crux nude* itself. See Du Cange, *Glossarium Mediae et Infimae Latinitatis* (1883-87; rpt. Graz: Akademische Druck- und Verlagsanstalt, 1954), 'titulus' 8.

16 Cf. *OED* 'tittle' 1.a.: '1483 *Cath. Angl.* 389/2 A Tytille (*A.* Titylle), *titulus, apex, epigrama*'; on *titulus* in this sense see, for instance Jean Gerson, *De modis titulandi*, no. 480 in: Glorieux (ed.) *Œuvres complètes*, vol. 9 (Paris: Desclée, 1973), 700-703.

17 *Title* is the spelling of Matt. 5: 18 in the 1562 edition of the Geneva Bible, the 1602 edition of the Bishops' Bible, and the AV.

18 *OED* 'title' 2a, 'the formal heading of a legal document'; 7a, 'Legal right to the possession of property ... ; title-deeds'; 8 '*Eccl.* A certificate of presentment to a benifice'.

19 See, for example, J.F. Niermeyer, *Mediae Latinitatis Lexicon Minus* (Leiden: E.J. Brill, 1976), 'titulus' 9.

20 See Mary Carruthers, *The Book of Memory: A Study of Memory in Medieval Culture* (Cambridge: Cambridge UP, 1990), 86 and 244-245. On p. 86 Carruthers quotes Richard of Auxerre's dictum that *titulus* is derived from *titan* 'because it is the illuminating "sun" of the entire text'.

21 For the most recent study of Herbert and the emblem see Bart Westerweel's contribution to this volume. Rosemary Freeman, *English Emblem Books* (London: Chatto & Windus, 1948) discusses several of Herbert's titles (pp. 168-171) but

surprisingly does not compare their function to those of inscriptions or *tituli* in emblem literature. John Hollander (pp. 223-224) refers to Herbert's 'emblem titles' but does not seem to regard the disparity between title and text as being analogous to the relation of *inscriptio* and *pictura*.

22 The tradition comprises, in the words of Douglas Gray, 'the inscription-poem used as *titulus*, carved or painted on tombs or the walls of buildings'. See 'The Five Wounds of Our Lord', *N&Q* 208 (1963), 166. *Titulus* could also denote a monument, 'whether with a legend or not' (Niermeyer, 'titulus' 1); according to Du Cange, another meaning (p. 7) was 'Versus lugubres de morte insigniorum personarum'.

23 See Ulrich Ernst, 'Ars memorativa und Ars poetica', *Ars memorativa: Zur kulturgeschichtlichen Bedeutung der Gedächtniskunst*, edited by Jörg Jochen Berns and Wolfgang Neuber (Tübingen: Niemeyer, 1993), 73-100, here 85.

24 Cf. Albrecht Schöne, *Emblematik und Drama im Zeitalter des Barock*, 3rd ed. (München: C.H. Beck, 1993), 20-21.

25 Samuel Daniel, *The Worthy tract of Paulus Iouius, contayning a Discourse of rare inuentions, both Militarie and Amorous called Imprese* (London, 1585), sig. Avii^r.

26 Examples are William Alabaster's sonnets 'Upon the Crucifix'.

27 This is confirmed by Samuel Daniel's use of the word *title* in *A Defence of Ryme*, where it denotes the name of a verse form or number: 'Onely what was our owne before, and the same but apparelled in forraine Titles, which had they come in their kinde and naturall attire of Ryme, wee should neuer haue suspected that they had affected to be other ...'. Samuel Daniel, *Poems and a Defence of Ryme*, edited by Arthur Colby Sprague (Chicago: U of Chicago P, 1965), 151.

28 An example is Raleigh's 'What is our life?' It should be noted that this is not a title but the beginning of the poem.

29 Robert B. Shaw has noted that Herbert's one-word titles appear to require 'the sort of elucidation which a set of definitions might supply. One might ask how Herbert's task as a poet compares with that of lexicographer. The analogy presents itself unavoidably in the case of "Prayer (I)"'. See his 'George Herbert: The Word of God and the Words of Man', *Ineffability: Naming the Unnamable from Dante to Beckett*, edited by Peter S. Hawkins and Anne Howland Schooter (New York: AMS Press, 1984), 81-93, here 84.

30 Another term is *paraphrasis*. See Lee A. Sonnino, *A Handbook to Sixteenth-Century Rhetoric* (London: Routledge, 1968), 116-117.

31 Synonymy cannot be separated from translation, its major field of application. A popular Anglo-Latin dictionary of Herbert's time, for example, was called *Synonymorum sylua*. In this work by Simon Pelegromius and 'H F', which went through thirteen editions between 1580 and 1639 (cf. *STC* 19556-19564), English headwords are printed as titles followed by a number of Latin (and Greek) equivalents.

32 Cf. Quintilian, *Institutio oratoria* 3: 6:5.

33 I am indebted to Professor Inge Leimberg for this delightful discovery. For 'dittie' as a form of verse, see Thomas Campion, *Observations in the Art of English Poesy* (1602), chapter 8 ('Of Ditties and Odes'), *Elizabethan Critical Essays*, edited by Gregory Smith, Vol. 2 (Oxford: Oxford UP, 1904), 346.

34   Ample documentation has recently been given by J.W. Binns, *Intellectual Culture in Elizabethan and Jacobean England: The Latin Writings of the Age* (Leeds: Francis Cairns, 1990), esp. chapter 1.

35   On Herbert's use of the letter T as a sign of the cross, see Inge Leimberg, 'The Letter Lost in George Herbert's "The Jews"', *SP* 90 (1993), 298-321, especially 317-321. Leimberg's interpretation of 'The Jews' is, at the same time, an exemplary study of one of Herbert's titles.

36   Yet another example is given by 'A Dialogue-Antheme,' where the title is neither prefixed to an anthem in the literal sense of the word nor to a poem about anthems. It is rather a metaphor of the musical structure of the poem, as well as of death's final transformation. It indicates that Death himself, in Christ's sacrifice, has been miraculously enabled to sing (cf. Herbert's 'Death'). See Inge Leimberg *et al.*, 'Annotating Baroque Poetry: George Herbert's "A Dialogue-Antheme"', *GHJ* 15 (1991), 49-67, especially 50.

37   Accordingly, I hesitate to share Rickey's opinion that 'the general significance of the name of *The Pulley* is perfectly clear' (p. 98).

38   Cf. *OED* pulley 3 fig: '1581 N. BURNE *Disput.* 109 The Cauuinist maist bauld of al vil afferme ... that ve be certane pilleis, or ingeyneis ar liftit vp to heauin be ane incomprehensible maner.' For the connection of 'rope' and 'pulling' cf. Herbert's *Outlandish Proverbs* 25 (Hutchinson, p. 322): 'Hee puls with a long rope, that waits for anothers death.'

39   Cf. *OED* 'ampul' 2: 'A vessel for holding consecrated oil, or for other sacred uses. (In this sense *ampulla* is now commonly used.)'

40   *OED* tire v^2 I †1; cf. French *tirer* and Italian *tirare*. M.M. Mahood was probably the first to draw attention to the technique of connecting different images by means of unspoken wordplay: 'Sometimes a word, the various meanings of which offer the poet a range of images, itself remains unexpressed. George Herbert's poem beginning 'Love bade me welcome' is built upon the ordinary and the Eucharistic meanings of the word *host* which nowhere occurs in the poem.' See her *Shakespeare's Wordplay* (London: Methuen, 1957; rpt. 1988), 24-25. For Donne's use of the technique, see Matthias Bauer, '*Paronomasia celata* in Donne's "A Valediction: forbidding mourning"', forthcoming in *ELR* 25 (1995).

41   Cf. Matt. 7: 14: 'arcta via est, quae ducit ad vitam' and John 14: 6: 'ego sum via et veritas et vita'. On the topos of the choice between the *via vitae* (being a *via virtutis*) and the *via mortis*, see Wolfgang Harms, *Homo viator in bivio: Studien zur Bildlichkeit des Weges* (München: Wilhelm Fink, 1970), e.g. 36, 46, 93. Augustine's wordplay also underlines the identity of *via* and *vita*. See, for instance, David Lenfant's *Concordantia Augustinianae* (Paris, 1665; rpt. Brussels: Culture et civilisation, 1963), *via*, esp. item 27: 'Vides viam, et quaeris quo ducat haec ipsa via? Ad veritatem et ad vitam ducit. Si amas veritatem et vitam, et cupis ad veritatem et vitam venire, a via noli errare. *Serm.* 46. *de temp.* cap 8. *Tom.* 10.' On paranomasia, see the essay by Judith Dundas elsewhere in this volume.

42   In 'The Flower', the speaker identifies himself with the heliotrope, which follows the motion of the sun and declines when the Lord turns away from him. The flower's *turning* and *troping* towards the light is related to the poet's own art in lines 38-39: 'I once more smell the dew and rain, / And relish *versing* ...' (my emphasis).

43 Cf. German *wittern*, which both means to decay and to trace by smelling.

44 *Send* as a noun, denoting the action of sending, is restricted to Scottish usage in the sixteenth century (*OED* n[1]).

45 The play on *sent* (sending) and *scent* in 'The Odour' is discussed by Heather Asals, *Equivocal Predication: George Herbert's Way to God* (Toronto: U of Toronto P, 1981), 28.

46 From 'Lent' we can go on to 'The Holdfast' which presents a logical paradox (cf. 9-10: 'But to have nought is ours, not to confesse / That we have naught. I stood amaz'd at this ...').

47 Cf. Isidor, *Etymologiae*, on the relationship between *vitis* and *vitta*: 'Vitta dicta quod ea pectus vincitur instar vitis ligantis' (edited by W.M. Lindsay [Oxford: Oxford UP, 1911], 19: 33:7; cf. 17: 5:2).

48 See Heather Ross' essay elsewhere in this volume.

49 The etymological play on 'more' and 'little', so consistent with the commercial imagery of the poem, is already to be found in '*My Master*': *Master* is derived from Latin *magister* and is thus the exact counterpart to *minister*. Cf. A. Walde and J.B. Hofmann, *Lateinisches etymologisches Wörterbuch*, 5th ed., vol. 2 (Heidelberg: Carl Winter, 1982), s.v. *minister* (p. 91): '... aus **minis-teros* für altes **minus-teros* mit *i* nach *magister*'. This goes together with an implied *minim* in the twice repeated 'my minde' (6, 7, 10).

50 *The Golden Legend*, edited by F.S. Ellis (London: J.M. Dent, 1900; rpt. New York: AMS Press), vol. 3: 110. I have checked this modern-spelling edition against an edition of Caxton's original version (London, 1521; *STC* 24879.5).

51 Cf. *Musae Responsoriae* XXXIII: 19-20 (Hutchinson, p. 398): '*Téque Deum* alternis cantans *Ambrosius* iram, / Immemor antiqui mellis, eundo coquit.'

52 *Golden Legend*, vol. 6: 140-141. The 'real' etymology of his name, 'gift of God', fits well with the imagery of mutual exchange. For a detailed interpretation of the poem and its imagery of mystical commerce, see Christiane Lang-Graumann's forthcoming Münster dissertation on the motif of the smallest particle in Herbert.

53 'Odore vero suavissimo omnes repleti sunt ...'. Jacobus a Voragine, *Legenda aurea*, edited by Th. Graesse (Dresden & Leipzig, 1841) cap. CLXV [160], p. 741.

54 Cf. 'That call' in line 25 of 'The Odour.'

55 Cf. 1 Cor. 3: 16 and 2 Cor. 6: 16 ('ye are the temple of the living God').

56 Hutchinson, p. 206, line 11.

'ALL WITHIN BE LIVELIER': ASPECTS OF HERBERT'S ART

9

MEATING GOD:
HERBERT'S POETRY AND THE DISCOURSE OF APPETITE

HEATHER ROSS

What we know as George Herbert's 'The Church' ends awkwardly with a word that seems hardly appropriate to the spiritual: the final word is 'eat', as most of us know, and that word is preceded by words suggesting an extremely ungraceful gesture: 'So I did sit and eat.' Throughout the entire group of poems there is a great deal of lexical preparation for the poem's closure; the language of eating, of hunger, of appetite indeed pervades the body of poetry from beginning to end. In 'The Church-Porch' the community of readers is proverbially instructed: 'Look on meat, think it dirt, then eat a bit; / And say withal, Earth to earth I commit' (pp. 131-132). Christ's Complaint from the Cross in 'The Sacrifice' accuses mankind of his original sin in terms that imply that it was, in part anyway, caused by excessive appetite: 'Man stole the fruit, but I must climb the tree' (p. 202). One hardly need be thorough in calling back to mind all the occurrences of lines and words that refer either literally or metaphorically to the notions of eating and appetite. Nevertheless, to continue with a few: 'As we at first did board with thee, / Now thou wouldst taste our misery' ('Affliction [5]'; 'To be in both worlds full/ Is more than God was, who was hungry here' ('The Size'); and 'Come ye hither all, whose taste / Is your waste; / Save your cost, and mend your fare' ('The Invitation').

Running along together with the doctrinal commands reminding Christians to curb their appetites are numerous references to God Himself as both food and the feeder of appetites: 'He leads me to the tender grass,/ Where I both feed and rest' ('The Twenty-third Psalm'); 'Prayer' is the 'Church's banquet'; and 'Man' has been given a universe created to provide man with his needs:

> Nothing we see, but means our good,
>   As our *delight*, or as our *treasure*:
> The whole is, either our cupboard of *food*,
>   Or cabinet of *pleasure*.

The 'food-hunger-appetite' complex in 'The Church' brings into the foreground the issue of the inequitable economic systems created by man (the gross differences in most systems between rich and poor) and their relationship to the ideal economic system built into the universe by God. 'Providence', particularly, focuses on the just economy of God: 'Bees work for man; and yet they never bruise / Their master's flower' (lines 65-66), 'Sheep eat the grass, and dung the ground for more' (line 69) and 'Springs vent their streams, and by expense get store' (line 71). The economy of God is one that provides for the hunger and appetites of his Church: 'The beasts say, Eat me ... / The trees say, Pull me' (lines 21, 23) and by praising God man pays his 'rent' for food and board.

In his chapter on the manners and courtliness of dining in *Prayer and Power*, Michael Schoenfeldt reads the ceremony of eating in 'Love (3)' in relationship to the punctiliousness worked out in Renaissance courtesy books of which Castiglione's *The Courtier* would be, for most of us, the most familiar. 'Love (3)', Schoenfeldt argues seemingly without difficulty, 'a superior's invitation to shelter and meat—presupposes a set of social conventions that Herbert's particular circumstances would have required him to know all too well.' Schoenfeldt speaks of the 'political pressures of courtesy' that necessitate the speaker's first refusal to dine in 'Love (3)': manners dictate that speaker first defer from accepting the invitation to 'taste my meat' too eagerly; the first refusal, Schoenfeldt argues, is 'socially determined'. While I appreciate greatly the accomplishment of Schoenfeldt in leading Herbert scholars away from the rut of the past three decades—a rut in which Herbert scholars are determined to speak as amateur theologians—I also believe that he has only begun to open up the poetry to other approaches that can be seen through the lenses of other discursive practices. And I might add at this point too that the speaker of 'The Pearl', anyway, dismisses the priority of the discursive practices of courtesy:

> I know the ways of honour, what maintains
> The quick returns of courtesy and wit:
> In vies of favours whether party gains,
> When glory swells the heart, and mouldeth it
> To all expressions both of hand and eye,
> Which on the world a true-love-knot may tie ...

There are now two claims that I would make in connection with the issue of discursive practices in *The Temple* and in 'The Church', neither are they unrelated to each other. Although Tzvetan Todorov's ideas about the possibilities presented by the differing conventions of a multiplicity of genres has not gone uncontested, his idea of *Genres in Discourse* makes an interesting starting point, especially when we remember the very large variety of

verse-forms, and genres, in Herbert's large body of poems. When Todorov
speaks of the 'system of genres', Todorov argues indeed that literary genres
'are nothing but such choices among discursive possibilities, choices that a
given society has made conventional': he continues,

> Three possibilities may be envisaged, in short, either the genre, like the
> sonnet, codifies discursive properties as any other speech act would; or
> else the genre coincides with a speech act that also has a nonliterary
> existence, like prayer; or else it derives from a speech act by way of a
> certain number of transformations and amplifications.

What I present as my argument, then, is this: that as there are a multiplicity
of genres in Herbert's 'The Church', so there are a multiplicity of discursive practices, and although courtesy, courtship, and restraint are the discursive practices clearly connected with the sonnet of the Early Modern
Period, 'Love (3)' is not a sonnet (unlike 'Love [1] and [2]') and, therefore,
its genre (if it has one) does not engage the discursive practices codified in
the sonnet. Furthermore, as I understand it, the historical Christ who lived
in a space and time with its own discursive practices, countered the discursive practices of his own world. If there has ever been the possibility of
counter-discourse, it was He who first dramatically presented it. Herbert's
Christ in 'The Sacrifice' complains explicitly that He was punished and put
to death for countering His own contemporary discourse: 'Then from one
ruler to another bound / They lead me; urging, that it was not sound / What
I taught: Comments would the text confound' (pp. 53-55).

'Love (3)' is a construct of three sixaines; for the most part it alternates
between iambic pentameter and iambic trimeter. There are minor irregularities—spondaic and trochaic substitutions for the iambic trimeter; there are
minor irregularities—spondaic and trochaic substitutions for the iambic
foot. The fact that each stanza is six lines long, put together with the fact
the rhyme scheme is consistently *ababcc* connects 'Love (3)' not with the
sonnet and the discursive practices implied by it but with a genre that is
sometimes called the 'counter-genre' of the sonnet: the epyllion, the Ovidian poem, bearing the form of what is known as the 'Venus and Adonis
stanza'. The conventions of this genre bring with it a discourse that promotes indulgence rather than restraint, and represents characters whose
actions are far from courteous and courtly. There are, of course, a good
number of poems at the end of 'The Church' that intensify the language of
eating, dining, feasting and banqueting. It is the poem entitled 'The Banquet' to which one can turn to explore Herbert's use of the principles of the
'counter-genre' and even, perhaps, a counter-discourse to the prevailing

discourse of the restraint of appetite and enjoyment of all the senses. Even
the title of the poem calls to mind an Ovidian poem written in 1595 by
George Chapman: 'Ovid's Banquet of Sence', and it is Chapman who best
explores in his 'Banquet' a discourse that argues the positive affects of total
immersion in the pleasures of all five senses. Ovid himself appears as one
of the two main characters in the poem; the other character, Corynna,
directs him in feeling all, including her and her body at the very end of the
poem. She invites:

> See Cupids Alps which now thou must goe over,
> Where snow that thawes the Sunne doth ever lye:
> Where thou maist plaine and feelingly discover
> The worlds fore-past, that flow'd with Milke and Honny.

'This sayd, hee layde his hand upon her side': 'So startled shee, not with a
coy retire, / But with the tender temper shee was blest.'

Much of Chapman's poem reads like a doctrinal presentation of a
counter-discourse that challenges the discourses of restraint imposed by the
prevailing contemporary mores imposed by the dual power and authority
imposed by Church and State. Corynna urges Ovid to indulge in each of the
senses and thus enjoy a banquet in all five senses; her argument and reason-
ing is absorbed by Ovid who represents it as follows:

> The sence is given us to excite the minde,
> And that can never be by sence excited
> But first the sence must her contentment finde,
> We therefore must procure the sence delighted.

After being instructed in the principles of the sonnet's counter-genre, which
enunciates the principles of a counter-discourse, 'Ovid' (or Chapman) concludes the poem with a political comment: the confinement of the senses
results in the confinement and even, perhaps, extinction of the self:

> In these dog-dayes how this contagion smoothers
> The purest bloods with vertues diet fined,
> Nothing thyr owne, unlesse they be some others,
> Spite of themselves are in themselves confined.

The 'lesson' argued in Chapman's 'Banquet' is paradoxical and problematic, turning around the prevailing idea that 'reason' should rule 'sence':
'Love is a wanton famine, rich in foode,/ But with a richer appetite con-

trold'—it 'hates all arguments: disputing still / For Sence, gainst Reason, with a sencelesse will.'

The language of Herbert's poem, 'The Banquet', subtly invokes Chapman's poem about the banquet of the senses. Even before the end of the first stanza of the poem, the invitation of 'taste' is fused with an invitation to indulge, thereby, in one of the other five senses—'sight'; and stanza three links the sense of 'taste' with the sense of 'smell' that culminates in the beautiful lines of stanza four: 'Only God, who gives perfumes, / Flesh assumes, / And with it perfumes my heart.' It is through the senses of this speaker, who '[I]n delights of earth was drowned,' that God finds him ('on the ground'): 'Having raised me to look up, / In a cup / Sweetly he doth meet my taste.' Human appetite, in this poem anyway, is hardly a negative need that should be curbed. Etymologically, 'appetite' is also a word that links hunger and desire with petition, perhaps, even, the petition that is acted out in prayer: 'Prayer the Church's banquet, Angels' age.' Feast, fast, and festival are all etymologically connected. And although I will turn shortly to broader definitions of discourse theory than Todorov's, which connects it with genre, one cannot leave Herbert's 'The Banquet' without mentioning that it is written, once again in a six-line form. This time the meter is predominantly trochaic (trochaic tetrameter with a truncated final foot succeeded irregularly by trochaic dimeter with a truncated final foot); its rhyme scheme is both regular and unusual (*aabccb*), suggesting, perhaps, the unconventionality of its own discursive practice.

To turn briefly to 'hard-core' discourse theory as it has been developed by Michel Foucault and others is to turn and end now with the most difficult questions about discourse and Herbert's poetry in relation to discourses of appetite. One might, perhaps, begin with a reasonably central statement by Foucault: truth, he argues, rests on institutional support: 'It is always possible that one might speak the truth in the space of a wild exteriority, but one is "in the true" only by obeying the rules of discursive "policing" that one has to reactivate in each of one's discourses' (*The Order of Discourse*). Discourse is 'control and repression': 'in every society the production of discourse is at once controlled, selected, organised and redistributed by a certain number of procedures whose role is to ward off its powers and dangers, to gain mastery over its chance events, to evade its ponderous, formidable materiality.' Power is at the centre of discourse theory, and it is power that produces knowledge. Paul Bove comments on the possibilities offered by discourse analysis:

'Discourse' provides a privileged entry into the post-structuralist mode of analysis precisely because it is the organized and regulated, as well as the regulating and constituting, functions of language that it studies.

That George Herbert wrote at a time and in a place where and when the power of the State was doubled by the fact that it was married to the power of the Church makes discourse analysis, as well as the possibility of counter-discourse (if there can be one) even more appropriate to the analysis of his poetry. The power and authority of the Church, and indeed its specific power over the control of appetite, is explored, as one might expect, in Herbert's poem entitled 'Lent'. This poem, like so many others that turn on the theme of eating, dining and banqueting is (once again) in a six-line stanza form. The rhyme scheme is also one that we have seen before, or, more correctly, will see later in 'The Banquet' (*aabccb*). In fact, the speaker begins oxymoronically: 'Welcome dear feast of Lent.' Immediately the speaker connects Lent with the dynamics of 'Authority'. But the 'Authority' to which the speaker is referring throughout is one in which individual Power is not taken away but given or, one might say, 'lent': 'True Christians should be glad of an occasion,' the speaker argues, 'To use their temperance':

> Unless Authority, which should increase
> The obligation in us, make it less,
> > And Power it self disable.

Curiously, the speaker himself understands what we now call 'discourse' and looks upon it positively not as disempowering the individual subject but as empowering that subject by enabling it to gain mastery over the self. Tentatively, then, I end (perhaps as Herbert would) with paradox: that it is through indulgence in the senses that one transcends them and finds God, whereas it is through the repression and denial of our senses, our appetites, that we find ourselves.

10

'ALL THINGS ARE BIG WITH JEST':
IRONY IN HERBERT'S 'TEMPLE'

HELEN WILCOX

Among the many wise sayings of Mr Walter Shandy in Sterne's novel *Tristram Shandy* (1761) is the following observation, aptly made during a meandering conversation with Uncle Toby, Mr Yorick and Corporal Trim:

> Everything in this world ... is big with jest,—and has wit in it, and instruction too,—if we can but find it out.[1]

Mr Shandy is, of course, attempting to 'find out' the 'wit' and 'instruction' hidden within his own chaotic circumstances, and in doing so he echoes— as readers will no doubt recognize—two lines from 'The Church-Porch', the introductory poem to George Herbert's *The Temple* (1633). In their original setting, without the whimsical quality added by Mr Shandy, Herbert's words confidently state that there is a natural wit which may be discerned even in the plainest of words or events:

> All things are big with jest: nothing that's plain,
> But may be witty, if thou hast the vein.

Despite their differences of context, style and emphasis, what both passages uphold is the potential for 'jest' in the ordinary things of life, whether these be the gestures of Corporal Trim which give rise to Mr Shandy's comment, or the legitimate Christian pleasures of good company and conversation outlined in Herbert's poem.

The discovery of Herbert's pastoral advice reworked in the secular context of Sterne's novel is very much in keeping with the theme of this collection. It is, first, a reminder of the easy interplay of the sacred and profane in the complex process of literary reception—the reading and re-reading, absorbing and recycling of texts—which takes place across and between traditions, periods and genres. In this case, the words of a seventeenth-century devotional poet have found their way, over a hundred years after their first publication, into the narrative labyrinths and beside the printed asterisks of a great but eccentric—and profane—text.[2] Second, and more significantly for the immediate purposes of this essay, the link between Herbert and Sterne highlights the fact that 'jest' is not the exclusive property of the profane world. The potential for wit, whether for amusement or for 'instruction', is a God-given quality which resides in 'all things' and, if handled appropriately, may be of service in the religious as well as the secular domain.

It is clear from a reading of *The Temple* that Herbert frequently found a 'vein' of 'wit' in his devotional experiences. Though he goes on to warn in 'The Church-Porch' that 'Wit's an unruly engine' (line 241), it was evidently an 'engine' which Herbert had under his control. My concern in this essay is to consider the creative and varied use Herbert made of one particular kind of witty 'jest'—that is, irony—in his English poetry. It is my contention that the range and importance of irony in Herbert's *Temple* may well lead us to gloss the phrase 'big with jest', in respect to Herbert's own poems, as 'pregnant with ironic potential'.

Irony is the mode of thinking and writing vividly defined in 1620 as that which 'with one eye looks two wayes at once'.[3] It is thus characterized by doubleness of vision, and is most frequently recognized as a rhetorical device whereby words can say one thing and mean another—whether that other is opposite to, or more or less important than, the superficial implication of the words. An ironic passage of writing, shining like silk which is shot through with a second colour, fits Herbert's description of 'jest' perfectly: it appears 'plain' but there is a 'vein' of wit to be discovered within it when the whole is viewed in a different light or seen from another perspective. In *The Temple* this new angle of vision is often a more heavenly perspective, leading not to a tragic irony (as is often the case in the drama of the period) but to a gently humorous reorientation. Irony in the hands of the devotional poet is a didactic tool; when lightly and subtly used, as by Herbert, it enables human concerns to be set wittily against the promise of redemption.

In the seventeenth-century context, however, the religious writer who used irony was choosing a rhetorical feature which was primarily associated not with benevolence but with profane characteristics such as scorn and mockery. In 1656 Reyner's *Rules for the Government of the Tongue* conjured up a picture of ironic speech as a creature with 'honey of pleasantnesse in its mouth, and a sting of rebuke in its taile'.[4] Both 'rebuke' and 'pleasantnesse', of course, have a place in religious writing, but the deliberate disguise of the one by the other may suggest a devilish duplicity. Puttenham, on the other hand, had in 1589 defined irony as the '*drye mock*',[5] a more neutral phrase which, though still including an element of mockery, might well suggest a useful rhetorical manner for the devotional poet. Puttenham's 'ironia' might be used 'sometime in sport, sometime in earnest', and was clearly distinguished from both the 'bitter taunt' and the 'mery skoffe' (pp. 189-190). The choice of this 'drye' rhetorical device, midway between bitterness and merriment, was no doubt perceived by Herbert as part of the challenge to take the secular traditions of poetic language and use them in the service of God. As he wrote in 'The Forerunners', the 'sweet phrases' and 'lovely metaphors' associated with profane love— hovering by the doors of 'stews and brothels'—were washed in the poet's tears and 'brought to Church well dressed and clad'. Among those worldy poetic techniques we may surely include the ironic jest, that playful doubleness of tone which Herbert found so expressive of his devotional experience. How better, for example, to show up the double contrast between the 'thin' reality of the apparently proud human condition and the sacrificial but soaring triumph of God than with irony ('Easter-Wings')? What more appropriate means could there be for the poet to point out the 'oblique' lines of the spiritual in the straighter 'diurnal' patterns of earthly life ('Colossians 3: 3') than with an ironic wit which points simultaneously in two directions?

This essay will outline five kinds of irony with which Herbert explored and expressed the double vision necessary to a devotional poet in a secular world. The opposition is not always between the poet and an imperfect world; the authorial voice may itself also be mocked. There are a number of poems, as we shall see, where the imperfect poet-speaker is tricked or 'cross-biased' ('Affliction [1]') by the Divine, as well as those in which the reader is surprised into faith by the ironies of the poet. The homely and the holy, the profane and sacred realms of reference, are thoroughly interwoven in the texture of Herbert's ironies.

The first of the five main varieties of irony which I perceive in Herbert's *Temple* may be located in the contrasts between voices within a lyric. A very clear instance of this is the sonnet 'Redemption', in which the main speaker appears at first to be efficient and businesslike, taking rational decisions and acting in a logical, purposeful manner:

> Having been tenant long to a rich Lord,
>   Not thriving, I resolved to be bold,
>   And make a suit unto him, to afford
> A new small-rented lease, and cancel th'old.
> In heaven at his manor I him sought:
>   They told me there, that he was lately gone
>   About some land, which he had dearly bought
> Long since on earth, to take possession.
> I straight returned, and knowing his great birth,
>   Sought him accordingly in great resorts;
>   In cities, theatres, gardens, parks, and courts:

The verbs are active—'resolved', 'sought', 'returned'—and every action in the narrative progression is carefully supported by explanatory phrases—'having been', 'not thriving', 'knowing'. This bustling, self-important speaker will admit of no uncertainty and moves 'straight' from one step to the next in the 'bold' plan of campaign. We may, however, already have picked up some textual hints of the ironic ignorance of a believer who wants singlehandedly to arrange a new 'small-rented' covenant, and seeks the Lord in all the wrong places through a misguided sense of what it means to be 'great'.

The remaining lines of the poem represent a radical and (for the speaker, at least) disturbing shift of perspective:

> At length I heard a ragged noise and mirth
>> Of thieves and murderers: there I him espied,
>> Who straight, *Your suit is granted*, said, and died.

The shock of seeing the Lord amongst 'thieves and murderers' renders the speaker's earlier self-confidence ironic; the phrase 'knowing his great birth', which had led the speaker to such false assumptions about the Lord, sounds hollow in retrospect. But the major irony of the poem comes with the entry of a second voice—that of Christ on the cross—in the last line of the poem. As soon as the speaker sees the dying Christ, but before the proposed 'suit' can be put to him, the Lord acts by speaking and then dying in order immediately to bring about the new covenant. The 'straight' used in the last line really means 'directly', unlike that which five lines earlier had been a part of the speaker's erroneous self-image of efficiency and promptness. The second use of the word 'straight' thus renders the first ironic; the second voice, brief and final, entirely undercuts the thirteen lines of the first speaker. The conclusion redefines the significance of 'great' when applied to God, and gives profound meaning to the phrase 'dearly bought'. The 'tenant' has indeed gained a new 'lease', at the great expense of Christ's blood but with no 'rent' to be paid, 'small' or otherwise, once redemption has been 'espied'.

The ironic contrast between the two voices in 'Redemption', particularly highlighted through repeated words which take on new significance precisely through ironic realization, is at the centre of the meaning of Herbert's sonnet. The folly of human beings who assume that they are self-sufficient is set against the self-sacrificing love of Christ, and the shock of discovery in the closing lines is simultaneously witty and serious. The intrusion of a second voice into the last line also represents a brief but intense drama, and this aspect of the ironic texture of *The Temple*, the counterpoint of verses, may perhaps best be termed dramatic irony.

This sort of irony can also be seen at work in 'Jordan (2)', one of Herbert's poetic considerations of the difficulty of writing devotional verse with the proper combination of love and skill. In the early days, he writes, the danger lay in seeking to 'excel' with 'trim invention' in describing 'heav'nly joys':

> My thoughts began to burnish, sprout, and swell,
> Curling with metaphors a plain intention,
> Decking the sense, as if it were to sell.

The poet's over-eagerness here leads to excess, expressed in metaphors of uncontrolled growth, unwanted complexity, and mercantile motivation, 'as if it were to sell'. By the end of the poem the only way out of the intractable problems facing the religious artist is offered in the advice of 'a friend' who is heard to

> Whisper, *How wide is all this long pretence!*
> *There is in love a sweetness ready penned:*
> *Copy out only that, and save expense.*

At first, the irony of the Christ-like voice here may seem similar to that in 'Redemption', for the poet-speaker again learns that all his activity has been wide of the mark. However, there is an additional element to the dramatic irony here in that the advice to 'save expense', the last words of the second voice (and of the poem), deliberately recalls the mercantile language of the first stanza. The poet had then been anxious about notions of spending and selling, which seemed inappropriate to writing about heaven; now the gentle heavenly voice at the conclusion of the poem urges the writer to follow the way of love, adding that this would be cheaper, too! This ironic link between the two voices suggests that when priorities are re-ordered— copying God rather than the self which was woven into the poem earlier— then everything else will fall into place, even the money or 'expense' of resources. The mercantile language of the poet-speaker is mocked by this irony, but the wise 'friend' is also shown to have a sense of humour. Since the voice here may be assumed to represent a divine intervention in the poem, the ironic wit which it demonstrates is a crucial sign of the suitability of irony, in Herbert's usage, for sacred issues and the dialogue with—or of—the Divine.

The second main type of irony to be found in *The Temple* may be called ironic allusion, since it is an ironic effect dependent upon intertextual links. In Herbert's lyrics this kind of irony generally re-enforces the devotional context (as opposed to making connections with the secular world) since it derives its impact from the poems' relation to religious source texts such as the Bible or the liturgy. Consider, for example, the lyric 'Easter', in which the magnificent polyphony of the opening stanzas (beginning 'Rise heart; thy Lord is risen') gives way in the second part of the poem to the achieved simplicity of the song, 'pleasant and long', composed by the trinity of heart, lute and the Holy Spirit. The song begins:

> I got me flowers to straw thy way;
> I got me boughs off many a tree:
> But thou wast up by break of day,
> And brought'st thy sweets along with thee.

The singer describes having made efforts to be ready to celebrate Easter, only to find that Christ is already 'up by break of day'—as is only natural since this is the resurrection day of the 'sun' of God. Once again, human responses, however well-intentioned, fall short of God's achievements; as ever, God has 'prevented' or gone before to show the way for Christians to follow. There is an ironic link here with the Collect for Easter Day, the prayer said publicly in all English parish churches on Easter Sunday morning:

> Almighty God, which through thy only begotten Son Jesus Christ, hast overcome death, and opened unto us the gate of everlasting life: We humbly beseech thee, that as by thy special grace preventing us, thou dost put in our minds good desires, so by thy continual help, we may bring the same to good effect ...[6]

The singer of the song in Herbert's 'Easter' is, ironically, surprised by Christ's 'preventing' him on Easter morning, while this is the very power and grace of God acknowledged and requested in the prayer. The collect as intertext also casts an ironic light on the singer's decision to pick 'flowers' and 'boughs off many a tree', since even that apparently independent purpose was, according to the collect, a 'good desire' which was 'put in our minds' by God's intervention.

The complexity of Herbert's intertextual ironies in this stanza may be more precisely illustrated by reference to the unusual word 'straw' which occurs in the opening line of the song: 'I got me flowers to straw thy way.' One of the other examples of this rare usage of 'straw' as a verb occurs in the Gospel account of the events of Palm Sunday (one week before Easter) in which it is said that 'others cut down branches from the trees, and strawed them in the way' (Matt. 21: 8). The combination of the similar action described in the opening lines of the song, and the echo of the same

rare verb, strongly suggests that Herbert had the biblical passage in his
mind at this point. The echo is, of course, deeply ironic, since Herbert's
singer thinks that the action of getting up and gathering branches to throw
down at Christ's feet is appropriate for Easter Sunday, whereas it is a week
out of date. The allusion to the Palm Sunday story, then, is a teasing one,
mocking the speaker who fondly imagines that everything is under control
while the reality is that, in following Christ, the believer is likely to be at
least a week (if not a lifetime) behind and always struggling to catch up.

At the opposite end of *The Temple* we find another brief example of
irony by allusion. In 'Love (3)', the speaker who is welcomed to Love's
banquet is reluctant to accept the invitation, uneasily conscious of the 'dust
and sin' which has 'marred' the life originally made by God. In an effort to
do anything rather than simply accept forgiveness and love, the speaker
offers to leave or, at the very least, just help others at the feast:

> ... let my shame
> Go where it doth deserve.
> And know you not, says Love, who bore the blame?
> My dear, then I will serve.
> You must sit down, says Love, and taste my meat:
> So I did sit, and eat.

The speaker's last moment of resistance before agreeing to 'sit, and eat' is
summed up in the word 'serve'; the idea of service seems to offer a chance
of staying to dinner but in the humble position of a waiter at the table rather
than simply a recipient of Love's overwhelming generosity. However, the
speaker has forgotten that in the Bible the concept of service has rich associations, from the suffering servant in Isaiah who prefigures Christ, to the
Pauline idea of Christians as 'servants to God' (Rom. 6: 22). The speaker's
excessive modesty (which can be a perverse form of pride) has led ironically through the vocabulary of service to an unexpected closeness to Christ,
who insisted upon serving his own disciples at the Last Supper (John 13: 4-
17). It is no coincidence that the words 'then I will serve' are the last
before the speaker's acceptance in 'Love (3)'; the ironic allusions have
awakened echoes which bring the speaker closer than ever to the model of
Christ.

Alongside Herbert's ironies of voice and allusion there is a third kind,
which might be termed irony of form since its wit largely derives from the
potential of the poetic form. While the types of irony which we have exam-
ined so far in *The Temple* draw on the dramatic and the intertextual as their
frames of reference, this third form of irony relies more closely on the
poetic context. There is a splendid irony, for example, in the opening poem

of 'The Church', which is entitled 'The Altar' and makes an immediate physical impact with its classical pillar or altar-like shape on the page. The visual impression precedes the reading of the words of the poem, which begin:

> A broken ALTAR, Lord, thy servant rears,
> Made of a heart, and cemented with tears:

The first words strangely contradict the formal impact of the poem as a whole; we know that, despite the opening statement, this is in fact no 'broken' altar but a completed and finely shaped work which has been 'reared' on the printed page. We seem to know more than the speaker and we read the opening words as ironic in their ignorance of the finished product which, we infer, represents in its completeness the work of the divine craftsman as well as the human poet. After all, the speaker later introduces the possibility of being silent ('if I chance to hold my peace') but the 'stones' of the constructed altar will not cease in their praise of God. However, the irony is ultimately at the readers' expense, since a too easy equation of the altar and the poem is a misreading of the poem's spiritual direction. The altar is indeed 'broken' because, as we read in the second line, it is made of 'a heart' which is imperfect through sin, broken in pieces (as also in Herbert's poem 'Jesu') but held together with a 'cement' of repentant 'tears'. The poetic form—a stone altar—and the inner focus of the devotion—a sorrowing human heart, where the most valuable sacrifices are made—are playfully in tension through the ironic doubleness of focus.

The poetic irony of 'The Altar' does not cease with the phrase 'a broken altar' which, as in Middleton and Rowley's definition of irony quoted earlier, 'looks two ways at once.' When the reader reaches the end of the poem, the altar shape is completed with a couplet:

> O let thy blessed SACRIFICE be mine,
> And sanctify this ALTAR to be thine.

The poem ends aptly for a devotional text which is also the first in a sequence; it turns into a prayer and seeks a blessing on 'The Sacrifice', which follows it, and all the other lyrics in 'The Church'. The irony is that the mode of reading itself runs counter to the process of building an altar. The builder 'rears' an altar from the ground upwards, whereas the reader works in the opposite direction, thereby reading last what should have come first—the 'ALTAR' with the 'SACRIFICE' of Christ placed in offering upon it. Thus the irony of form alerts us to the imperfection of the linguistic altar even while asserting the primacy of Christ's self-offering which is the foundation of *The Temple*.

Many more examples of Herbert's poetic irony may be found in the witty relation (or sometimes the apparent lack of connection) between the titles of his poems and the texts they are expected to enlighten. It may (ironically) be observed that some of Herbert's titles are not at all 'big with jest' on a first reading, and certainly do not reveal their 'vein' of wit until one reaches the final lines of the lyrics in question.[7] Herbert's titles seem to work on a principle of deferred revelation, and when the connection with the poem is analysed, it is often revealed to function through irony. The essential mistake of the speaker in 'The Collar', for instance, is compressed into the title: what the complainant angrily perceives as a slave's collar is in fact the easy yoke of service to Christ (Matt. 11: 30), and while the speaker seems to be the one who is calling out, in the end the crucial call is that of God to the 'child'. The poem is an expansive gloss on the ironies of Christian life which are contained in its title, both in the ambiguities of the written word 'collar' and in the heard words 'choler' and 'caller'. After reading the poem we are able to discern that the title was 'big with jest' after all.

'The Quiddity' is a fine example of Herbert's poetic irony fully at work, teasing the reader through both title and poetic form.

> My God, a verse is not a crown,
> No point of honour, or gay suit,
> No hawk, or banquet, or renown,
> Nor a good sword, nor yet a lute:
>
> It cannot vault, or dance, or play;
> It never was in *France* or *Spain*;
> Nor can it entertain the day
> With a great stable or demesne:
>
> It is no office, art, or news,
> Nor the Exchange, or busy Hall;
> But it is that which while I use
> I am with thee, and *Most take all*.

As a poem offering (and in itself representing) a definition of poetry, this is perhaps rather a disappointment. The title, suggesting the quintessence or true meaning of something, raises our hopes, as does the opening statement, 'A verse is ...'. We are led to expect something grand, witty or beautiful; we are given instead a simple poetic form, a list of denials and a mockery of everyday courtly or city matters. We expect the positive and we are supplied with negatives, what poetry is not; we expect the aesthetic and we are confronted with the practical. The poem casts an unrelentingly ironic and teasing light on our expectations as readers of poetry (as well as on the accomplishments of courtiers).

Perhaps, then, this short lyric is a fulfilment of the other meaning of its title, a quibble or playful argument? Just as we arrive at this conclusion, and prepare to accept the lyric in this light-hearted spirit, the poem reaches its own conclusion and forces us to revert to the original idea of the 'quiddity' as a quintessence. In the last two lines the speaker comes to the essence of verse: 'that which while I use / I am with thee'. Suddenly poetry is defined not by absences but by presence—the closeness of God—and the simplicity of the poem's form and language is shown in all its transparency and is rendered sacred. Despite (or maybe because of) the fact that the closing phrase, 'Most take all', is an echo of a gambling call, its inclusive vocabulary of 'most' and 'all' reveals the basis of Herbert's spiritual aesthetics. Poetry in the service of God is not to be defined by a particular style or perfection, but by its use as a route to transcendence. The modest 'Quiddity' has, by its ironic ambiguity of title and apparent negativity which is ultimately positive, surprised us into a new understanding of verse. Once again, poetic form has been used by Herbert to ironic effect: in the plainness of title and form a richness has been discovered, and a profane phrase has opened up a sacred ideal at the close of the poem.

The process of reading a Herbert poem may be described as a cycle of expectation, surprise and reorientation, made possible by ironic relationships between speakers, related texts and our shifting positions as readers. The fourth kind of irony which I identify in *The Temple* is also dependent on a cyclical pattern, in this case a pattern set up by the poet through the circumstances of the lyric sequence. To read a Herbert lyric in isolation is to lose the very special type of irony which is at work within and between the poems. This irony, which may be termed sequential or circumstantial, is that which deliberately and creatively undermines some of the strongest moments of triumph or serenity in *The Temple*. It is a didactic irony reminding us of the transience even of confident conclusions like that of 'The Temper (1)':

Whether I fly with angels, fall with dust,
    Thy hands made both, and I am there:
    Thy power and love, my love and trust
        Make one place ev'ry where.

This vision of an all-embracing love which will unite the high and the low, the spiritual and the material, is immediately shattered by the opening lines of the subsequent poem, 'The Temper (2)'. The effect is particularly striking since the next poem shares the same title yet defeats any expectation that it will form a continuation of its predecessor. Instead, it stands in complete contrast: the tone is despairing and the mood bewildered:

> It cannot be. Where is that mighty joy,
>   Which just now took up all my heart?
>   Lord, if thou must needs use thy dart,
> Save that, and me; or sin for both destroy.

Juxtaposed, the two 'Temper' poems gain a quality of irony, suggesting the cyclical nature of devotional moods and the tentative quality of human certainties. In particular, the speaker of 'The Temper (1)', who seemed so joyously confident in the concluding stanza, may not have been so secure after all; the prospect of an all-encompassing love creating 'one place ev'ry where' was dependent not only on God's 'power and love' but also on the speaker's reciprocal 'love and trust'. The contrasting beginning to 'The Temper (2)' casts an ironic light on the human capacity for such 'love and trust'—that is, for faith without the support of grace.

The pattern of *The Temple* as a sequence sustains the understandable wish for linear development and growth experienced by most readers and/or believers; this need is satisfied, for example, in the clustering of poems according to the sequence of the church's year. However, the arrangement of the sequence also counters such hopeful or end-focused spiritual desires with inbuilt reminders of the recurring nature of human sin. While individual poems such as 'The Temper (1)' may seem to conquer or resolve devotional crises, the sequence as a whole gives, through its ironic recognitions and juxtapositions, no simple pattern of improvement. Instead *The Temple* presents an image of fluctuating moods and events, a cycle of moments set in the wider realm of eternity. Another clear instance of this irony of circumstance in Herbert's sequence may be found in the last line of the last poem, 'Love (3)', which closes (as we have seen earlier) with a gloriously simple statement of response to God's love: 'So I did sit and eat'. It would seem that all is here concluded and settled; the instinct for a linear pattern in the poems and in devotional experience has been fulfilled. But if we read this in terms of a sequence, then what comes next? Where will the believer 'sit' to 'eat'? The answer is, of course, at the altar—or rather, at 'The Altar', the opening poem of the sequence—and so we are back where we began. The irony of the structure of 'The Church' encourages us to read the poems as a circle rather than (or as well as) a line of development. For

'Love (3)' is not just about a heavenly banquet but also the Eucharist and its repeated pattern of liturgical contact on earth; 'The Church' functions, through its ironies of structure and cross-reference, as (so to speak) a circulator of devotional energies; its end is its beginning.

This brings me to my end, too, in the sense of the last of the five kinds of Herbertian irony with which this essay is concerned. The fifth is perhaps the most familiar, and most easily identifiable, type: the small-scale ironic effect located in the single word with a double impact, a rhetorical feature which we might call the irony of wit. The samples of the four broader types of irony referred to earlier have in several instances also encompassed this witty turn of meaning in one word: the double use of 'straight' in 'Redemption', for example, or the biblical echoes in 'straw' ('Easter') and 'serve' ('Love [3]'). Further instances may be found throughout *The Temple* and no doubt most readers will have their own favourite examples. Among the most striking is the boldly ironic last line of 'Affliction (1)' in which the speaker risks everything on the multiple meanings of 'love': 'Let me not love thee, if I love thee not.' This famous statement plays on the many contrasts between superficial and genuine devotion contained in the word 'love', setting them in ironic opposition to one another. The line is, further, in its own right a poignant and ironic outburst of exasperated affection, seeming to reject the way of devotion while at the same time reclaiming it.

The witty irony found in the poem immediately following 'Affliction (1)', 'Repentance', is more playful than moving, and is located in the phrase 'a well-set song'. On the one hand this refers to the fine combination of music and words which Herbert's lyrics always seek to achieve, both symbolically and in practice; on the other hand it evokes the idea of the 'broken bones' of the sinful individual whose repentance can result in the new strength of 'fractures well cured'. The ironic twist here is that the 'song' suggested by the first meaning of the phrase can only result from the experience of the suffering implied in the second. In this instance the ironic rhetoric does not work by opposition or the superceding of one view by another, but by the surprising combination of the two.

A further variety of the irony of localized wit is to be seen in Herbert's poem 'Home', where the human race is rebuked for not even leaving 'one poor apple for thy love'. The homely practicality of tone gives the comment an ordinariness and an element of understatement; in our careless selfishness we have, it simply suggests, eaten everything and left nothing at the 'feast' for the son of God. The ironic second level of meaning, centred on the word 'apple' with all its significance in the narrative of human disobedience, then strikes home with the force of human shame. The phrase 'one poor apple' does not imply the last dregs of the feast which might have been left, but the first splendour of Eden and the perfection of creation which has been lost. The irony of understatement, and the choice of such a resonant word as 'apple' to be the focal point of the ironic wit, together give this apparently nonchalant line a power beyond its simplicity.

These, then, are five aspects of the multi-faceted irony which may be seen at work in *The Temple*. In addition to alerting us to a significant element in the wit of Herbert's poetry, this discussion has indirectly drawn attention to several important features of his art. It reminds us that Herbert was an exceptional rhetorician, in control of the twists and turns of his lyrics, didactic in his use of the 'cross-bias' ('Affliction [1]'). This bowling term refers to a 'double motion' ('Colossians 3: 3') by which the ball moves forward yet travels obliquely; the metaphor suggests not just that the poet is ultimately 'biased' towards and by the 'cross' of Christ, but also that he is aware of the need to 'cross' or challenge the reader with oblique as well as simple meanings. This ironic doubleness is not the same as 'catching the sense at two removes', a reading process to which Herbert objected in 'Jordan (1)'. It is, rather, catching two senses in one, a proper aesthetic of duality for poetry which explores the interplay of earthly and higher existences.

An awareness of the varieties of irony in *The Temple* can remind us of the range of modes at work in Herbert's poetry. We have seen ironic effects which draw on narrative patterns and constructed voices, on the interaction of the poems with each other and with their sources, on the visual dimension and on the impact of verbal wit. We are also made to remember that though the subject of *The Temple* is serious, it is not humourless. Even in 'The Church-Porch', when Herbert is berating the English for their 'sloth', he manages to be ironic in his mockery:

> Thy gentry bleats, as if thy native cloth
> Transfused a sheepishness into thy story:
>> Not that they all are so; but that the most
>> Are gone to grass, and in the pasture lost.   (93-96)

The mockery lies initially in linking the attitude of the English gentry with the weak timidity of the sheep whose wool they wear as clothing. The irony deepens, however, as the grassy English countryside becomes a biblical landscape with the use of the word 'pasture'; in this spiritual terrain we are all sheep, but this particular flock is no longer close to its shepherd, Christ, and thus is 'in the pasture lost'. The contemporary world is shown up here with the clarity of an ironic wit, just as elsewhere in *The Temple* speakers and readers are tricked into new insights. The source of this irony, however, is never mere contempt, and its end is a return to the spiritual with sharpened perception.

The study of Herbert's irony, lastly, makes clear that the capacity to create ironic overtones in an apparently simple statement is not just a human quality in *The Temple* but a divine one, too. We know that Herbert's God is witty—punning, for example, on 'eye' and 'I' in 'Love (3)'—so it should not be difficult to see the God configured in these poems as ironic. God is depicted, for example, in 'The Pulley' as hoping for the return of sinners but knowing that, in the end, a bit of 'repining restlessness' may be necessary to help them to holiness. The prevailing atmosphere of a sympathetic and sometimes amused irony, always an aspect of love rather than of disaffection, is very important to the working of *The Temple* as a devotional text. The ironic twinkle in the poetic eye is a reflection of that in the eye of the poet's God—and, true to the nature of irony (and of eyes), it has two effects in one: a twinkle of humour, and a sparkle of transcendence. Irony is the rhetorical mode for the condition of being between two worlds.

If everything is, thus, 'big with jest'—as Mr Shandy, in addition to George Herbert, well knew—then it is, as Sterne's character wisely added, for 'instruction too'. In Herbert's poetry this ironic instruction leads, as we have seen, to a new perception of both the immediate and the transcendent. And though *The Temple* is not quite as chaotic and mirthful as Tristram's ideal kingdom—full of 'hearty laughing subjects' with 'grace to be as wise as they were merry'[8]—yet it is appropriate to recall such 'Shandeism' as we celebrate the capacity of Herbert's poetry to mock us, subtly and thoroughly, into the kingdom of heaven.

Notes

1   Laurence Sterne, *The Life and Opinions of Tristram Shandy, Gentleman* (London: Dent, 1912), 289 [5: 32].

2   See Cedric Brown's essay later in this volume for further discussion of the phenomenon of Herbert's words taken out of a devotional context and echoed in an entirely different setting and period.

3   Thomas Middleton and William Rowley, *A Courtly Masque: The Device Called The World Tost at Tennis* (1620), 124.

4   Edward Reyner, *Rules for the Government of the Tongue* (1656), 227.

5   George Puttenham, *The Arte of English Poesie*, edited by Gladys D. Willcock and Alice Walker (Cambridge: Cambridge UP, 1936), 189.

6   Collect for Easter Day, *The Book of Common Prayer 1559: The Elizabethan Prayer Book* , edited by John E. Booty, Charlottesville: UP of Virginia, for the Folger Shakespeare Library, 1976), 152-153.

7   See Matthias Bauer's discussion of Herbert's titles elsewhere in this collection.

8   Sterne, *Tristram Shandy*, p. 248 [4: 32].

11

GEORGE HERBERT'S APOCALYPTICISM:
SECULAR AND SACRED

TED-LARRY PEBWORTH

Late Renaissance figures such as George Herbert were certainly aware of living and acting in two worlds, the sacred and the profane, but the boundaries of these two spheres were less distinct for them than they are for most modern readers, and not necessarily discrete and impermeable. Hence, in 1619, Herbert could protest in a letter to his stepfather, Sir John Danvers, that Sir Francis Nethersole is mistaken in fearing that a position Herbert then earnestly sought—the Oratorship of Cambridge University—'being civil may divert me too much from Divinity, at which, not without cause, he thinks, I aim'. For, as Herbert contends, 'this dignity, hath no such earthiness in it, but it may very well be joined with Heaven; or if it had to others, yet to me it should not'.[1] To Herbert, the sacred and the profane, especially the latter's ultimate and overarching manifestation in political concerns, were largely inseparable.

Thus it is that, from the beginning of his public career to the end of his brief life, Herbert sought and found religious answers to political as well as religious problems. Most strikingly, when faced with difficulties in either state or church, he characteristically abjured present human violence as an appropriate response in favour of divine intervention 'In the end'.[2] That is, in both arenas—the sacred and the profane—he espoused an apocalyptic view of history that relies not upon present conflict but instead upon the Last Judgement to set things right.

To say that Herbert espoused an apocalyptic view of history is by no means to aver that he was a millenarian. Harold Toliver is indeed correct in stressing Herbert's 'anti-millennial historicity'.[3] But as Claude J. Summers argues in an essay on the poetry of Robert Herrick and Henry Vaughan, seventeenth-century Anglican apocalypticism was of a different nature entirely from that espoused by Puritans, the more zealous of whom emphasized and looked forward to the thousand-year reign of the saints foretold in the book of Revelation (with themselves as the saints) as the just reward for undergoing persecution at the hands of the Established Church. Rather, the apocalypticism of the English Church in the seventeenth century focused on two other events that, according to St John of Patmos, were to take place during the Last Days: the mystical marriage of the Lamb of God and the Last Judgement. For Anglicans such as Herbert, Herrick, and Vaughan, the reliance on apocalyptic answers to present problems is 'fundamentally an attempt to escape history'—and its reversals—'by means of an appeal to a vision of eternity and an expression of faith in God's eventual intervention in human affairs.' As Summers concludes, this Anglican eschatological perspective 'facilitates an acceptance of the current afflictions as trials to be endured and as injustices to be redressed in the fullness of God's time'.[4]

This appeal to the Last Judgement is the method that, in secular poems written early in his career, Herbert uses to console and compensate the Queen of Bohemia for her political losses. It is the same appeal that, in sacred poems written both early and late in his career, Herbert uses to deal with the perceived enemies of the Church of England. This hitherto unremarked continuity between Herbert's secular poetry and his devotional poetry casts a revealing light on each and on Herbert's characteristic way of comprehending the world, that is, on his wit.

Sometime between the spring of 1621 and the fall of 1622, Herbert wrote two poems to the recently exiled Elizabeth Stuart, Queen of Bohemia. Born in 1597, she was the daughter of King James and his consort Anne of Denmark. Early in 1613, Elizabeth, then Princess Royal of England, married Frederick V, the Elector Palatine, a leading Protestant among the German princes. In 1619, shortly after the outbreak of the Thirty Years War, Frederick unwisely accepted election to the throne of the largely Protestant kingdom of Bohemia, thereby incurring the enmity of the Hapsburg Roman Catholic emperor Ferdinand II, who claimed the Bohemian crown by hereditary right. By force of arms, Ferdinand drove Frederick from Bohemia; and in short order, the Roman Catholic Maximillian of Bavaria, a client of the emperor, occupied the Upper Palatinate, and the Spanish Hapsburgs conquered the Lower (or Rhenish) Palatinate. The erstwhile and now homeless King and Queen of Bohemia sought refuge in Protestant Holland, where they established a court-in-exile in The Hague. Though Frederick and Elizabeth were immediately dubbed the Winter King and Queen by Ferdinand's Jesuit supporters, Elizabeth herself was quickly styled the Queen of Hearts by her English admirers, who saw her as 'a kind of martyr' to the Protestant cause.[5] Both as an individual and as Public Orator of Cambridge, Herbert no doubt wished to console the Winter Queen, for whom on an earlier, happier occasion he had written an epithalamion.

His two poems addressed to the Queen of Bohemia are, in fact, poems of consolation. Composed at the nadir of Elizabeth's fortunes, soon after the loss in quick succession of both Bohemia and the Palatinate, they are designed to comfort the Winter Queen in her adversity. Without disguising the extent of her present misfortunes, the poems look forward to better times, and they seize the unhappy occasion of her recent exile to praise

Elizabeth's dignity in defeat. The faith in which the poems are securely grounded permits them to be simultaneously realistic and tactful. They are fine examples of a certain kind of political poetry in which art transforms objective loss into subjective gain. Informed with topical reality, they incorporate the immediate circumstances of defeat into a larger, apocalyptic vision of ultimate victory.

The longer of the two poems, 'To the Lady Elizabeth Queen of Bohemia', is divided into three parts. In the first twenty-two lines, Elizabeth's loss of 'two clods of earth'—that is, Bohemia and the Palatinate—is translated into evidence of her innate personal superiority: 'Those that rule in clay / Stick fast therein; but thy transcendent soul / Doth for two clods of earth ten spheres control' (6-8). Moreover, the 'black tiffany' (the cloth of which mourning scarves were made), ostensibly symbolic of her defeat and exile, actually serves as a 'foil' to set off the true richness of her innate worth and to distinguish it from the accidents of fortune or chance (17, 16). The second section of the poem (23-54) expands on this theme. With the artificial panoply of state removed, Elizabeth's 'native beauty' shines in its own right, proclaiming her 'undivided majesty' (30, 34). And the darkness of her present misery actually makes her individual splendour more apparent. Moreover, God has given Elizabeth children who will grow up to conquer new kingdoms for her, sending her Catholic enemies to a punishment where neither their incense nor their Spanish saints can aid them. The final section of the poem (55-66) is in a quieter mood. The poet addresses the Queen of Hearts with great tenderness. Her chief government now is 'to manage woe, / To curb some rebel tears, which fain would flow' (57-58). But, Herbert consoles her, in some 'better season' that 'hand divine, / Which mingles water with thy Rhenish wine,' will punish her enemies and restore her to happiness (60, 63-64). The poem is remarkable chiefly for its careful modulation of tone, its blend of righteous indignation with tact and tenderness, and for the daring of its conceits.

The second, briefer poem, 'To the Same. Another'—written in shorter, quicker lines—is an apostrophe to Elizabeth's 'majestic soul', urging it to 'abide / Like David's tree planted beside / The Flemish rivers' (1-3). As Herbert's modern editors note, the primary allusion here is to Ps. 1: 3, where the godly man is likened to 'a tree planted by the rivers of water, that bringeth forth his fruit in his season; his leaf also shall not wither; and whatsoever he doeth shall prosper' (AV). But these opening lines also suggest another psalm, one of exile and sorrow beside a foreign river, a psalm which looks forward to the defeat of enemies and the restoration of the righteous to their homeland: 'By the rivers of Babylon, there we sat down, yea, we wept, when we remembered Zion. We hanged our harps upon the

willows in the midst thereof' (Ps. 137: 1-2). Herbert's second poem to Elizabeth does not dwell on present defeat, however. It goes on to promise
justice 'In the end' (3). In a metaphor reminiscent of Ben Jonson's earlier
poem on the union of England and Scotland under a single monarch (Epigram 5) and looking forward to Henry Vaughan's 'The World', Herbert
turns a circumnavigation of the globe into a great ring wedding Elizabeth's
fame to eternity. This triumphant conclusion is all the more touching for
the poet's having revealed his awareness of the queen's present perilous
circumstances.

What is remarkable about these two poems is that, while the first
glances at Elizabeth's children as future avenging forces, they both ultimately rely on God, not men, to exact vengeance for her political reversals.
Many Englishmen in the early 1620s saw the defeat of Elizabeth and Frederick at the hands of the Emperor and the King of Spain as a clarion call to
military action in a holy war against Roman Catholicism. But this is
emphatically not Herbert's position. In effect, he counsels patience in adversity, secure in the religiously grounded expectation that Elizabeth's
goodness—and the Protestantism she represents—will finally be rewarded
and that the evil acts of her enemies—who are also the enemies of Protestantism—will ultimately be punished through divine intervention. This perspective is articulated through subtle but certain allusions to the Last Judgement. In the longer poem, Herbert comforts Elizabeth with an appeal to a
'better season' in the future, when a 'hand divine' will 'pour full joys to
thee, but dregs to those / (And meet their taste) who are thy bitter foes' (60,
63, 65-66). In the shorter poem, it is 'In the end' (3)—a phrase redolent
with overtones of the Last Judgement—that 'Our God will surely dry those
tears / Which now that moist land to thee bears' (5-6). Obviously, Herbert
is here alluding to the promise of Rev. 21: 3-4 that in the New Jerusalem
the blessed will dwell with God and 'God shall wipe away all tears from
their eyes; and there shall be no more death, neither sorrow, nor crying,
neither shall there be any more pain: for the former things are passed
away'. Moreover, the 'ring' in the shorter poem—the circumnavigation of
the globe by which Elizabeth's 'fame shall wed / Eternity into one bed'
(13-14)—evokes that second event important in Anglican apocalypticism,
the Wedding of the Lamb, at which Christ marries his true Church. Inas-
much as Elizabeth has come to represent—if not embody—the Protestant
cause, which Herbert by implication identifies here as the true Church, the
marriage of her 'fame' to 'Eternity' at a time 'In the end' will parallel—if
it does not equal—the marriage of Christ to the true Church as foretold in
St John's Revelation.

In the two poems addressed to the Queen of Bohemia, Herbert looks forward to an apocalyptic answer to a present political problem that has religious consequences. If F.E. Hutchinson is correct in dating at least the 'inception' of 'The Church Militant'—the long poem that closes *The Temple*—to the early 1620s (p. 543), then about the time that Herbert wrote the poems to the Queen of Bohemia, he began composing an apocalyptic answer to a religious problem that has political consequences. 'The Church Militant' chronicles the history of the earthly church, always beset by sin and falling short of its professed ideals, as one long progress toward that 'time and place, where judgement shall appear' (277). The implication is, of course, that at that Last Judgement, the earthly church will be purged of its sinful elements and then wed to the Lamb as the Church Triumphant; but the emphasis in Herbert's poem is not on future glory but on the past, present, and even future sinfulness in the earthly institution that necessitates that final judgement.

Especially notable in the poem is a lengthy indictment of Roman Catholicism (157-234), which is couched largely in terms drawn from St John's Revelation. Rome is the 'Western Babylon' (211), and 'As new and old Rome did one Empire twist; / So both together are one Antichrist' (205-206). The allusions to the Apocalypse throughout this passage are numerous, and in employing them Herbert subscribes to an established and popular Protestant tradition definitively set forth in the annotations to the Geneva Bible, first issued in 1560. According to that tradition, Rome is the Babylon of St John's Revelation. In that vision, the city is dominated by a Whore sitting on a seven-headed beast. The Geneva commentators identify the beast as 'ancient Rome'—the 'old Rome' of Herbert's poem—while they identify the Whore herself as 'the newe Rome which is the Papistrie ... the Antichrist, that is, the Pope with the whole bodie of his filthie creatures' (Rev. 17, notes *d* and *f*). Interestingly, Herbert never uses St John's figure of the Whore of Babylon in 'The Church Militant'. Instead, he has 'Sin' itself bravely resolving 'To be a Churchman ... and wear a Mitre' (161, 163). But the reactions of the princes of the earth to 'Sin' as the Bishop of Rome in Herbert's poem are equivalent to those of the 'kings of the earth' toward the Whore in Revelation. In St John's vision, 'the kings of the earth have committed fornication' with the Whore for secular, political gain (Rev. 17: 2); in 'The Church Militant', 'Princes' haste to Rome to 'submit their necks' either to the Pope's 'public foot or private tricks' from the same motive (195, 196).

In an apocalyptic poem such as 'The Church Militant', the Last Judgement is, of course, the final act. In the poems to the Queen of Bohemia, Herbert had been explicit as to the fate of Elizabeth's enemies. In 'The

Church Militant' he is less explicit as to the fate of the Church of Rome. Near the beginning of the passage on that church, Herbert speaks of a truth that 'Rome will one day find unto her cost' (160), but he is not otherwise forthcoming as to the details of her ultimate fate. By alluding throughout to passages in the Book of Revelation, however, he does not have to be explicit; St John of Patmos is explicit for him. In the Last Days, according to Rev. 18: 8, the Whore will be judged, and her fate will be terrible: 'Therefore shall her plagues come in one day, death, and mourning, and famine; and she shall be utterly burnt with fire'. A decade later this rhetoric of allusion will serve Herbert well in writing the religio-political lyrics of 'The Church' section of *The Temple*.

In commenting on 'The Church Militant', Hutchinson noted that the poem's 'anti-Roman animus is characteristic of Herbert's early and more controversial mind' (p. 543), implying that the poet's later stance—as reflected in the lyrics of 'The Church'—was less controversial. Such, however, is simply not the case. Herbert never eschewed controversy. He did, however, alter his strategic approach to controversial subjects. In his later lyrics, he avoided the overt and impassioned rhetoric of controversy, preferring to maintain a gentle, even sweet surface while continuing to make judgements on controversial issues through a rhetoric of allusion. A central component of this rhetoric of allusion is an implied apocalypticism and a characteristic doubleness. Much of Herbert's poetry and many of his most acclaimed techniques depend on a double vision, an ability to focus simultaneously on two perspectives, often including the sacred and the profane or the temporal and the eternal. Herbert's implied apocalypticism is itself one version of his doubleness, for it allows him to evoke simultaneously a moment in history and the end of history itself.

This implied apocalypticism is to be found in several of the lyrics in 'The Church' section of *The Temple*, especially those having to do with the perceived enemies to the peace of the English Establishment. By the late 1620s and the early 1630s, those enemies included not only Roman Catholicism from without but also increasingly zealous purifiers from within who drew their ecclesiology ultimately from Geneva. In such poems as 'Divinity', 'The Family', and 'Church-Rents and Schisms', Herbert relies on allusions to Last Things—both the Wedding of the Lamb and the Last Judgement—as the ultimate answers to present squabbles and tears in the Established Church. Such allusions in 'The Family', for example, help transform a personal expression of an individual's internal conflicts into a plea for peace and harmony in the Church; as so often in Herbert, the perspective is double, simultaneously private and public. But the most striking and sustained use of the rhetoric of allusion to evoke a double perspective and to resolve ecclesiastic strife by means of apocalyptic solutions occurs in his poem entitled 'The British Church'.[6]

That poem is, on the surface, a joyous hymn celebrating the form and liturgy of Herbert's 'dearest Mother' (23), the Church of England, as the divinely favoured compromise between Roman Catholicism's luxurious trappings and Genevan Calvinism's austere nakedness, 'the middle way between superstition, and slovenliness,' as he remarks in *The Countrey Parson* (Hutchinson, p. 246). As Joseph Summers suggests, the poem is a fine example of Herbert's 'marvelous wit and playfulness', and its tone perfectly matches its theme, expressing that 'middle way' of emotion between 'the extremes of agony and ecstasy' that are to be found elsewhere in *The Temple*.[7] But the poem is more than witty and playful; and the assured, gentle tone in which it celebrates the maternal English Establishment and criticizes wanton Rome and slovenly Geneva is deceptive. Informing Herbert's descriptions of the three earthly churches are Biblical passages that place the poem within a broad context of Christian history, culminating in the Apocalypse, and that infuse it with an authority and a force that go far beyond one poet-priest's calm, disarmingly witty preference in form and liturgy.

In Herbert's poem, three churches—those of Britain, Rome, and Geneva—are presented as three women who are characterised primarily by their dress. The 'array' of the British Church is 'fit ... , / Neither too mean, nor yet too gay' (7-8); Roman Catholicism is 'wantonly' attired (13); and Geneva 'nothing wears' (24). All three descriptions allude to events of the Last Days.

Underlying Herbert's description of the 'fine aspect in fit array' of the Church of England (7) is the account of the bridal raiment in St John's vision of the marriage of Christ the Lamb to his cleansed and completed Church: 'for the marriage of the Lamb is come, and his wife hath made herself ready. And to her was granted that she should be arrayed in fine linen, clean and white: for the fine linen is the righteousness of saints' (Rev. 19: 7b-8). The bride's raiment is of 'fine' workmanship, and it is costly, having been purchased with blood—both the blood of the sacrificed Lamb and the blood of those who have been martyred for belief in him (see Rev. 6: 9 and 7: 14). Yet the garment is of essentially modest material—linen, rather than of a showy, exotic fabric—and its only adornment is the dazzling whiteness of its dearly-purchased purity. In alluding to this Biblical passage in his description of Anglicanism, Herbert ingeniously but clearly identifies the localized and historical British Church with the universal and eternal Church Triumphant, whose members will populate the New Jerusalem.

For his picture of Counter-Reformation Rome, Herbert turns again to the passage in Revelation that he had employed for the whole history of the Roman Church in 'The Church Militant', but this time he alludes specifically to the Whore of Babylon: 'She on the hills, which wantonly / Allureth all in hope to be / By her preferr'd' (13-15). Relevantly for the overall structure of Herbert's poem in terms of human dress, St John pictures the Whore as lewdly 'arrayed in purple and scarlet colour, and decked with gold and precious stones and pearls' (17: 4a). But the contrast between the English Establishment and Roman Catholicism is not merely one of outward show, as the surface of the poem might indicate. Just as the identification of the English Establishment with the Bride of the Lamb looks forward to its eventual triumph, so the identification of Roman Catholicism with the Whore of Babylon looks forward, as we have seen in 'The Church Militant', to its eventual destruction at the Last Judgement.

While Herbert shares with Genevans a scorn of the painted temptress Rome, he convicts Calvinist ecclesiology in its turn for an inverted pride in deliberate bareness: she 'nothing wears' (24). St John's Revelation offers no apposite context for this picture of Geneva as the underdressed woman of the valley, but one of Christ's parables referring to Last Things does. Significantly, that parable—recounted in Matt. 22: 1-14 and concerned with the feast that a king prepares to celebrate his son's marriage—is connected by marginal cross-references to St John's account of the Wedding of the Lamb in the most popularly used Bibles of Herbert's day, both Protestant and Catholic, namely, the Geneva translation, the edition of the Vulgate promulgated by Sixtus V in 1590, and the Authorized Version of 1611. Concerned with the Second Coming, the parable speaks primarily to the rejection of Christ by the Jewish nation and his acceptance by Gentile nations; but one of its incidents is stated in terms of human grooming and is relevant to Herbert's poem. While presiding over his son's marriage feast, the king is angered by the appearance of a guest not properly attired in 'a wedding garment' (v. 11). Although the major point of the incident is a warning against spiritual unpreparedness, the improper dress of the wedding guest is perceived as a mark of disrespect towards both the host and the occasion, a dramatic context that perfectly fits Herbert's attitude towards Genevan ecclesiology in 'The British Church'. Again, without sacrificing his calm and sweet tone, Herbert is able through allusive context to convey an authoritative rebuke. Moreover, just as the identification of Roman Catholicism with the Whore of Babylon inevitably looks forward to that church's divinely appointed destruction, so the linking of Genevan Calvinism with the improperly garbed wedding guest of Christ's parable implies that reformed church's equally unpleasant fate at the hands of an angry

God. The judgement against the disrespectful guest is swift and terrible: 'Then said the king to the servants, Bind him hand and foot, and take him away, and cast him into outer darkness; there shall be weeping and gnashing of teeth' (Matt. 22: 13).

Like many other poems in *The Temple*—and like the two outwardly secular poems to the Queen of Bohemia—Herbert's 'The British Church' reflects a double perspective. Ostensibly rooted in its speaker's present, the poem playfully comments on a particular historical controversy from a personal point of view. But its pattern of scriptural allusions carries the poem forward to the final days of human history as foretold by both Christ and St John the Divine, and that anticipated future completes the poem's fragment of the present in judgements that are neither playful nor personal. The exaltation of the English Establishment and the destruction of Roman Catholicism and of Genevan Calvinism are subtly but firmly revealed as God's judgements, not those of the apparently naive speaker. From this double perspective, the institution Herbert celebrates indeed becomes 'double-moat[ed]' (29), in a literal as well as a figurative sense. In the poem's present, the British Church, like the nation it ministers to, is protected—in the words of Shakespeare's John of Gaunt—by 'the silver sea, / Which serves it in the office of a wall, / Or as a moat defensive' (*R2*, 2: 1:46-48), shielding it from the horrors of the continent's religious wars. And in the future, the British Church will be 'moted' by the walls of the New Jerusalem (see 'Mote' *sb.*[2], *OED*). Confidence in that future allows Herbert to view the present and comment on it with equanimity. Anticipating her apotheosis, he can praise his present church uncritically; and placing her antagonists within the context of their future damnation, he can charitably afford them present gentleness of tone.

Achsah Guibbory has recently observed that many Renaissance writers subscribed to more than one concept of time, simultaneously viewing the movement of the individual life as cyclical while seeing the broader pattern of history as linear. Herbert had just such a double perspective. He saw the individual's spiritual life as consisting of 'cycles of affliction and renewal',[8] while he viewed the whole of human history as a Providential line drawn from creation to the Last Judgement, from Genesis to Revelation. Such a perspective enabled Herbert to accept temporal crises with equanimity. He applied this perspective not only to the religio-political crises of his time, but also to more personal ones. When his mother was gravely ill in 1622, for instance, he counselled her to adopt the kind of double vision that would later sustain him. 'As the Earth is but a point in respect of the heavens, so are earthly Troubles compar'd to heavenly Joyes,' he reflected, and added: 'consider what advantage you have over *Youth* and *Health*, who are so near those true Comforts. ... I have alwaies observ'd the thred of Life to be like other threds or skenes of silk, full of snarles and incumbrances: Happy is he, whose bottom is wound up and laid ready for work in the New *Jerusalem*' (Hutchinson, pp. 372-373). The faith that enabled him to accept the approaching death of his mother also sustained Herbert in the face of the crises that confronted church and state in the turbulent years of the earlier seventeenth century. Just as he counselled his mother to look forward to the New Jerusalem, so he took his own advice and found solace in his ability to juxtapose earthly troubles with heavenly joys and worldly reversals to apocalyptic justice.

Michael C. Schoenfeldt has tellingly observed that 'Herbert's reputation as an Anglican saint has ... hindered our understanding of his poetry by diverting attention from the amount of time and energy he invested in the world'.[9] As evidenced by a close reading of his poetry and prose, Herbert was always conscious of worldly affairs, especially the conflicts present in state and church. A part of what has blinded us to that fact is that he consistently refuses to accept worldly, violent answers to those sacred and profane conflicts, preferring instead to trust in divine, apocalyptic retribution. Moreover, he has manifested that apocalypticism primarily through the rhetoric of allusion rather than through direct statement, thereby in effect concealing it from all but the most attentive readers. Yet recognition of Herbert's apocalypticism enables us to discern both the doubleness of his thought—his constant consciousness of the interplay of the sacred and the profane—and its unity in a vision that collapses such distinctions altogether. Indeed, Herbert's double vision, especially his simultaneous awareness of the temporal and the eternal, is a function of his most characteristic quality, his wit. It is a means of comprehending the world through the lens of eschatology.

Notes

1   Hutchinson, p. 370. Further quotations from Herbert's prose letters and *The Countrey Parson* are from this edition and cited parenthetically in the text above.
2   Herbert, 'To the Same [i.e., the Queen of Bohemia]. Another' (3), in Tobin, p. 198. Subsequent quotations from Tobin's edition are given with line numbers cited parenthetically in the text above. Hutchinson edited Herbert's two poems to the Queen of Bohemia from an inferior manuscript source and placed them among 'Doubtful Poems' (Hutchinson, pp. 211-213). Arguments for Herbert's authorship may be found in Ted-Larry Pebworth, 'George Herbert's Poems to the Queen of Bohemia: A Rediscovered Text and a New Edition', *ELR* 9 (1979), 108-120; and in Kenneth Alan Hovey, 'George Herbert's Authorship of "To the Queene of

Bohemia"', *RQ* 30 (1977), 43-50. Tobin places these poems among the canonical works and bases his modernized texts on the Pebworth edition.

3   *George Herbert's Christian Narrative* (University Park: Pennsylvania State UP, 1993), 190.

4   'Herrick, Vaughan, and the Poetry of Anglican Survivalism', *New Perspectives on the Seventeenth-Century English Religious Lyric*, edited by John R. Roberts (Columbia: U of Missouri P, 1994), 46-74; the quotations are from 51-52.

5   A[dolphus] W[ard], 'Elizabeth, Queen of Bohemia', *DNB*.

6   For a full discussion of 'The Family', see Claude J. Summers and Ted-Larry Pebworth, 'The Politics of *The Temple*: "The British Church" and "The Familie"', *GHJ* 8 (1984), 1-15. The following discussion of 'The British Church' is indebted to the lengthier treatment of the poem in Claude J. Summers and Ted-Larry Pebworth, 'Herbert, Vaughan, and Public Concerns in Private Modes', *GHJ* 3 (1979-80), 1-21.

7   *George Herbert: His Religion and Art* (Cambridge, MA/London: Harvard U.P/Chatto & Windus, 1984), 189.

8   *The Map of Time: Seventeenth-Century English Literature and Ideas of Pattern in History* (Urbana & Chicago: U of Illinois P, 1986), 265.

9   *Prayer and Power: George Herbert and Renaissance Courtship* (Chicago & London: U of Chicago P, 1991), 8.

INTERTEXTUALITY

12

'THE SWEET CEMENT ... IS LOVE':
GEORGE HERBERT AND THE EMBLEM BOOKS

BART WESTERWEEL

I placed a jar in Tennessee,
And round it was, upon a hill.
It made the slovenly wilderness
Surround that hill.

The wilderness rose up to it,
And sprawled around, no longer wild.
The jar was round upon the ground
And tall and of a port in air.

It took dominion everywhere.
The jar was gray and bare.
It did not give of bird or bush,
Like nothing else in Tennessee.

Wallace Stevens, 'The Anecdote of the Jar'

'Herbert and emblems' is a combination that has been alive in Herbert scholarship ever since Mario Praz called Herbert's poetry 'a conspicuous case of a mute emblem book (i.e. wanting only the plates)',[1] and Rosemary Freeman included a whole chapter on Herbert in her pioneering study *English Emblem Books* (1948).[2] In 1973 Rosalie Colie persuaded us that Herbert's collection of poems 'is, among other things, a "school of the heart", much like continental devotional emblem books'.[3] As early as 1942 Eleanor James wrote an unpublished dissertation entitled 'The Emblem as an Image-Pattern in Some Metaphysical Poets',[4] in which she devotes generous portions to Herbert's assumed relationship with the devotional emblem books of the seventeenth century.

More recently Barbara Lewalski has made a thorough and persuasive, although not unchallenged, attempt to outline the indebtedness of the seventeenth-century religious lyric to the Protestant emblem book in a chapter of her book *Protestant Poetics and the Seventeenth-Century Religious Lyric* (1979)[5] and in 1981 Mary Cole Sloane published a book-length study, *The Visual in Metaphysical Poetry*,[6] in which the emblem book is a central issue throughout. In numerous articles and books or parts of books critics and scholars have followed the leads provided, especially those by Freeman, Praz, Colie and Lewalski. In what I consider one of the soundest accounts of 'Herbert and emblems' in recent years, Richard Todd, in his book *The Opacity of Signs* (1986), comments rather wrily on all these activities:

> No reader of *The Temple* will need to be told that to assert that Herbert's poetic is related to that of the emblem writers is to propose something of a critical commonplace.[7]

Freeman's approach to the emblem's influence on Herbert's poetry is mainly literary and concentrates on the emblematic conceit. Having stated that no other poet in the English language has made such an extensive use of the emblematic conceits as Herbert did, she concludes that:

> ... Herbert's work as a whole constitutes the transformation of the methods of the emblematists into a form for poetry ... characterized by a simplicity of image, an extreme unobtrusiveness, and a concentration of meaning in which the complexity becomes only gradually apparent (Freeman, p. 157).

Since most emblem writers, at least outside the Low Countries, were not among the foremost literary figures of their day it comes as no surprise that the emblem looks rather wan besides the brightness of Herbert's verse.

Colie's approach is generic and the virtue of her account is that she establishes the extent to which Herbert's poetry avails itself of images of the heart, images that are parallelled by the pictures found in the *schola cordis* type of emblem book. What most 'emblematic' accounts of Herbert's poetry have in common, and my own 1984 study is no exception, I am afraid,[8] is that they are on the one hand inclusive as regards the claimed influence of the emblem and the emblem book, but reductive on the other in that the emblem book is invariably reduced to the status of a storehouse of images and that it is reduced, moreover, to a picture or a series of pictures.

A revealing case in point is John Tobin's 1991 Penguin edition of *George Herbert: The Complete English Poems*. The front cover of that edition shows the *pictura* of one of the emblems from the first published emblem book, the 1531 *Emblematum Liber* by Andrea Alciati (see Fig. 1). However carefully edited the main body of Tobin's text, the choice of and reference to the emblem that adorns the cover in such a conspicuous way does insufficient justice to the qualities of the volume. That the illustration is taken from the first edition (Augsburg, 1531), not from a 1536 (presumably Paris) edition, as the back cover of the book indicates may represent a conspicuous mistake but a minor issue, but a more important question is: why this particular emblem and why from Alciati's book of emblems? The motto that belongs to the emblem reads: '*Prvdentes Vino Abstinent*' ('The wise will abstain from wine'). The *pictura* shows an olive tree with a vine clinging to it. In the two-line epigram the tree addresses the reader, explaining that it is the tree of Pallas Athena, and that it feels oppressed by the vine and grapes since the virgin, its mistress, hates anything to do with Bacchus ('*Quid me uexatis rami? sum Palladis arbor, / Auferte hinc botros, uirgo fugit bromium*').

The emblem is perhaps intended to illustrate those stanzas in 'The Church-Porch', that exhort the reader to 'Stay at the third glass' (41), but the relevance of the emblem as an introduction to *The Temple* as a whole eludes me. And why an emblem from Alciati, the connection of whose emblem book to Herbert is tenuous at best? If an emblem is called for at all, why not one from the many devotional emblem books that were not only relevant, but available and well-known to Herbert as well? I am afraid that the emblem—or, to be more precise, the mutilated emblem, since the *pictura* only is reproduced—was simply added by the publisher as a pleasant illustration to allure the reader, quite in line with the precept of *utile dulci*, or, to misquote Herbert: 'An emblem may find him, who a sermon flies, / And turn delight into a sacrifice'. Or should we grant whoever selected the illustration more subtlety than we have allowed for so far? Geffrey Whitney, the author of the first printed emblem book in English, *A Choice of Emblemes* (Leyden, 1586), defines the scope of the emblem thus:

> ... all Emblemes for the most parte, maie be reduced into these three kindes, which is *Historicall, Naturall, & Morall. Historicall*, as representing the actes of some noble persons, being matter of historie. *Naturall*, as in expressing the natures of creatures, for example the loue of the yonge Storkes, to the oulde, or of suche like. *Morall*, pertaining to vertue and instruction of life, which is the chiefe of the three, and the other two maye bee in some sorte drawen into this head. For, all doe tende vnto discipline, and morall preceptes of liuing ('To the reader', sig. ** 4).

Is the emblem supposed to indicate that the prime function of Herbert's poetry is to present us with a mixture of 'Naturall' matter, used for 'Morall' purposes? Partly true, but only very partly, any reader of Herbert would agree. In brief, the juxtaposition of a mutilated emblem and Herbert's poetry is suggestive but detrimental to both, since it reduces both to a caricature.

The purpose of this article is to provide a corrective to what I see as the reductive effect of the indiscriminate usage in Herbert criticism of the words *emblem* and *emblematic*. Let me begin by sketching a couple of tendencies in the use of emblems in critical discourse.

Firstly, many scholars, although they acknowledge that the emblem is usually a tripartite form, consisting of motto, *pictura*, and epigram or *subscriptio*, reproduce and discuss their *picturae* only. It is also common practice to emphasize the visual nature of the emblem form and use that assumed visual nature to explicate the imagery and conceits of Herbert's verse. What Mary Cole Sloane writes seems symptomatic in this respect: 'There are striking parallels between the prints Quarles used and some of the imagery found in the poetry of Donne and Herbert' (Sloane, p. 25). In most books and articles discussing Herbert and emblems the prints of the emblems are reproduced, without the texts that are an integral part of the emblem. In this way the emblem is reduced to the position of a mere illustration of a verbal image. Perhaps it is useful to refer once again to the Preface of Whitney's book of emblems, where he refers to his emblems as *texts*, first and foremost: '... there are divers Emblemes *written* of one matter ... although the *worde* [that is, emblem] doth comprehende manie thinges ...' (emphasis added). Francis Quarles, author of the most popular of the English emblem books, *Emblemes* (London, 1635), wishes his reader 'as much pleasure in the *reading*, as I had in the writing' (sig. A3) of his emblems. Alciati, the *pater princeps* of the emblem book, considered his book a collection of illustrated epigrams.

Secondly, the words emblem and emblematic are used as if the emblem either belongs to a well-defined, almost monolithic genre, or has a well-defined, unique meaning. This position is summed up nicely by Chana Bloch in her 1985 *Spelling the Word*,[9] where she regards attempts to find fruitful connections between Herbert's verse and the emblem book disappointing because of the stiffness and lifelessness attributed to the emblem on the one hand and the supple flexibility of Herbert's verse on the other. I shall return to this issue later. As a genre the phenomenon of the emblem and the emblem book is not stiff or lifeless at all, however; on the contrary, it is remarkably unstable and varied, especially if, again, one considers not only the history of the *picturae* separately but in their context, as part of a complete emblem with a motto and a *subscriptio*, but also as part of an emblem *book*, that is, a collection of emblems that was produced under specific historical and cultural circumstances. The same *pictura* and even the same motto may be used for entirely different purposes in different emblem collections. For Herbert's poem 'Easter Wings', for instance, the emblem with the motto *'Paupertatem summis ingeniis obesse ne prouehantur'* ('Poverty mars the development of the greatest talents') in Alciati's collection, imitated in England by Geffrey Whitney in 1586 and George Wither in 1635,[10] is hardly relevant, whereas the analogous *pictura* as we find it in Hugo's *Pia desideria* (1624)[11] and Quarles's *Emblemes* (1635) is highly relevant (see Figs 2, 3 and 4). The emblem from Alciati's collection, a sixteenth-century humanist venture, refers to the poverty that prevents talented men to flourish; the emblem in Hugo and Quarles refers to man's sins, which prevent him from reaching his heavenly destination. Christian emulation has changed the profane emblem into a sacred one.

When critics refer to Herbert's 'emblematic' imagery the word 'emblem' or 'emblematic' is frequently used to cover multiple meanings such as the 'hieroglyph(ic)' or the 'allegory/-ical' or the *'technopaegnion'* (pattern poem). In view of the inconsistent and variable way in which the word 'emblem' was used even by emblem writers themselves it seems better to avoid the use of the word emblem unless one refers to a specific emblem or a specific emblem book or unless the specific meaning of the word emblem is defined in the context where it is used. Quarles—and he was by no means unique in this respect—writes in the same brief Preface ('To the Reader', A3) from which I have already quoted:

An Embleme is but a silent Parable .... Before the knowledge of letters, God was known by *Hierogliphicks*; And indeed, what are the Heavens, the Earth, nay every Creature, but *Hierogliphicks* and *Emblems* of His Glory?

We should not forget, either, notwithstanding Praz's reference to Herbert's poetry as a 'mute' emblem book that Herbert did not choose to either incorporate *picturae* or to present his poems as *emblemata nuda*, as Francis Thynne had done.[12] Again this is a point I shall return to later.

In the remainder of this essay I wish to offer a tentative emblematic account of Herbert's poetry, bearing in mind what has been said so far, by means of a comparative analysis of some of Herbert's poems with the emblems of Francis Quarles, Herbert's contemporary. The purpose of the exercise is not to try to prove once again the extent to which Herbert was indebted to the emblem writers but to demonstrate how the emblematic mode as one of the rhetorical means at his disposal was analyzed critically rather than simply applied in Herbert's poetics of sacred love. The discussion will also demonstrate that Quarles himself shared some of Herbert's doubts about earlier assumptions that the emblem gave direct access to important moral and religious truths.

In a persuasive and mostly convincing account Richard Todd elaborated the relationship between Herbert and the *schola cordis* emblem tradition, originally outlined by Rosalie Colie in 1973. Todd relates the school of the heart type of emblem book to Herbert's 'Passion' poems and presents useful comparative analyses between emblems from the continental *schola cordis* collections of emblems, notably those 1620s collections of Daniel Cramer and Benedictus van Haeften.[13] Todd's argument regarding the reader's share in 'beholding' and 'considering' the details of the Passion is particularly illuminating. All the illustrations in Todd's chapter are either from Cramer's or van Haeften's emblem books. In the text he occasionally refers to and quotes from Harvey's *School of the Heart* (1648), the English reworking (not strictly speaking a 'translation' as Todd claims) of van Haeften's collection.[14]

Although a more detailed analysis of the texts of Harvey's emblems *vis à vis* Herbert's poetry seems called for, the territory of Herbert and the *schola cordis* tradition is pretty well covered on the whole. As I have argued elsewhere, the *schola cordis* tradition is a mixed subgenre, however. It is part and parcel of the category of the emblem books dealing with the exploits of Divine Amor and Anima, the human soul. Also, I tend to agree, up to a point, with Lewalski and with Mary Cole Sloane, that Herbert's concerns are reflected most closely in the protestant English collections contemporary with him. I propose to single out one such emblem book for closer scrutiny: the *Emblemes* by Francis Quarles (1635). Quarles' book of emblems consists of five books that are based on two continental devotional emblem books: the anonymous *Typus Mundi* (Antwerp, 1627) for Books 1 and 2, and Hugo's *Pia Desideria* (Antwerp, 1624) for Books 3, 4, and 5. The latter is one of the most influential and most widely imitated collections of devotional emblems of the seventeenth century. I would like to consider a number of aspects of some of these emblems.

The first poem of Book 3 in Quarles' emblem book parallels the very first emblem in its model, Hugo's *Pia Desideria* (see Fig. 5). A telling difference between Quarles and his Jesuit predecessor is the fact that Hugo added titles to each of the three books that emphasize the devotional nature of his collection: Book 1: *Gemitus Animae Poenitentis*, Book 2: *Vota Animae Sanctae*, and Book 3: *Suspiria Animae Amantis*; that is: the groaning of the penitent soul, the prayers of the pious soul, and the sighs of the loving soul respectively. This structure reflects a love relationship between the human soul and Christ as it had been developed in the bride and bridegroom imagery of Bernardian love mysticism in the format of the three stages of the sequential meditation. This is the kind of structuring also found in Catholic English emblem books such as those by Henry Hawkins. In his *Partheneia Sacra* (Rouen, 1633) the pattern of the meditative scheme is provided by the twenty-four acts of devotion represented by the twenty-four plants in the garden of the sacred Parthenes. In *The Devout Hart* (Rouen, 1634) a translation, without the *picturae*, of the Latin edition of *Le Cœur Devot*, a *schola cordis* by Etienne Luzvic (Paris, 1626), each emblem consists of a series of meditative exercises, called successively *The Incentive*, the *Preamble to the Meditation*, the *Meditation*, and a *Colloquy*. There is nothing like this in the protestantized emblem book by Quarles, although the number of emblems in each book, fifteen, imitates the *Pia Desideria* in suggesting the number of steps to the Temple and of the 'Psalms of Degree'. As Ernest B. Gilman put it in 1980 in an article on Quarles' emblems:

> Far less sure than the meditative steps of the Jesuits, these 'trembling paces' between pain and comfort, doubt and resolution, mark the larger rhythms of Quarles' book'.[15]

The first emblem is a case in point. Whereas in Hugo the ecstatic sighs, prayers and groans, pictured in the engraving as arrows with little scrolls attached to them ('Ah!', 'Utinam', and 'Heu!'), shooting upwards from the breast of the seated Anima towards the eye and ears of God, depicted in the middle of the rays of the sun, set the tone of the collection as a whole, in Quarles it is turned into an introductory exhortation to the individual reader (p. 126):

> Dart up thy Soule in Groanes: Thy secret Grone
> Shall pierce his Eare, shall pierce his Eare, alone:
> Dart up thy Soule in vowes; thy sacred Vow
> Shall find him out, where heav'n alone shall know:
> Dart up thy soule in sighs: Thy whispring sigh
> Shall rouze his eares, and feare no listner nigh:
> ...
> Shoot up the bosome Shafts of thy desire,
> Feather'd with Faith, and double forkt with Fire,

Quarles' 'Entertainement' is parallelled in the title of one of Herbert's poems, 'Sighs and Groans', and in a much more complex form in the opening lines of Herbert's 'Artillery':

As I one ev'ning sat before my cell,
Methoughts a star did shoot into my lap.

This unusual thought leads to an elaborate conceit in the third and fourth
stanzas:

But I have also stars and shooters too,
Born where thy servants both artilleries use,
My tears and prayers night and day do woo,
And work up to thee; yet thou dost refuse.
...

Then we are shooters both, and thou dost deign
To enter combat with us, and contest
With thine own clay. But I would parley fain:
Shun not my arrows, and behold my breast.   (17-20, 25-28)

The meditative exhortation of Quarles's emblem appears as a dramatic
battle in Herbert's poem.
    In emblem 3: 14 the engraving exhibits a major difference compared to
the original in Hugo's *Pia Desideria* (see Figs 8 and 9). Next to Anima,
who is observing the Apocalypse through a telescope, a second figure has
been added, a naked woman, hair loose, a mirror in her hand, who addresses Anima. The figure represents Flesh and the accompanying poem is
a debate between Body and Soul:

Fl. What meanes my sisters eyes so oft to passe
       Through the long entry of that Optick glasse?
       Tell me; what secret virtue does invite
       Thy wrinckled eye to such unknowne delight?
Sp. It helps the sight; makes things remote appeare
       In perfect view; It drawes the object neare.
Fl. What sense-delighting objects doest thou spie?
       What does that Glasse present before thine eye?
Sp. I see thy foe, my reconciled friend,
       Grim death, even standing at the Glasses end;
       His left hand holds a branch of Palme; his right
       Holds forth a two-edg'd sword.
Fl. A proper sight!
       And is this all? does thy Prospective please
       Th'abused fancy with no shapes but these?   (177)

Concerning the emblem Gilman has this to say:

> The condition of sight has become a kind of agon between Flesh and
> Spirit for the eye of the viewer, who is made to feel the pull on him
> from two directions (Gilman, p. 397).

And Karl Josef Höltgen and John Horden, editors of the recently published
facsimile edition of Quarles' *Emblemes*, indicate that most alterations in the
plates as compared to the originals are related to Quarles' text and 'intro-
duce additional figures, personifications and objects'. Höltgen and Horden
conclude that these alterations 'make Quarles' emblem pictures look less
like compositions of static symbols and more like semi-dramatic, masque-
like *tableaux vivants* or allegorical scenes'.[16]

Gilman, Höltgen and Horden all touch on a crucial issue here. Both
picture and text of Quarles' emblem invite the reader/spectator to exercise
his/her powers of observation and perception to the full and to participate
actively in the implications of the scene in front of him. In this respect
Quarles' emblems are far removed from the monolithic type of emblem that
was mentioned previously.

Our next example is the first emblem of Book 4 (see Fig. 10). In this
case, too, the *pictura* activates the observer's mind rather than presenting a
static truth. Anima is seen in a quandary; she is in the process of making a
choice between Amor Divinus, who holds the Tables of the Law, on the
one hand, and Amor Mundanus, with the traditional attributes of bow and
arrows, on the other. The latter tries to deflect Anima's attention from his
rival by touching her shoulder (the scene is reminiscent of a similar but
much more famous representation, in this case of Aphrodite and her two
sons, Eros and Anteros, in Titian's painting 'The Education of Cupid').

The scene is set *in medias res*. The movement suggested by the figure
of Anima is reinforced by the text of the accompanying poem:

> O How my will is hurried to and fro,
>   And how my unresolv'd resolves do varie!
> I know not where to fix; sometimes I goe
>   This way; then that; and then the quite contrary:

In stanza six Quarles adds:

> I know the nature of my wav'ring mind;
>   I know the frailty of my fleshly will:
> My Passion's Eagle-ey'd; my Iudgement, blind ...

The active participation of the viewer in the scene depicted is enhanced by the background scene of the *pictura* that emphasizes the contrast between the two Cupids: the unbridled rearing horse is the symbol of unrestrained passion, whereas the ox signifies the patience and strength of the true Christian and is often used to symbolize Christ's sacrifice.

In the intriguing third stanza of the text Quarles pursues the idea of human penmanship in contrast with the divine writing of the Commandments:

> The curious Penman, having trim'd his Page
>   With the dead language of his dabled Quill,
> Lets fall heedlesse drop, then, in a Rage,
>   Cashieres the fruits of his unlucky skill;

Gilman comments on this emblem:

> 'Unregarded' language is heedless language, like the penman's spilled ink. Its plea is apparently not heeded, yet love comes unexpectedly, and unseen—that is, 'unregarded'—before the blinded eye of the poet. Divine Love reverses the order and logic of the poet's language ... , saves it from the sad tautologies of unresolved repetition, and so subtly cancels the penman's original error: his words are 'regarded' after all (Gilman, p. 395).

The true vision for the Protestant emblem writer is in the observation of the Word. Any reader of Herbert's verse will be reminded of the lines in his often anthologized poem 'Jordan (2)':

> Thousands of notions in my brain did run,
> Off'ring their service, if I were not sped:
> I often blotted what I had begun.

For our two final examples we first turn to Book 3, emblem 2 (see Fig. 6). The emblem revolves around the conceit of the stigma of Christ's hand, a small but significant detail added by Quarles to the original engraving of the *Pia Desideria*. The wound becomes a peephole through which God can observe man's foolishness:

... O, canst Thou choose but see,
That mad'st the Eye? Can ought be hid from Thee?
Thou seest our persons, Lord, and not our Guilt;
Thou seest not what thou maist; but what thou wilt:
The Hand, that form's us, is enforc'd to be
A Screene set up betwixt thy Work and Thee:
Looke, looke upon that Hand, and thou shalt spy
An open wound, a Thoroughfare for thine Eye;
Or if that wound be clos'd, that passage be
Deny'd betweene Thy gracious eyes, and me,
Yet view the Scarre; That Scarre will countermand
Thy Wrath: O read my Fortune in thy Hand.   (p. 134)

Herbert, too, employs the *topos* of the stigmata for the extravagant conceit of Christ's side wound in 'The Bag':

He, who came hither all alone,
Bringing nor man, nor arms, nor fear,
Received the blow upon his side,
And straight he turned, and to his brethren cried,

If ye have any thing to send or write,
(I have no bag, but here is room)
Unto my father's hands and sight
(Believe me) it shall safely come.
That I shall mind, what you impart;
Look, you may put it very near my heart.

The dramatic impact of the image is underscored by the deictic presentation: 'Look, you may put ...'. Once again, in both the emblem and in Herbert's poem the true vision lies in writing.

In Book 3, emblem 10, finally, the stage is occupied by three actors, who conduct a debate about the fate of the human soul upon its arrival at Heaven's gate (see Fig. 7). The emblem is strongly reminiscent of the final poem of *The Church*, 'Love (3)'. Whereas in Herbert's poem the eucharistic debate between God and the human soul is conducted within the allegorical setting of a host and a guest at Heaven's inn, the scene in the emblem book is that of the final reckoning. Quarles adds the figure of Justice to emphasize that human Justice and Divine Grace are incompatible categories. Whereas Justice pleads throughout the poem to be allowed 'to strike the blow', the guilty but repentant soul is forgiven in the end. Neither

Justice's blindfold nor the downcast eyes of Anima are trustworthy instruments in the face of God's grace nor is the speaker's protest in 'Love (3)' that he is unable to look at God sufficient to countermand God's gracious invitation to partake of the Heavenly meal:

> Love bade me welcome: yet my soul drew back,
>> Guilty of dust and sin.
> But quick-eyed Love, observing me grow slack
>> From my first entrance in,
> Drew nearer to me, sweetly questioning,
>> If I lacked anything.
>
> A guest, I answered, worthy to be here:
>> Love said, You shall be he,
> I the unkind, ungrateful? Ah my dear,
>> I cannot look on thee.
> Love took my hand, and smiling did reply,
>> Who made the eyes but I?
>
> Truth Lord, but I have marred them: let my shame
>> Go where it doth deserve.
> And know you not, says Love, who bore the blame?
>> My dear, then I will serve.
> You must sit down, says Love, and taste my meat:
>> So I did sit and eat.

Quarles, too, reminds us throughout the emblem book that the human eye is an untrustworthy agent. The eye is 'benighted' (1: 14), 'deluded' (3: 2), 'Leprous' (3: 13), and the eyes are called 'Faithless Opticks' (1: 7); 'all these cast doubt on the very faculty we must exercise in a collection of emblems' (Gilman, p. 398). As Gilman puts it:

> Quarles' solutions reflect more sharply than do purely literary forms a Protestant strategy for accommodating—or rather, for creating the failure to accommodate—the visual image: destruction of the image (1: 14), mortification of the viewer (1: 15), and lifting the burden of sight (3: 2 and 10) (Gilman, p. 402).

We have come a long way from the world of correspondences of which the earlier form of the emblem was one offshoot. In Herbert's verse and in the emblem book by Quarles the emblem functions as the 'jar' does in 'The

Anecdote of the Jar' by Wallace Stevens. Herbert does not write emblems, but he 'places' (in the rhetorical sense of '*dispositio*') the material from the emblem books into a context in which it is no longer fits naturally. The emblem can no longer be said to give access to important truths *per se*; the truth always lies beyond or runs counter to what is expected. The world of the senses and thus the emblem world, is a playground for experiments, but the experiments lead invariably to frustration, deception and denial. All these have to be observed and perceived, by the participants in the emblems and the poetry and by their readers in order to attain a glimpse of another reality. No longer does a Grecian urn teach us that beauty is truth, truth beauty; the urn has turned into a 'jar' that clashes with its surroundings. While, as a result of the development of the new science in the early part of the seventeenth century and of the new epistemology that went hand in hand with it, the senses as a means of attaining truth became the only trustworthy agents in the world of science, their role in the world of the spirit grew more ambivalent and precarious. Hence it is not surprising that we find this process reflected in the changing role assigned to the senses both in the earlier, continental sacred emblem books as compared with some of its later, English offshoots, and in the religious verse of the same period.

The devotional emblem developed from a monolithic form into what Michael Bakhtin would call a 'dialogic' one,[17] in which opposing views are presented, without being resolved, sometimes in a conflict between *pictura* and text, sometimes within the text or the *pictura* itself, in the case of Quarles, or in the presentation of opposing viewpoints within the imagery and/or structure of the poetry, as in the case of Herbert's poetry. From that conflict truth may emerge, for the emblematist, for the poet, for the reader, whose active participation in the deciphering of the text has become essential, since that truth lies beyond the text or the *pictura* that is observed and read. It might be concluded that from an epistemological point of view the poem by Wallace Stevens which serves as an epigraph to this paper is to its model, Keats' 'Ode to a Grecian Urn', as Herbert's poetry is to the emblem tradition.

fig. 1

The Church.

¶ Eafter wings.

The Church.

¶ Eafter wings.

Lord, who createdft man in wealth and ftore,
Though foolishly he loft the fame,
Decaying more and more,
Till he became
Moft poore:
With thee
O let me rife
As larks, harmonioufly,
And fing this day thy victories:
Then fhall the fall further the flight in me.

My tender age in forrow did beginne
And ftill with ficknefles and fhame.
Thou didft fo punifh finne,
That I became
Moft thinne.
With thee
Let me combine,
And feel this day thy victorie:
For, if I imp my wing on thine,
Affliction fhall advance the flight in me.

fig. 2   Eafter

PAVPERTATEM SVMMIS
ingenijs obeffe ne prouehantur.

Dextra tenet lapidem, manus altera fuftinet alas.
Vt me pluma leuat, fic graue mergit onus
Ingenio poteram fuperas uolitare per arces
Me nifi paupertas inuida deprimeret.

fig. 3

H; Ba:

*I am in a Straight betwixt two haueing a
Desire to Depart & to be wth Christ .
Phil: j.23* *Will: Simpson . Sculpsit .*

fig. 4

W. Simpson Sculp

*Lord all my Desire is before Thee & my
groaning is not hid from Thee: P. 38*

fig. 5

*Oh that they were wise, then they would
Vnderstand this; they would consider
their latter end. Deeteron: 32 . I Payne scul,*

fig. 6

*Vtinam saperent et intelligerent ac nouissima
prouiderent ! Deuteron . 32.*

fig. 7

My soule hath coueted to desire thy
Iudgements· psal·11g· will simpson

fig. 8

O Lord Thou knowest my Foolishnesse.
& my Sins are not hid fro Thee Ps:
W. Simpson fec: 49 3.

fig. 9

Enter not into iudgment with thy
seruant for no man liuing shall be
iustified in thy sight   Will·simpson

fig. 10

Notes

1   Mario Praz, *Studies in Seventeenth-century Imagery*, 2nd ed. (Rome: Edizioni di Storia e Letteratura, 1964), 220.

2   Rosemary Freeman, *English Emblem Books* (London: Chatto & Windus, 1948).

3   Rosalie Colie, *The Resources of Kind: Genre-Theory in the Renaissance*, edited by Barbara K. Lewalski (Berkeley: U of California P, 1973), 53, 57.

4   Eleanor James, 'The Emblem as an Image-Pattern in Some Metaphysical Poets' (University of Wisconsin, 1942), unpublished dissertation.

5   Barbara Lewalski, *Protestant Poetics and the Seventeenth-Century Religious Lyric* (Princeton: Princeton UP, 1979).

6   Mary Cole Sloane, *The Visual in Metaphysical Poetry* (Atlantic Highlands, NJ: Humanities Press, 1981).

7   Richard Todd, *The Opacity of Signs: Forms of Interpretative Activity in George Herbert's* The Temple (Columbia: U of Missouri P, 1986), 122.

8   Bart Westerweel, *Patterns and Patterning: A Study of Four Poems by George Herbert* (Amsterdam: Rodopi, 1984).

9   Chana Bloch, *Spelling the Word: George Herbert and the Bible* (U of California P, 1985).

10 George Wither, *A Collection of Emblemes* (London, 1635).

11 Hermannus Hugo, *Pia Desideria* (Antwerp, 1624).

12 Francis Thynne, *Emblemes and Epigrammes*. MS presented to Sir Thomas Egerton (1600). Reprint edited by F.J. Furnivall (EETS, London: N. Trübner, 1876).

13 Daniel Cramer, *Emblematum Sacrorum* (Frankfurt, 1629) and Benedictus van Haeften, *Schola Cordis* (Antwerp, 1629).

14 Christopher Harvey, *Schola Cordis* (London, 1647).

15 Ernest B. Gilman, 'Word and Image in Quarles' *Emblemes*', *Critical Inquiry* 6 (1980), 394.

16 Karl Josef Höltgen and John Horden, eds & introduction, Francis Quarles, *Emblemes* (1635) and *Hieroglyphikes of the Life of Man* (1638) (Hildesheim: Georg Olms), sig. 20*. See also Höltgen, 'The Devotional Quality of Quarles' Emblemes', in *Aspects of the Emblem*, edited by K.J. Höltgen (Kassel: Edition Reichenberger, 1986), 31-65.

17 Michael Bakhtin, *The Dialogic Imagination: Four Essays by M.M. Bakhtin*, edited by Michael Holquist, translated by Caryl Emerson and Michael Holquist (Austin: U of Texas P, 1981); see also Bart Westerweel, 'The Dialogic Imagination: The European Discovery of Time and Shakespeare', in *Renaissance Culture in Context: Theory and Practice*, edited by Jean R. Brink and William F. Gentrup (Aldershot: Scolar Press, 1993), 54-74.

13

EMBLEMATIC AND INCREMENTAL IMAGERY:
RABELAIS, SPENSER, MILTON, HERBERT, CATS

KAY GILLILAND STEVENSON

In the phrase 'the interplay of the spiritual and the secular' which unifies contributions to this volume, the active word 'interplay' sets one musing. What are the dynamics of the imagery which brings together religious and sexual experience? Varied examples from continental and English writers— Rabelais, Spenser, Milton, Cats, as well as Herbert—may illuminate the question. The range of practice invites consideration of poetry's affiliations with other arts, affecting an audience immediately or unfolding in time, and to the movements of the mind which Locke defines as wit and judgement.

In chapter 8 of *Gargantua*, Rabelais describes the hat-emblem designed for his infant giant: a copulating couple whose union produces a shape nearly spherical, the original form of mankind in the tale Aristophanes recounts in the *Symposium*, surrounded by a motto in Ionic script: ΑΓΑΠΗ ΟΥ ΖΗΤΕΙ ΤΑ ΈΑΥΤΗΣ.[1] Quoting from 1 Corinthians 13 in its original language is more than humanistic precision; Rabelais wittily emphasizes the link between Plato and Paul, the Greek philosopher and the Greek New Testament, simultaneously producing a neat opposition between them. Aristophanes' comic 'just so' story to explain the urgency and satisfactions of love, through the tale of the once-round humans split in two and now looking for their other half, is set in a frame of St Paul's 'love seeketh not her own'. The wit of the emblem is in the clash between picture and motto.

Like puns, parodies can give particular emphasis to the coincidence of dissimilar things, but in other cases, parody provides gradual illumination of differences. In *The Faerie Queene*, Spenser makes symmetries, and invitations to compare paired scenes, especially prominent in Book I, 'Contayning the Legend of the Knight of the Red Crosse, or of Holinesse.' This opening book is ostentatiously, insistently, built on repetitions and inversion, such as visits to antithetical infernal and heavenly houses. Characters with similar names but opposed natures—Fidessa and Fidelia—are common. In organizing the plot, Spenser arranges episodes so that the first and last open battles of his hero, the Redcrosse Knight, are against dragons; the first and last of the more covert traps are set by Archimago. Although Book III, 'Contayning the Legend of Britomartis, or of Chastitie,' is far harder to reduce to neat diagrams, in the 1590 edition of the poem the full span of the three-book organization calls attention to tellingly placed comparable

episodes. Spenser makes the first defeat of the Redcrosse Knight a dis-
mayed flight from the dubious vision he is given of carnal disport, but
Book III culminates with Britomart gazing unoffended—and indeed with
longing—at the impassioned embrace of the lovers she has reunited. At one
point in Book III, Spenser speaks directly to readers about the process of
distinguishing between things apparently similar:

> But never let th'ensample of the bad
> Offend the good: for good by paragone
> Of evill, may more notably be rad.   (3:9:2)

Spenser's description of Error, the first dragon the Redcrosse Knight meets,
is clearly the model for Milton's picture of Sin, woman above and serpent
below, in *Paradise Lost*. At the door of Hell, Satan meets his daughter Sin,
and Death who was born of their incestuous union:

> The one seemed woman to the waist, and fair,
> But ended foul in many a scaly fold
> Voluminous and vast, a serpent armed
> With mortal sting: about her middle round
> A cry of hell hounds never ceasing barked
> With wide Cerberian mouths full loud, and run
> A hideous peal: yet when they list, would creep,
> If aught disturbed their noise, into her womb,
> And kindle there unseen.   (2: 650-659)[2]

More interesting than specific borrowings is the process by which Milton,
like Spenser, works through cumulative parody. In *The Faerie Queene*, the
offspring of Error creep into her mouth when they sense danger (as young
vipers were thought to shelter within their mothers' mouths); as when Error
vomits books and pamphlets, emphasis is on the oral orifice and on verbal
perversions. In *Paradise Lost* Milton modifies the behaviour of the dragon's brood in order to link their place of refuge to another pattern of
imagery. The hell hounds were engendered in a violent assault on his
mother by the newborn Death; now 'hourly conceived / And hourly born,
with sorrow infinite' (2: 796-797) they multiply her pain. Monstrous as the
story is, it foreshadows Eve's punishment as pronounced by the Lord in
Genesis and in closely paraphrased form in *Paradise Lost*:

Thy sorrow I will greatly multiply
By thy conception; children thou shalt bring
In sorrow forth.   (10: 193-195)

These passages from the second and tenth book are, however, only part of a complex pattern of parallels. The range of sexual experience in *Paradise Lost* extends from incest and rape in the complicated relations of Satan, Sin, and Death, through the prelapsarian delight of Adam and Eve, to the blissfully complete angelic unions described by Raphael (8: 614-629). Eve's parallels, not only with Sin but also with Mary, are crucial to the imagery of Milton's narrative; the story moves on past curse to redemption, and in the final line given to Eve, 'By me the promised seed shall all restore' (12: 623), emphasizes the positive affiliation.

Although making connections and making distinctions are primary activities in poets and in their readers, in any particular author or critic one or another of these activities may be given prominence. The examples chosen from Rabelais on the one hand, and from Spenser and Milton on the other, suggest a division, or polarity, between kinds of imagery. One works through immediate surprise and recognition, the other through progressive discrimination. Emblematic and incremental we might call the extremes.

Combining and distinguishing are together so basic to the working of imagery that it seems a ponderous explicitness to comment on the fact—but given a critical climate in which making one's methods explicit has become routine, let us pause or plod for a moment: Imagery exists in the gaps between identity and categorical definition or literal assertion (Mary is Mary; Mary is female; Mary walks) and random collocations (Mary is ampersand; Mary postmarks). I note, however, in the difficulty of finding an example, how easily one takes the wildest connection of words as a challenge for finding connections, how easy it is to read a series of words as metaphor rather than as nonsense. Experiments in generating poetry by computer demonstrated the point; given a lexicon sorted as nouns, verbs, and other parts of speech, along with grammatical constructions, the machine delivered lines which seemed highly evocative; one might have said 'highly imaginative' if ignorant of the source. The same thing happens with academic jokes, such as the Ern Malley spoof, an attempt to write nonsensical poems by piecing together phrases from newspapers.[3] The mind does not treat two things or words presented together without making either a connection or a distinction; a neutral collocation seems almost impossible. How pervasive the active search is for relationships among words and ideas has been demonstrated by linguistic experiments leading to the conclusion that 'within chunks of language which are conventionally presented as texts, the hearer/reader will make every effort to impose a coherent interpretation'.[4]

Although it is an activity of all speakers and listeners, the gift for linking disparate ideas or images is often seen as a particularly poetic talent. Among critics, Aristotle is pre-eminent in emphasizing the process of making connections. He asserts, in an often quoted passage of the *Poetics*, that mastery of metaphor is 'a sign of genius, since a good metaphor implies an intuitive perception of the similarity in dissimilars'.[5] In *An Essay Concerning Human Understanding* (1690) John Locke defines wit and judgement as contrasting or complementary movements of thought, conveniently and crisply providing a theoretical explanation of both activities of the mind.

> For *wit* lying most in the assemblage of ideas, and putting those together with quickness and variety, wherein can be found any resemblance or congruity, thereby to make up pleasant pictures and agreeable visions in the fancy; *judgment*, on the contrary, lies quite on the other side, in separating carefully, one from another, ideas wherein can be found the least difference, thereby to avoid being misled by similitude, and by affinity to take one thing for another.[6]

While Pope in 'An Essay on Criticism' wishes for a happy marriage between wit and judgement, Locke writes of judgement as 'a way of proceeding quite contrary to metaphor and allusion.'[7] He seems to exclude from consideration images which take part of their interest from progressive discrimination.

Earlier, in *The Arte of English Poesie* (1589), due attention is paid to recognition both of resemblance and differences as part of artistic pleasure, and to an exercise of the mind (not Locke's pejorative 'no labour of mind') in perceiving both. Discussing the interpretation of emblems, George Puttenham praises those outstanding 'both for subtilitie and multiplicitie of sense' such as the use of the sun as an emblem for the queen, apt as indicating her bounty and glory yet also a *simile dissimile*, 'which is also a subtilitie, likening her Majestie to the Sunne for his brightnesse, but not to him for his passion, which is ordinarily to go to glade, and sometime to suffer eclypse'.[8]

In the ordinary course of reading, there is an almost automatic screening out of the *dissimile* in poetic metaphors. (The same is true, and functional, in non-literary language, for while a pun may be telling, amusing, pleasurable in a joke or poem, it would be all too tedious to suspect *double entendre* in every single occurrence of the number two.) This selective attention to congruence, involving either semi-conscious or wilful suppression of incongruity, is sometimes tested by the conceits of the most extreme metaphysical or baroque poetry, by Crashaw's lines, for example, on Mary Magdalene's eyes as portable baths, compendious oceans. If we concentrate on individual images, we are apt to attend particularly to the play of mind that sorts out and selects the points of resemblance, and here a great deal of interesting work has been done, not least by scholars in religious studies. Walter Brueggeman, in an article exploring one particular image, that of exile, comments on the way 'metaphor proceeds by having only an odd, playful, and ill-fitting match to its reality',[9] and on the way in which these flickers of connection illuminate experience. Other studies of reading, notably those of Wolfgang Iser, concentrate on another sort of play of mind, the play of retrospection and readjustment which is particularly important for what I am here calling incremental metaphors. Speaking in grammatical terms, we might call the difference in emphasis a matter primarily of selection or of syntax.

Semi-grotesque engravings in some emblem books emphasize the curious readiness of an interpreter to concentrate on a far-fetched point of similarity. The emblem books have a second quality, especially important here: a kind of hermetic seal between emblems, forbidding contamination of one by the other, a process by which memory of what an image meant a few pages back has no effect on interpretation of the current image. This is a kind of reading completely different from the cumulative, progressive building of associations and of distinctions in what I called incremental metaphors.

Meditating on, and denying, the Horatian dictum *ut pictura poesis*, G.E. Lessing considered the fundamental differences between arts of time and space.[10] The distinctions he made have some affinities with those contrasts on which I am insisting. But while he concentrates on the differences between poetry and the visual arts, the examples on which I am musing are mainly poetic, though from poems which make differing demands on the mind and imagination of the reader. One sort of image is, in itself, static like a piece of sculpture—though a responsive audience must move about it, considering both the oddity and appropriateness of metaphorical yokings. Responding to incremental imagery, developed serially, is more like listening to music, recognizing repetitions and modifications of a theme.

Is there a clear division between writers particularly attracted to emblematic wit or to judicious discrimination? It is tempting to think so, and to sort poets into one category or another, with Donne in the first. He considers the matter of metaphor in *Devotions upon Emergent Occasions*, addressing God first as 'a *direct* God, may I not say a literall *God*, a God that wouldest bee understood *literally*, and according to the *plaine sense* of all that thou saist.' He nonetheless moves rapidly on to more flamboyant expressions:

> thou art ... a *figurative*, a *metaphoricall God* too: A *God* in whose words there is such a height of *figures*, such *voyages*, such peregrinations to fetch remote and precious *metaphors*, such *extentions*, such *spreadings*, such *Curtaines* of *Allegories*, such *third Heavens* of *Hyperboles*, so *harmonious eloquutions* ... as all *prophane Authors*, seeme of the seed of the *Serpent*, that *creepes*; thou art the *dove*, that flies.[11]

One might venture that the emblem is most easily developed in short works, such as lyrics, or highly episodic narratives, and incremental imagery in highly organized longer narratives. There is no difficulty here if the authors selected as examples are as different as Rabelais, who builds even a long text from discrete sections, and Milton, who works through intricate patterns of repetition and variation.

Some poets work in both modes. Spenser, in *The Faerie Queene*, educates his readers in hermeneutic alertness and flexibility. He demands that we be able to disregard some similarities, taking the ass on which Una rides and the ass on which Idlenesse rides as very different, or leaping from one Biblical allusion to serpents to another, not confusing the serpent in Charissa's cup with those reptiles against which the Redcrosse Knight does battle.

As in many other matters, Herbert offers a teasing test-case, making it clear that the suggested division between emblematic and incremental is not so much a matter of categorizing two methods but of identifying the polar positions between which the practice of various writers, or of one writer in various works, can be situated. Rather than concentrate on a poem such as the early sonnet 'My God, where is that ancient heat towards thee' (Tobin, p. 194), in which he explicitly contrasts human eroticism and divine love, or the relationship between 'Jordan (2)' and Sidney's *Astrophel and Stella* 1, or on other poems which parody secular lyrics,[12] I would like briefly to suggest three points. Two arise from *The Temple*. First, although it is possible to read individual poems as discrete lyrics, the collection invites reading them as a series, architecturally unified, with recurrent or pervasive image-patterns, the repetitions enriching interpretation of individual poems. Second, a number of the lyrics, such as 'Love-Joy', include interpreters, thus dramatizing the process of interpretation and reinterpretation of images. Finally, Herbert's comments on reading the Old and New Testaments emphasize the play of memory and understanding.

Taking these points in reverse order, starting with the most general, one notes that Medieval and Renaissance habits of reading the Scriptures encouraged interpretative agility, both in keeping separate various alternative meanings of a text, and in bringing together disparate materials. In the elaborations of fourfold exegesis, there are sharp shifts between what a Biblical passage means literally, and what it can mean morally, allegorically, or anagogically. The practice of typology, on the other hand, rests on seeing Old Testament and New Testament materials as versions of the same thing.

To learn to read with the Bible as the central text of all texts is, for anyone working in the Augustinian tradition of *De doctrina Christiana*, a great training in recognition of both similarities and differences. As Augustine teaches, what is meant, everywhere in the Scriptures, is charity; nonetheless, a reader should attend to local meanings and their diversity.[13] Herbert sums up a long tradition when in Chapter 4 of *The Country Parson* he writes of 'a diligent Collation of Scripture with Scripture' which leads to understanding not only of how dissimilar texts come together, a unity dependent on 'Truth being consonant to it self', but also of habitual discriminations and attention to context: 'For the Law required one thing, and the Gospel another: yet as diverse, not as repugnant: therefore the spirit of both is to be considered, and weighed' (Hutchinson, p. 229). In poetry, notably in 'The Holy Scriptures (2)' Herbert emphasizes this sense of a network of associations, with verse speaking to verse, building toward understanding. The process is akin to the use of incremental imagery in Spenser and Milton.

A striking number of poems in *The Temple* are concerned with the reading or, more pointedly, with the misreading of metaphor. These lyrics place stress on the pleasures or dangers in interpreting a sign (natural or verbal), the pleasure of recognition on the one hand and the pitfalls of similarity on the other. Discrimination in reading images which can, and often do in Herbert's poems, represent diametrically opposed values is the central point, for example, of the poem called 'Artillery', whose narrator misinterprets the star which falls into his lap, prudently brushing it away to avoid 'mishap'. In this and in a large number of other poems, including 'Love Unknown', Herbert includes an authoritative interpreter, explaining the metaphors the narrator has himself not rightly understood.

One of the texts from *The Temple* centred on imagery is, of course, 'Prayer (1)', a poem made up entirely of a series of metaphors. There is no full sentence in the poem, no assertion, only the phrases, which may—or may not—imply ellipsis. Should a reader supply 'is' or 'is like' between the opening word 'Prayer' and the cluster, almost clutter, of phrases after it? Though 'Prayer' ends with the phrase 'something understood', that phrase itself is a riddling one—what is that something? And who is it that understands, God or man? The problem of understanding is further complicated by the fact that many of the phrases that make up the poem are illogical, literally incomprehensible, absurd: 'Angels' age ... Engine against th'Almighty' (1, 5). It is both tempting and difficult to see them as condensed similes; prayer 'is like (and also unlike)' each one. Individually teasing, they provide what, one might argue, is a demonstration of incremental enlightenment; 'Heaven in ordinary' and 'man well dressed' work together to establish one interpretation based on relative plainness and relative adornment, which bring heaven and earth closer together, and another interpretation which evokes the preparation of food for a set meal in an inn.

Early in *The Temple*, Herbert's recurrent image of the stony heart invites attention to certain qualities of stone: in 'The Altar' as a shapable building material, though one so intractable that only God's power can cut it; in 'The Sacrifice' as notably unresponsive matter, unlikely to melt (90). Occasionally, as in 'Sepulchre', he reviews some accumulated connotations for the image: 'cold, hard, foul' (23). An ambiguity, or complication in my reading of the image, and in my thinking about the ways in which he handles imagery, occurs in 'The Sinner' where, after the word 'quarries' (5) reintroduces the metaphor, it becomes prominent in the sonnet's concluding lines: 'Yet Lord restore thine image, hear my call: / And though my hard heart scarce to thee can groan, / Remember that thou once didst write in stone.' The immediate context invites a positive reading, encouragement to the praying sinner (or the reading sinners) for though the hardness of the heart is a challenge to God, the lines are the reminder that God has—in this poetic sequence as well as in Biblical history—been a cutter of stone. To be reminded here, however, of the Ten Commandments, as the text cut in stone, produces a tension between consolation and conviction of sin, undercutting the reassurance of the prayer with stress on what there is to repent. This is, I think, an example of the progressive or cumulative force of images, acquiring a variety of meanings which invite simultaneous consideration.

No ambiguities about whether the meaning of an image earlier in a volume is to be kept alive in the reader's mind arises in my last example, taken from the Dutch poet Jacob Cats. Much admired both in his native country and in England (Joshua Sylvester contributed a commendatory sonnet to the volume in question), Cats demonstrates an emphatically non-cumulative, a pronounced, discreteness in imagery. Some testing of generalizations about emblematic *versus* incremental is possible in one of the most interesting of all the formal emblem-books, Cats' *Silenus Alcibiadis*. An elaborate title-page defines its multiple approach:

> Silenus Alcibiadis sive Proteus, Humanae vitae ideam, Emblemate trifariam variato, oculis subjiciens. Iconibus artificiose in aes incisis, ac trium linguarum explicatione eleganter elustratus. Deus nobis haec otia fecit.[14]

Englished, this comes out as:

> Alicibiades' Silenus, or Proteus, placing under the eyes an image of human life, emblematically varied in three parts. With pictures artfully cut in bronze and elegantly explained with commentary in three languages. God made this leisure for us [Eclog. I.6 ... NOT WEARIED BY ACTIVITY]

It is possible that *elustratus*, that is, 'fully illuminated, or revealed,' where *illustratus* might be expected instead, emphasizes the drawing out of the meanings. There are other interesting details in the title-page: the clash between the quotation from Virgil (leisure) and the motto from Hercules (activity); and another clash, unless the phrase 'Alcibiades' Silenus' is meant simply as an identifying tag, between the notorious attractiveness of Alcibiades and the grotesqueness of Silenus.

In three parts, the book runs through 51 emblems, interpreted first according to Love and manners, then according to morals and finally according to Christian doctrine. A monkey holding its offspring (a particularly ugly monkey, incidentally) is in Part I accompanied with the motto AMOR, FORMAE CONDIMENTUM (love the seasoning of beauty) and verses emphasizing that for the lover there is no ugly beloved; in Part II, more wryly, the motto becomes QUALIS MATER, TALIS FILIA (like mother, like daughter); in Part III it is DELICTA OPERIT CHARITAS (love conceals offences), with a quotation from 1 Cor. 13: 5: 'Charitas non praesumit malum'. Here, in Cats' series of poems in different languages, the French one reads:

> Le Singe son Petit, combien que laid, ne laisse,
> Mais, sans s'en offenser, l'embrasse et le caresse.
> Si de Chrestien le nom ne veux porter en vain,
> Couvrir tousiours te faut les fautes du Prochain.

There is no question in this collection of incremental reading. Secular and profane interpretations of a single image are equally, temporarily possible, but with no pollution or cross-pollination of ideas.

Although protean transformations give Cats' emblem-book as a whole its richness, the sections are self-contained, each emblem dependent on temporary attention to selected possible connections of ideas, screening out earlier associations. Circling back to the examples with which we began, we might note that the emblem for Gargantua's hat is a special case, or extreme case, of balancing similarity and difference with oxymoronic neatness, holding together for a moment the opposing ideas of copulation and Pauline charity, of finding oneself and seeking not one's own. The modulations and discriminations operative in reading an image in Spenser or Milton, in contrast, operate over a period of time. Puns, like parodies, give particular emphasis to the coincidence of dissimilar things, though the one does so immediately, the other through the exercise of memory and gradual discrimination.

Notes

1   *Œuvres complètes,* edited by Pierre Jurda (Paris: Editions Garnier Frères, 1962), 1: 38.

2   John Milton, *Paradise Lost,* edited by Alastair Fowler (London: Longman, 1971).

3   Marie Boroff, 'Computer as Poet', *Yale Alumni Magazine* (January 1971), 22-25; *Ern Malley's Poems* with an introduction by Max Harris (Melbourne: Lansdowne Press, 1961).

4   Gillian Brown and George Yule, *Discourse Analysis* (Cambridge: Cambridge UP, 1983), 199.

5   *Poetics* 1459a, cf. *Rhetoric,* 1405a. *The Complete Works of Aristotle,* The Revised Oxford Translation, edited by Jonathan Barnes (Princeton: Princeton UP, 1984).

6   John Locke, *An Essay Concerning Human Understanding,* edited by Alexander Campbell Fraser (Oxford: Clarendon, 1874), 1: 203.

7   The context of the words quoted makes his point even stronger: 'This is a way of proceeding quite contrary to metaphor and allusion; wherein for the most part lies that entertainment and pleasantry of wit, which strikes so lively on the fancy, and therefore is so acceptable to all people, because its beauty appears at first sight, and there is required no labour of thought to examine what truth or reason there is in it' (1: 203).

8   George Puttenham, 'Of the device or embleme', *The Arte of English Poesie,* edited by Gladys D. Willcock and Alice Walker (Cambridge: Cambridge UP, 1936), 103.

9   Walter Brueggeman, 'Preaching to Exiles', *Journal for Preachers* 16/4 (1993), 3. For another interesting discussion, see Sandra M. Schneiders, 'Scripture as the Word of God', *The Princeton Seminary Bulletin* 14 (1993), 18-35.

10   Gotthold Ephraim Lessing, 'Laocoon or On the Limits of Painting and Poetry' (1766), translated by W.A. Steel, in *German Aesthetic and Literary Criticism,* edited by H.B. Nisbet (Cambridge: Cambridge UP, 1985).

11   *Devotions upon Emergent Occasions,* edited by Antony Raspa (Montreal: McGill-Queen's UP, 1975), 99.

12 In a convenient appendix to the Everyman edition of *The English Poems of George Herbert* (London: Dent, 1974), C.A. Patrides provides the texts of 'Some Secular Poems parodied by Herbert' (pp. 209-213).

13 Augustine, *On Christian Doctrine*, translated by D.W. Robertson Jr. (Indianapolis: The Liberal Arts Press, 1958), 31.

14 Amsterdam, 1622. These words are accompanied by engraved figures: one with scythe and winged hourglass, another a Hercules with the motto INDEFESSUS AGENDO. An earlier edition, which I have not yet had a chance to see, was published in 1618. There were many reprints, with the engravings in different formats. The large round engravings of this edition are, for example, replaced in the *Werke* of 1710-11 by small rectangular engravings.

14

'THE PRESENT TIMES ARE NOT / TO SNUDGE IN':
HENRY VAUGHAN, *THE TEMPLE*, AND
THE PRESSURE OF HISTORY

ROBERT WILCHER

It is a commonplace of criticism that, in the words of E.C. Pettet, 'without the inspiration and model of *The Temple* there would certainly have been no *Silex Scintillans*'.[1] More recently, the relationship with Herbert has been placed 'at the center' of Vaughan's 'poetic life', and an attempt has been made to free 'the younger poet from the shadow of his master' by demonstrating that Herbert 'shaped rather than overwhelmed or displaced the Welsh poet's creative energies'.[2] Another critic has argued that Vaughan's 'admiration for Herbert was a troubled one' and that the two parts of *Silex Scintillans* embody the artistic conflict he underwent in 'freeing himself from the tyranny of Herbert's words'.[3] One of the issues raised by Henry Vaughan's manifold debts to George Herbert, which range from the adoption and adaptation of titles and stanza forms to the copying of images, phrases and even entire lines, is that of their status and significance.[4] Pointing out that Vaughan had always had an 'unusual reliance upon prior texts', Thomas Calhoun argues that 'Recognition of the old in the new, like the recognition of distinct lines in polyphony, is an act of discovery (nowadays editorially preempted) that Vaughan must have anticipated from his readers'.[5] But the function of this act of discovery may be difficult to pin down. Gerald Hammond goes so far as to claim that what Vaughan takes from Herbert can be disconcertingly limited in its allusive value: 'Where Biblical echoes are precise and purposeful, Herbert's lines, images, and words often have no relevance to the Vaughan poem they find themselves in' (Hammond, p. 1).

A comparison of appropriated materials with their sources in *The Temple* may sometimes prompt the conclusion that the disciple was merely paying homage to the master or even that he was writing under the unconscious spell of a body of work that had been completely assimilated to his own imaginative needs.[6] Nevertheless, there are occasions when some more deliberate and complex exploitation of Herbert's poetic idiom seems to be taking place under pressure from the particular historical circumstances in which Vaughan found himself. Graeme Watson, for example, has argued that because of the historical context in which he was writing, Vaughan 'resolutely avoids Herbert's device of the temple of the heart';

and that when he does bring heart and temple together in 'Jacob's Pillow, and Pillar', in a passage which derives its basic idea from Herbert's 'Decay', it is with much sharper awareness of the contemporary situation, so that 'rejection of the temple is not just a sign of the renunciation of the law, it is a strategy to escape actual persecution'.[7] In the present paper, I shall discuss a single example of this process.

Jonathan Post includes 'Misery' in a list of poems from *Silex Scintillans* which share with 'their prototypes in *The Temple*' the project of exploring 'the inner configurations of the Christian life' (Post, p. 98). It is useful for my purposes because its title connects it with a specific Herbert model and Vaughan's editors have identified within its 114 lines an extraordinary array of reminiscences from elsewhere in Herbert's work—from, among other poems, 'The Church-Porch', 'Sighs and Groans', 'Church-Monuments', 'The Glimpse', 'Mortification', 'Giddiness', 'Nature', 'Jordan (2)', 'The Collar', 'Sion', 'The Star', 'The Glance', and 'Love (2)'. The central debt to Herbert's 'Misery' is thematic rather than formal: the earlier poem is in six-line stanzas and Vaughan uses octosyllabic couplets; but both poets are concerned with the human tendency to rebel against the service owed to God. From the start, however, there are important differences of approach. Until the very last line, in which he applies everything he has said about Man to his own predicament, Herbert conducts an apparently objective survey of the effects of 'Folly and Sin' on the behaviour of human beings, who are only kept from the disaster of wilfully rejecting their Maker by His own unfailing love for them:

> They quarrel thee, and would give over
> The bargain made to serve thee: but thy love
> Holds them unto it, and doth cover
> Their follies with the wing of thy mild Dove,
> Not suff'ring those
> Who would, to be thy foes.   (25-30)

Vaughan picks up the words 'serve', 'hold', and 'quarrel' in his opening lines, but presents the situation in more explicitly personal terms:

> Lord, bind me up, and let me lie
> A prisoner to my liberty,
> If such a state at all can be
> As an impris'ment serving thee;
> The wind, though gathered in thy fist,
> Yet doth it blow still where it list,

> And yet shouldst thou let go thy hold
> Those gusts might quarrel and grow bold.   (1-8)[8]

In his account of the way in which his 'spilt thoughts ... / Take the down-road to vanity,' Vaughan's speaker enacts in his own person the follies that Herbert lays at the door of Man, who is 'a foolish thing, a foolish thing' (2). Herbert, adopting the role of an advocate for God, is scornful of the creature's stubborn obtuseness before an all-seeing Creator—'No man shall beat into his head, / That thou within his curtains drawn canst see' (15-16)—and censures his commitment to his own pleasures:

> Why, he'll not lose a cup of drink for thee:
> Bid him but temper his excess;
> Not he ...   (8-10)

Vaughan, glancing obliquely at Herbert's lines, assimilates this folly and self-indulgence to his own experience:

> Some fig-leaves still I do devise
> As if thou hadst nor ears, nor eyes.
> Excess of friends, of words, and wine
> Take up my day ...   (23-26)

Borrowings from elsewhere in *The Temple* follow a similar pattern, transforming the objective into the subjective, drawing the individual out of the general. For example, the line 'I break the fence my own hands made' (21) derives from the phrase 'Man breaks the fence' in 'Perirrhanterium' (22); and another observation from the same poem—'The drunkard forfeits Man, and doth devest / All worldly right, save what he hath by beast' (35-36)—is expanded into Vaughan's climactic confession of slavery to appetite:

> But I go on, haste to devest
> My self of reason, till oppressed
> And buried in my surfeits I
> Prove my own shame and misery.   (41-44)

Up to this point, the difference between the two poems has been one of approach to the common theme of obedience: Herbert examines the misery of a race of creatures that betrays its own best interests in refusing to serve the God who made and sustains it; and Vaughan expresses the 'shame and misery' of one who is only too aware of his own foolishness and ingratitude in excluding God from his mind, 'who of that cell / Would make a court, should he there dwell' (35-36)—an image that goes back to the idea of imprisonment in the opening lines and owes something to an image in Herbert's 'The Glimpse':

> Thou knowst how grief and sin
> Disturb the work. O make me not their sport,
> Who by thy coming may be made a court!   (28-30)

Vaughan's next series of borrowings, however, take his poem into another dimension of experience.

An interlude, in which God responds to his cry, pours 'a shower / Of healing sweets' into the sinner's self-inflicted wounds, and 'fills all the place' with His grace, culminates in an evocation of the peace that comes with self-discipline:

> I school my eyes, and strictly dwell
> Within the circle of my cell,
> That calm and silence are my joys
> Which to thy peace are but mere noise.   (57-60)

By accepting his confinement to the cell of service in which he can 'lie / A prisoner to my liberty,' he opens himself to the transforming power of that divine love which is able to 'make a court' of the mind that admits it. But the passage from Herbert's 'Mortification' which lies behind Vaughan's lines prompts a more specific reading of the later poet's situation. It is the fourth stanza of six in a meditation on human mortality and the journey from infancy to old age:

> When man grows staid and wise,
> Getting a house and home, where he may move
>   Within the circle of his breath,
>   Schooling his eyes;
>   That dumb inclosure maketh love
> Unto the coffin, that attends his death.   (19-24)

The man of mature years in Herbert's poem, after the 'frank and free' season of youth, reads the inclosure of his own 'house and home' as an emblem of the coffin that will be his final resting-place, and schools his eyes to accept the inevitability of death. Vaughan must school himself not to face the fact of mortality but to accept his strict confinement in the cell or dwelling-place in which God has appointed him to live in peace. That this cell is the 'house or home' to which he retired to enjoy 'calm and si- lence' after the more active service of the civil wars is strongly suggested by what follows. Impatience at being bound up and fenced in erupts once more, and he delivers a speech ringing with echoes of Herbert:

> At length I feel my head to ache,
> My fingers itch, and burn to take
> Some new employment, I begin
> To swell and foam and fret within.
>> *'The age, the present times are not*
>> *To snudge in, and embrace a cot,*
>> *Action and blood now get the game,*
>> *Disdain treads on the peaceful name,*
>> *Who sits at home too bears a load*
>> *Greater than those that gad abroad.'*   (61-70)

The unusual word 'snudge' is picked up from 'Giddiness', another of Her- bert's objective meditations on Man, in which the inconstancy and way- wardness of his temperament are highlighted. But the word brings its immediate context with it into Vaughan's poem:

> Now he will fight it out, and to the wars;
>> Now eat his bread in peace,
> And snudge in quiet ...   (9-11)

In Herbert's 'Misery', Man is 'a foolish thing' because he allows 'Folly and Sin' to 'play all his game' (3). Vaughan, in the Wales of the late 1640s, knows that *'Action and blood now get the game'* and that there is a more specific pressure upon him not to 'snudge in quiet' than the mere fickleness of human nature. 'Wars' and 'peace' are metaphors for contradictory im- pulses in 'Giddiness'; in Vaughan's poem, there is a topical context that gives political force to the line *'Disdain treads on the peaceful name'*.[9]

The final couplet of the rebellious speech transforms the spiritual mutiny of another Herbert poem into a Royalist commentary on the politi- cal realities of *'the present times'*. In 'The Collar', a rebellious Herbert had repudiated his apparently fruitless obedience to God with the repeated cry, 'I will abroad'. Towards the end of the poem, this line had been paired in rhyme with the same word that Vaughan uses in 'Misery':

> I will abroad.
> Call in thy death's head there: tie up thy fears.
> He that forbears
> To suit and serve his need,
> Deserves his load.   (29-32)

Vaughan's complaint seems to be that those who curb their impulse to 'take / Some new employment'—who accept the Christian discipline of dwelling strictly within the circle of peace—are in danger of being charged with cowardice or indifference, as if they were content to *'embrace a cot'* rather than endure the hardships of action or exile with their king. But the fretful speaker knows the weight of the burden he bears by staying *'at home'* and not (like Herbert's rebel in 'The Collar') choosing to 'suit and serve his need' for more positive engagement.

Another of Herbert's expressions of resistance to God's control of his life contributes phrases to the later stages of 'Misery' and as before they gain a political edge from the specific context which Vaughan has established for them. 'Nature' begins by invoking four possible acts of defiance against God's sovereignty:

> Full of rebellion, I would die,
> Or fight, or travel, or deny
> That thou hast ought to do with me.   (1-3)

Vaughan's comment on the mutinous speech that he sets apart as a quotation in 'Misery' takes up three of these options, each of which has more than the rhetorical value invested in it by Herbert:

> Thus do I make thy gifts given me
> The only quarrellers with thee,
> I'd loose those knots thy hands did tie,
> Then would go travel, fight or die.   (71-74)

In the final stanza of 'Nature', Herbert prays that God will 'smooth my rugged heart, and there / Engrave thy rev'rend law and fear' (13-14). Vaughan brings the analysis of his particular brand of politically generated misery towards its conclusion with a similar prayer, but one in which he pleads not merely that he may respect God's law in general but that his heart may be strong enough to do whatever God requires of it:

> O send me from thy holy hill
> So much of strength, as may fulfil
> All thy delights (what e'er they be)
> And sacred institutes in me;
> Open my rocky heart, and fill
> It with obedience to thy will ...   (97-102)

The specific nature of that obedience, in relation to what he had earlier called 'these mutinies'—times when, 'wilded by a peevish heart,' he had stormed at God, 'calling my peace / A lethargy, and mere disease' (81-84)—becomes even more evident when 'Misery' is read in the context provided for it by the three poems that precede it in *Silex Scintillans* and by the allusions to Herbert's poetry that bind the four together as a group. The first of them, entitled 'The Mutiny', is a typological rendering of the plight of a defeated Royalist and Anglican in terms of the captivity of the Israelites in Egypt. Pondering on the 'after-burdens, and griefs yet to come,' the captive in this Old Testament analogue to the 'impris'ment' to God's will explored in 'Misery', recounts how his thoughts 'quit their troubled channel' and stormed at the banks that confined them in the same way that the 'spilt thoughts' of the later poem rush 'headlong and loose' to seek the 'lower grounds'. Like the 'prisoner' who burns for some 'new employment' in 'Misery', this Israelite pleads with God to let him 'strive and struggle with thy foes / (Not thine alone, but mine too,)' (15-16). He also begs that his eye and ear may be sealed up against 'all this foam / And frothy noise which up and down doth fly' (24-25)—an image which is connected with Vaughan's 'foam and fret within' in 'Misery' but which needs the context supplied by another poem by Herbert for its full significance to be released. 'The Family' begins with the question, 'What doth this noise of thoughts within my heart / As if they had a part?' Then, after a prayer that the Lord will 'Turn out these wranglers, which defile thy seat,' it goes on to celebrate the 'Peace and Silence', 'Order', and 'Humble Obedience' that should characterize the 'house and family' of God. Claude J. Summers and Ted-Larry Pebworth have convincingly argued that the poem has 'a public dimension', which is anti-Puritan in emphasis, and have suggested that it 'may glance approvingly at the practice of ejecting non-conforming ministers from their livings'.[10]

That the 'foam / And frothy noise' in 'The Mutiny' are related to the noise of the Puritan wranglers who disturb the peace of the Church in 'The Family' is confirmed by the next poem in *Silex Scintillans*. 'The Constellation' contemplates the 'exact obedience' with which the 'ordered lights' of the stars move in their 'vast progressions' across the night sky. In contrast, the British nation is 'disordered into wars'; and those who cry 'zeal' to justify the destruction of their father and mother (king and church), unable to conceal their true nature behind a show of piety, 'Seem mild, but are known by their noise.' A closing petition alludes unmistakably to two more of Herbert's poems, 'The British Church' and 'Church-Rents and Schisms'—poems which are among his most overt treatments of the state of the contemporary world:

> Give to thy spouse her perfect, and pure dress,
> > *Beauty* and *holiness*,
> And so repair these rents, that men may see
> > And say, *Where God is, all agree.*   (57-60)

In 'The British Church' and 'Church-Rents and Schisms', Herbert person-ifies the Church of England as 'dear Mother' (1) and 'Mother dear and kind' (24); in 'The Constellation', one of Vaughan's images for the effects of civil war is an obvious allusion to these contexts in Herbert:

> The children chase the mother, and would heal
> > The wounds they give, by crying, zeal.   (39-40)

Vaughan's alternative image of the church as the spouse of Christ draws upon details of Herbert's portrait of his 'dear Mother' in 'The British Church': her 'perfect lineaments, and hue', her 'Beauty', and her 'fit array'.[11]

The setting for Vaughan's 'Misery' is completed by 'The Shepherds', a Nativity poem which begins by evoking a biblical golden age when the national leaders were '*patriarchs*, saints, and kings'—in sharp contrast to the guides who 'prove wandering stars' in 'The Constellation'. But by the time of the birth of Christ that age was long past, and the true faith was sustained in the 'humble cots' of '*Bethlem*' rather than the 'stately piles' of Jerusalem. Vaughan's description of the homes of the shepherds contains various details which reach backwards and forwards to neighbouring poems in *Silex Scintillans*:

> No costly pride, no soft-clothed luxury
> > In those thin cells could lie,
> Each stirring wind and storm blew through their cots
> > Which never harboured plots,
> Only content, and love, and humble joys
> > Lived there without all noise.   (31-36)

The reader may be tempted to speculate whether the 'cot' where the poet sat discontentedly *'at home'*, snudging *'in quiet'* during those dangerous times of *'Action and blood'*, ever 'harboured plots'.

In the context of these three companion poems, which explore from a variety of perspectives the difficulty of maintaining a Christian stance of peace and humility in a period of disorder and successful rebellion, Vaughan's 'Misery' emerges as a powerful and subtle statement of the political as well as the spiritual predicament of a 'fierce soul' that 'bustles about / And never rests till all be out' (79-80). And a great part of its subtlety lies in the complex tissue of allusions by means of which it draws both inspiration and authority from the work of a great poet whose name, by the end of the 1640s, had become firmly associated with the cause of an outlawed church and the king who had died for it.[12]

Notes

1   E.C. Pettet, *Of Paradise and Light: A Study of Vaughan's* Silex Scintillans (Cambridge: Cambridge UP, 1960), 51.

2   Jonathan F.S. Post, *Henry Vaughan: The Unfolding Vision* (Princeton: Princeton UP, 1982), xvii, xx.

3   Gerald Hammond, '"Poor dust should lie still low": George Herbert and Henry Vaughan', *English* 35 (1986), 12, 20.

4   See Pettet (pp. 51-70) for a detailed categorization of the different kinds of borrowing from Herbert in *Silex Scintillans*.

5   Thomas O. Calhoun, *Henry Vaughan: The Achievement of* Silex Scintillans (Newark: U of Delaware P, 1981), 67, 72.

6   Pettet (p. 62) suggests that on occasion Herbert's phrasing and imagery appeared as 'vague subconscious material' in *Silex Scintillans*.

7   Graeme J. Watson, '*The Temple* in "The Night": Henry Vaughan and the Collapse of the Established Church', *MP* 84 (1986), 148-149.

8   Quotations from Vaughan's poetry are from *Henry Vaughan: The Complete Poems*, edited by Alan Rudrum (London: Penguin Books, 1976).

9   For the situation of Royalists and faithful members of the Church of England in the Wales of the late 1640s and early 1650s, see Noel Kennedy Thomas, *Henry Vaughan: Poet of Revelation* (Worthing: Churchman Publishing, 1986), 27-36.

10 Claude J. Summers and Ted-Larry Pebworth, 'The Politics of *The Temple*: "The British Church" and "The Familie"', *GHJ* 8 (1984), 7, 9-10.

11 Summers and Pebworth have discussed the political dimensions of these two poems by Herbert, and compared 'The British Church' with the poem to which Vaughan gave the same title, in 'Herbert, Vaughan, and Public Concerns in Private Modes', *GHJ* 3 (1979-80), 1-21.

12   In 'Herbert's Seventeenth-Century Reputation: A Summary and New Consider-
     ations', *GHJ* 9 (1986), 1-15, Ray points out that 70% of the texts catalogued in his
     Herbert Allusion Book can be identified as written by loyal Anglicans and Royal-
     ists.

15

MYSTERY, IMITATION, CRAFT:
FROM GEORGE HERBERT TO SYLVIA PLATH

CEDRIC BROWN

Thinking about this event over the past months, I felt I did not want to reach into my bag and read out the latest thing I happened to be writing. Scholars of Renaissance literature should have a sense of occasion, and most of all should students of the work of George Herbert, rhetorician supreme to his university and to the readers of *The Temple*. So, this being an anniversary of the birth of a poet whose work we wish to remember 400 years later, I am going to use some of my time to celebrate Herbert's much-imitated craft, but to do it in an unexpected and very specific way.

The lens through which I shall view the compelling skill of George Herbert is provided by the work of a mid-twentieth-century woman poet, whom no-one would normally think of connecting with our man. (The best encomia have indirection.) I am going to point to an instructive case of imitation of one of Herbert's most beautifully turned and often antholo-gized poems, the sonnet 'Prayer (1)'. The craft of Sylvia Plath's poem of early 1960, 'You're', about her unborn first child, will be seen in the con-text of comparisons with three other imitations of 'Prayer (1)' by mid-seventeenth-century poets. The comparisons reveal a somewhat mechanical quality in the seventeenth-century examples and a much more interesting grasp of a poetic idea in the twentieth-century example. As we shall see, Plath's poem changes the apparent subject of the sonnet, but comes much closer than the other examples to its sense of mystery.

I say apparent subject, because there is of course more than one subject in both poems, and as it turns out the contrast between a religious subject in the hands of a male priest and a secular one in the hands of a impending mother is not so very large in terms of the *kind* of experience being imi-tated. What is more, both poets have in common (whilst the other com-parators do not) a concern, visible in the poems themselves, for the making the poetry itself.

I will not insult the present audience by offering to say too much about the wonderful, verb-less sonnet, 'Prayer (1)', but I need to pick out one or two features of the poem. On an obvious level, it is an affectionate medita-tion, attempting definition, of something extremely familiar yet eluding easy description. Prayer is considered in the poem in many aspects, as both public and private act, as both group and single activity, and as both praise and petition. It is also shown as subject to many moods, from harmonious communion to angry unthankfulness (which might even stretch to the betrayal indicated in the re-crucifying of 'Christ-side-piercing spear'), but the key idea throughout is one of *communication* between man and God, between earth and heaven, as it often is in *The Temple*. That a main concern is communication is indicated by the last phrase of the poem, which mischievously rewrites the priorities: the most useful thing to be appreciated is not man's incomplete and wondering grasp of prayer, or his divergent uses of it, but the fact that it is heard and understood at the other end:

Prayer (1)

Prayer the Church's banquet, Angels' age,
    God's breath in man returning to his birth,
    The soul in paraphrase, heart in pilgrimage,
The Christian plummet sounding heav'n and earth;
Engine against th'Almighty, sinners' tower,
    Reversed thunder, Christ-side-piercing spear,
    The six-days world-transposing in an hour,
A kind of tune, which all things hear and fear;
Softness, and peace, and joy, and love, and bliss,
    Exalted Manna, gladness of the best,
    Heaven in ordinary, man well dressed,
The milky way, the bird of Paradise,
    Church-bells beyond the stars heard, the soul's blood,
    The land of spices; something understood.

That which is most useful comes clear at the end, and so a structure is established in the closing of the tight form of the sonnet. As we shall see, it was most clearly Plath who took from the poem the idea of communication, so as to structure a series of laconic, celebratory descriptive phrases.

Another related structure both Christopher Harvey and Henry Vaughan saw in the sonnet and tried to preserve. In the varying moods and definitions of Herbert's poem, there is a turning of thoughts towards heaven at the end. The poem admits discontented and unreconciled uses of prayer in the opening of second quatrain, showing attitudes of aggression, attempts to coerce God or acts of pride (like the tower of Babel), then turns to images of sabbath peace and harmony, until it is recorded that prayer can give a glimpse of a heavenly order, where praise might be reckoned to be unproblematic and communication easy. In the last part of the third quatrain through to the concluding couplet we find a series of phrases about heaven which, as we shall see, Harvey dutifully echoed for rather a lot of his poem and understood as his ending, whilst in Vaughan's poem, too, the idea of 'Heaven here' runs through the text and furnishes the close. But we shall also see that the sense of a sequence into an ending is much more interesting in 'You're', because Plath like Herbert contrives a final clarification which is the recognition of something other, of a perspective clarified by recognizing that the main thing is beyond the incomplete definition of the speaker.

So much to set up some terms of reference. I want to turn now to the Plath poem, which will be the least familiar to you, I imagine, and I shall want to offer some contextualization as well as an interpretation, because there are references to occasion in it which help appreciation once they are explained.

Plath and her English poet husband, Ted Hughes, had been married since 1956. They spent the summer of 1959 touring the United States by car, going as far as the West Coast and coming back via New Orleans before returning to her home state, Massachusetts, at the end of August. Thereafter in the Autumn of 1959 they were to have a period of writing at Yaddo, a big house at Saratoga Springs in upstate New York which functioned as a study centre. By late November the community of artists was dispersing. They spent Thanksgiving at Plath's mother's house, and then set out for a new home in England in England in December. The rest of December was in fact spent in the Hughes house in Yorkshire, but then came the move to London, arriving on January 2. And flat hunting.[1]

They did not find a place of their own until 1 February. The baby was due at the end of March 1960. By the time she left America Plath was noticeably pregnant, and she was large by the time of setting up the flat. The child, Frieda, her first, was born at the beginning of April. So, 'You're' is not only a poem about carrying the embryo; it is also about moving to England, to a new home in London. At beginning of the second stanza, 'Vague as fog and looked for like mail' records the experience of a London winter a long way from her American East Coast home; a nervous sense of distance may help to explain the reference to Australia in the next line; the prawn in the line after has travelled round America and across the Atlantic; and one gets the impression that the new arrival, the clean slate' with its own identity which is to be the child, has something to do with making brave new beginnings in new places. The poem was written in January or February 1960, when she was seven or eight months pregnant.

You're

Clownlike, happiest on your hands,
Feet to the stars, and moon-skulled,
Gilled like a fish. A common-sense
Thumbs-down on the dodo's mode.
Wrapped up in yourself like a spool,
Trawling your dark as owls do.
Mute as a turnip from the Fourth
Of July to All Fool's Day,
O high-riser, my little loaf.

Vague as fog and looked for like mail.
Farther off than Australia.
Bent-backed Atlas, and traveled prawn.
Snug as a bud and at home
Like a sprat in a pickle jug.
A creel of eels, all rippled.
Jumpy as a Mexican bean.
Right, like a well-done sum.
A clean slate, with your own face on.[2]

Plath wrote a number of so-called riddling poems from an early age, and in some of them her models were modern American poets, Wallace Stevens and Elizabeth Bishop, perhaps, and from the more distant past, Emily Dickinson, but some critics have sensed that in 'You're' there is a quality of metaphysical wit. When I started to dig around for what commentators had said on this poem, I was mischievously delighted to find one solemnly discussing the influence of Donne on this poem and another also to be published in the *Ariel* volume,[3] a poem called 'Cut'. (The inappropriate comparison was with another well-known anthology piece, 'A Valediction Forbidding Mourning'.) Well, Plath *was* a constant echoer of other poet's voices, especially in her earlier years—that in itself is no surprise—and her well-educated range of reading in poetry was large. What signals the imitation of Herbert and not Donne in this case is the assimilation of a kind of experience to an appropriate poetic form, or idea.

As prayer is something well-known, to be looked at in different ways, part of daily life yet always resisting easy definition, a mystery embedded in the everyday, so the baby in the womb is also a constant companion, something intimately present and yet distant, unknowable, and the subject of many different ideas and fantasies. The greatest mysteries may be closest to home. The first stanza begins a series of playful but disconcertingly vivid images of the foetus in the dark amniotic fluid, this way up and that, grotesquely imagined in its early stages of development, some kind of curled up fish or prawn. It is understood as a triumph for new life—thumbs down to dodos—and the loaf rises in a satisfying way; but still this living thing is as vague as fog, it might as well be in Australia as far as distance is concerned, and waiting for its appearance is like waiting for letters from home. The playfulness of these lines may owe something to Herbert's teasing definitions; both poets provide entertainment by contriving surprises and odd juxtapositions in the train of conceits. And then, just as Herbert's poem finally makes its way heavenward, until in that land of spices something comes clear, as prayer is 'understood', so Plath's poem follows the development of the foetus now jumping inside her to the point at which all comes clear, too, when 'like a well done sum' the baby will appear not as series of grotesque imaginings but as 'A clean slate, with (its) own face on'. A revelation at the end of time. Just as what is imitated in Herbert's poem is the realization that the full understanding of the mystery of prayer is only finally with God, to whom the matter must finally be referred, so too with Plath's baby what will eventually matter is not the mother's half playful, half anxious attempt to compass it, but the fact of its appearance. There will be a new face and a new personality to whom the mother must allow complete being. In both cases the speaker must ultimately refer to an 'other' for the mystery to be revealed.

For the reader, the poem presents a kind of riddle, and a game has been entered into. Plath just shows by her title that she is defining something— you are—then takes the reader on a journey of widely-flung comparisons until a cumulative sense dawns. Herbert's poem has a true title, of course, he *tells* the reader his subject, but the same kind of journey of definition has taken place, with similar virtuoso display, until the most instructive definition is reached in the very end.

As I said, Plath's baby had been on a real journey, across America and the Atlantic, at home in the womb yet awaiting, like the poet, a place of fresh beginnings in London. The difference between this riddling poem and other Plath riddling poems is I think in its shaping, in the way it comes like 'Prayer (1)' to a simple clarity at the end, and if this is indeed a sign that the Herbert poem was somewhere in her mind, then we have here also, perhaps, another symbolic meaning in the writing of the poem: for all the well-known recognition of Herbert in White Anglo-Saxon Protestant culture in America, the new beginnings are signalled here through *English* culture, through a very *English* poet, for the American woman married to another English poet setting up flat in the foggy capital of England.

In fact, this poem held a special place in her poetic production, about which she worried so incessantly. Since leaving Yaddo in November until the birth of little Frieda at the beginning of April, 'You're' was in her mind her only successful composition. Most of her time in this period was spent in making a fair copy of the typescript for her first collection of poems (in Yorkshire) or in searching for a flat and setting up house (in London) in early 1960, another kind of making (Wagner-Martin, pp. 172-173). Yet, as we shall see, the compulsion to be making poetry is not absent from this apparently light-hearted, celebratory piece.

* * *

I want now to turn briefly to the three obvious seventeenth-century imitations of Herbert's sonnet, before returning to the Herbert/Plath inter-reading, having tried to create a better perspective by this method.

As you will all know, Christopher Harvey's *The Synagogue*, a collection of lyrics closely modelled on *The Temple*, was first printed with *The Temple* in an edition of 1640, and then regularly again thereafter, new poems being added to it in successive editions. Many mid-seventeenth-century readers would therefore have had both *The Temple* and *The Synagogue* in one book. As you will also know, Herbert's poems had a very wide appeal to different religious constituencies in the middle and latter parts of the seventeenth century, but the fact that Harvey's poems regularly accompanied them in editions of the middle part of the century put a slant on the apparent churchmanship. One commendatory poem to Harvey written in 1654 by a certain A.S. says that reading his poems is like going back to the old, pre-revolutionary church:

> While I read your lines, methinks I spie
> Churches, and churchmen, and the old hierarchie:
> What potent charms are these! You have the knack
> To make men young again, and fetch time back.[4]

Harvey was a traditional churchman. Son of a Cheshire preacher and schoolmaster, he was educated at Brasenose College in Oxford from 1613 to 1620. He held a living in Herefordshire from 1630 to 1639, where he had also been for a short period a schoolteacher, then held another living in Warwickshire from 1639. He was a firm royalist during the Civil War and wrote books against the rebels. As far as the poems of *The Synagogue* are concerned, one symptom of his determined institutionalism appears in the fact that most poems are about the fabric, furniture, books, officers and feast-days of the church. It is no surprise, then, that Herbert's general poem about prayer, having a strong psychological dimension as well as an institutional one, produces the wholly institutionalized 'Church-Festivals'. This poem comes close to suggesting that communion with God is confined to those special occasions in the calendar.

Church-Festivals

Marrow of time, Eternity in brief
Compendiums Epitomiz'd, the chief
Contents, the Indices, the Title-pages
Of all past, present, and succeeding ages,
Sublimate graces, antidated glories,
      The cream of holiness,
      The inventories
      Of future blessedness,
The Florilegia of celestial stories,
Spirits of joyes, the relishes and closes
Of Angels musick, pearls dissolved, roses
Perfumed, sugar'd honey-combs, delights
      Never too highly priz'd,
      The marriage rites,
      Which duly solemnis'd
Usher espoused souls to bridal nights,
Gilded sun-beams, refined Elixars,
And quintessential extracts of stars;
Who loves not you, doth but in vain profess
That he loves God, or heaven, or happiness.[5]

The correspondence of Harvey's poem with Herbert's wonderfully taut sonnet is on the basis of a general idea: church festivals are celebrated as a special holy time, savouring of heaven. Harvey tries repeatedly to convey the quintessence of something valued, but the wonderful compression of Herbert is lost, and individual ideas and images are allowed to expand for too long: arranging things in threes was I think a mistake, and the idea of books, for example, spreads out too long, over the first four lines, descending to contents pages and indexes. (Its later appearance with inventories and florilegia is perhaps more interesting.) There is some ingenuity in using many images of things distilled in the latter half of the poem, and he takes from Herbert, as I have already said, the idea of rising towards heaven at the end, but the effect is somewhat lost in the final emphatic *sententia*. To read Harvey's imitation makes one realize what agility in technique and variation in attitude there was in Herbert's original.

To be fair, it may not be appropriate even to *look* for the representation of varying individual experience in poems in *The Synagogue*: that may be to expect the wrong appeal. There must have been a political appeal connecting with the picturing of the old churchmanship. This poem was first published in the edition of 1640; it celebrated the festivals that were to be abolished with the abolition of the Book of Common Prayer in 1645; by 1652 A.S. and others could see in Harvey's volume a celebration of a whole past age.

We might also note that the frame of reference in the poem has become one of time, of specific moments in time as they might seem to preview eternal bliss. That might be kept in mind was we turn to the next imitation. To judge from his handling of the time dimension and his picking up of the image of the honeycomb, Vaughan seem to have recollected Harvey's poem as well as 'Prayer (1)', as he wrote his poem, called 'Son-dayes':

1.

Bright shadows of true Rest! some shoots of blisse,
         Heaven once a week;
The next worlds gladnes prepossest in this;
         A day to seek
Eternity in time; the steps by which
We Climb above all ages; Lamps that light
Man through his heap of dark days; and the rich,
And full redemption of the whole weeks flight.

2.

The Pulleys unto headlong man; times bower;
         The narrow way;
Transplanted Paradise; Gods walking houre;
         The Cool o'th'day;
The Creatures Jubile; Gods parle with dust;
Heaven here; Man on those hills of Myrrh, and flowres;
Angels descending; the Returns of Trust;
A Gleam of glory, after six-days-showres.

3.

The Churches love-feasts; Times Prerogative,
          And Interest
Deducted from the whole; The Combs, and hive,
          And home of rest.
The milky way Chalkt out with Suns; a Clue
That guides through erring hours; and in full story
A taste of Heav'n on earth; the pledge, and Cue
Of a full feast; And the Out Courts of glory.[6]

Vaughan's poem is more inventive than Harvey's. He gets some sense of
the interesting contrary movements and unexpected juxtapositions in Herbert's sonnet. He has the skill which Harvey did not, of knowing that he
should not hold on to lines of images too long. Nevertheless, there is something slightly too easy in the progression in the second stanza, say, from
'transplanted paradise' to 'Gods walking houre' to 'The Cool o'th'day',
even if those phrases are rather good. Vaughan follows Herbert, like Harvey, in taking his poem towards heaven at the end, in the last four lines,
and he doesn't do it badly. But the whole poem is looser and more repetitive than Herbert's poem, and it is rather simply fixed on a general notion
of Sundays as a preview of heaven, a bit of heaven here, and a means to
eternity. Also, although Vaughan is not so institution-bound as Harvey,
nevertheless the shift from prayer as subject to the whole sabbath day takes
away the sense of personal communication which is at the heart of Herbert's poem and which furnishes many of the varieties and surprises. Yet
this, too, may need political contextualization. The cherished festivals of
Herbert and Harvey no longer exist in the post-Civil War period of the
1650s; there are for Vaughan no specific times of ritual worship, only
undifferentiated Sundays which may stand as glimpses of eternity. Nevertheless, however ingeniously wrought, Vaughan's poem has no psychological centre, whereas Plath in her baby riddle touches more of the mysteries
of the knowable and unknowable.
     What happens when Herbert's poem is converted for wholly public
voice can be demonstrated by the version for congregational singing of
1697, where much of the riddling disappears into repetitive exposition:

Prayer

Prayer the Churches Banquet is,
        Prayer the Angels Age,
Prayer the Soul in Paraphrase,
        The Heart in Pilgrimage.

God's breath in Man returning thither
        From whence it had its Birth;
Prayer the Christian Plummet is
        That soundeth Heav'n and Earth.

Prayer reversed Thunder is,
        And Christ's side-peircing Spear,
Prayer's a kind of heav'nly Tune
        Which all things hear and fear.

Engine against the Almighty One.
        It is the Sinners Tower,
The World that was a Six-days Work
        Transposing in an Hour.

Softness and Peace, and Spiritual Joy,
        Prayer is Love and Bliss,
It is as 'twere the Milky way,
        The Bird of Paradice.

Prayer exalted Manna is,
        And gladness of the best,
Heaven in Ordinary 'tis,
        Prayer is Man well drest.

The Church-Bell's heard beyond the Stars,
        It is the Souls Heart-blood,
A kind of Land of Spices 'tis,
        And something understood.[7]

Here, the introduction of verbs, mainly the repetition of 'is', does nothing
for the sense of mystery in Herbert's poem, but then you don't expect much
enigmatic compression in a hymn for Dissenters. They were, I take it, after
togetherness.

Now, considering all these poems against their original, one might conclude that in matters of imitation to run in parallel in form and subject is not necessarily to imitate the spirit; paradoxically, to recreate poetic form in another context, on another subject, may be to produce something like the spirit of the original.

* * *

As so back to the way that Herbert and Plath use similar poetic form to encapsulate some similar kinds of experience, in celebration of a mystery very much fitted into the thoughts of the individual. I have mentioned the self-reflexivity of both poets. We might notice that one of the next poems which Hughes (*Collected Poems*, p. 142) records Plath writing, a few months after 'You're', was one called 'Still-born'. This is not about a failure of live birth but about the failure of being able to make poems come to life. The comparison is significant. She was evidently full of anxiety about being able to write, and she felt restless when she could not. During the time of pregnancy and birth, the creation of the baby and the creation of poems seem to have have come into association; each was a metaphor for the other, though one was crowding the other out. In 'You're' the baby comes to birth and something is completed, like a sum well done, and it is almost as if the baby writes the poem for her, just as the clarifying completion of many a Herbert poem is attributed to the hand of God. The journey to birth and the journey of the poem have been fashioned in the ending of a celebratory text in which, as often in Herbert, a shaping of a text has been made to stand for a realization. But the baby was the boss, the baby finally dictated the terms.

Plath's fellow poet Anne Sexton went with her to Robert Lowell's poetry workshop in Boston in the spring of 1959. Lowell said that he saw directness and promise in Plath's work, but Sexton, the colloquial and much less academic poet than Plath, remarked to him that she felt on the contrary that Plath

> dodged the point and did so perhaps because of her preoccupation with form. ... Sylvia hadn't then found a form that belonged to her. Those early poems were all in a cage (and not even her own cage at that). I felt that she hadn't a voice of her own ... (*Bitter Fame*, pp. 150-151).

Of course we know, from much cumulative evidence, that Plath was frequently put in despair by a sense of having to compete with poetic voices from past and present, and that her considerable knowledge of literature was as much a problem to her as a poet as an asset, but in this particular case, in 'You're', she found someone else's form, or cage, and it worked. In this poem she did her imitation with all the Renaissance arts of discovering fit rhetorical means.

Herbert, too, was a ventriloquist, and wonderfully resourceful as a ventriloquist. He, too, mastered other poets through the use of their forms. There are plenty of earlier secular sonnets which have passages of accumulated conceits, but I think only Herbert refined this figuration into such meaningful shape as 'Prayer (1)' has, so as to create a mimesis, to tease the reader with various impression until an understanding is sealed at the end. With Harvey and Vaughan imitation made possible celebrations of holy times, and those celebrations may have had some urgency in their context, but in terms of agility of technique it led to not much more than elaborated statement. Plath seems to have sensed a teasing game which could be done in her own way. Both Herbert and Plath prove themselves by fashioning more and more triumphant appropriations of this kind; both seem possessed by the need to show this mastery in the working of their poems. In this case, Plath, as Herbert often does, writes a poem which shows that it is partly about poetry-making, responding to that self-conscious art in Herbert which has attracted so many other poets, like Helen Vendler and Seamus Heaney, in this century. Herbert is a poet's poet in terms of technical virtuosity, but also a poet's poet in terms of showing that self-consciousness about poetry-making which so appeals to twentieth-century attitudes.

Though by 1960 she may have reached less maturity of technique than Herbert in *The Temple*, Plath is in this happy case the liveliest imitator, because she seems to have intuited that Herbert's method made best sense if in some way the riddling bore upon the matter of communication itself, between mother and baby, as between man and God. So the reader, too, is more fully drawn into the business of triumphant fashioning. Both poems are about mysterious forces close to the heart, and in that sense are similar, but the sacred and the profane have spanned, and the craft itself has become a kind of mystery. Hence my title. Babies and God, known yet unknown, near yet far, have been mastered into form, but remain rival centres of authority. Playfully, or anxiously, and concerned with making, both texts show that their speakers must finally defer to authorities outside themselves.

Notes

1   Ann Stevenson, *Bitter Fame: A Life of Sylvia Plath* (London & New York: Houghton Mifflin, 1989), 172-183; Linda W. Wagner-Martin, *Sylvia Plath: A Biography* (London: Chatto & Windus, 1988), 162-169.
2   Sylvia Plath, *Collected Poems*, edited by Ted Hughes (London & Boston: Faber & Faber, 1981), 141.
3   J.D. O'Hara, 'Plath's Comedy', in *Sylvia Plath: New Views on the Poetry*, edited by Gary Lane (Baltimore & London: Johns Hopkins UP, 1979), 76-77. For another observation of 'metaphysical' influence see for example Sr Bernetta Quinn, 'Medusan Imagery in Sylvia Plath', in Lane, p. 99.
4   *The Complete Works of Christopher Harvey*, edited by A.B. Grosart (London, 1874), 88-89.
5   Harvey, *Complete Works*, p. 43.
6   *The Works of Henry Vaughan*, edited by L.C. Martin, 2nd ed. (Oxford: Clarendon, 1957), 447-448.
7   *Select Hymns taken out of Mr. Herbert's Temple* (London, 1697), 10-11.

LIST OF CONTRIBUTORS

MATTHIAS BAUER is a Postdoctoral Fellow at the Westfälische Wilhelms-Universität, Münster. He is co-editor of *Connotations: A Journal for Critical Debate* and is currently working on a study of the mystical linguistics of metaphysical poetry. His most recent publication is '*Paronomasia celata* in Donne's "A Valediction: forbidding mourning"' in *ELR* (1995).

CEDRIC BROWN is currently Head of English in the University of Reading. He is author of *John Milton's Aristocratic Entertainments* (Cambridge: Cambridge University Press, 1985) and *John Milton: a literary life* (London: Macmillan, 1995), editor of *Patronage, Politics and Literary Traditions in England, 1558-1658* (Detroit: Wayne State University Press, 1993) and has written widely on seventeenth-century poetry and the literature of patronage. He is currently working on the social history of texts.

DIANE KELSEY MCCOLLEY is a Professor of English at Rutgers University. She has published widely on seventeenth-century poetry and its relations with music and the visual arts. Among her books are *Milton's Eve* (Urbana: University of Illinois Press, 1983), and a more recent study, *A Gust for Paradise: Milton's Eden and the Visual Arts* (Urbana: University of Illinois Press, 1993), which was awarded the Milton Society's James Holly Hanford Award.

MARIO DI CESARE is Distinguished Professor of English and Comparative Literature at the State University of New York, Binghamton and Founder and Director of MRTS (Medieval and Renaissance Texts and Studies). Among his many publications are his edition, with Rigo Mignani, of *A Concordance to the Complete Writings of George Herbert* (Ithaca: Cornell University Press, 1977) and a facsimile edition, with the late Amy Charles, of the Bodleian Manuscript (MS Tanner 307) of *The Temple*. He has just completed *A Diplomatic Edition of the Bodleian Manuscript* (Binghamton: MRTS, 1995).

ELIZABETH CLARKE, Senior Lecturer in English at Westminster College, Oxford, is the author of a book forthcoming with Oxford University Press, provisionally entitled '*Divinitie, and Poesie, Met*': Theory and Theology in George Herbert's Poetry*.

ROBERT CUMMINGS teaches English at the University of Glasgow. He has published mainly on sixteenth- and seventeenth-poetry, and co-edits the journal *Translation and Literature*.

JUDITH DUNDAS is Professor of English, University of Illinois at Urbana-Champaign. Her publications include *The Spider and the Bee: The Artistry of Spenser's* Faerie Queene (Urbana: University of Illinois Press, 1985), *Pencils Rhetorique: Renaissance Poets and the Art of Painting* (Newark: University of Delaware Press, 1993), and articles on wit in sixteenth- and seventeenth-century poetry in English.

JOHN OTTENHOFF is Associate Professor of English at Alma College, Alma, Michigan. His publications include articles on Herbert's sonnets, typology and the devotional sonnet, and Anne Locke; he is at work on a larger study of Donne and Herbert's sixteenth-century devotional forerunners.

TED-LARRY PEBWORTH is William E. Stirton Professor in the Humanities and Professor of Literature at The University of Michigan-Dearborn. He has published critical and textual studies on a variety of seventeenth-century British authors and is a senior textual editor of *The Variorum Edition of the Poetry of John Donne* (Bloomington: Indiana University Press, 1995ff).

HEATHER ROSS is Associate Professor of English at York University, Toronto, Canada. She has published, as Heather [Ross] Asals, *Equivocal Predication: George Herbert's Way to God* (Toronto/Buffalo/London: University of Toronto Press, 1981) and co-edited, with P.G. Stanwood, *John Donne and the Theology of Language* (Columbia: University of Missouri Press, 1985).

KAY GILLILAND STEVENSON, Lecturer in the Department of Literature, University of Essex, is the co-author (with Clive Hart) of *Heaven and the Flesh: Desire and Ascension from the Renaissance to the Rococo* (Cambridge: Cambridge University Press, 1995). She is now editing an eighteenth-century oratorio based on *Paradise Lost*.

RICHARD TODD teaches English literature at the Vrije Universiteit Amsterdam. His publications in the field of early modern literature include *The Opacity of Signs: Forms of Interpretative Activity in George Herbert's* The Temple (Columbia: University of Missouri Press, 1986) and articles on the

Sidney-Pembroke psalter and Dutch analogues, and on Carew's epitaph on Donne.

BART WESTERWEEL is Professor of English Renaissance Literature at the University of Leiden. He is author of *Patterns and Patterning: A Study of Four Poems by George Herbert* (Amsterdam: Rodopi, 1984) and has also co-edited, with Theo D'haen, *Something Understood: Studies in Anglo-Dutch Literary Translation* (Amsterdam: Rodopi, 1990). Other publications include articles on emblems and iconography in sixteenth- and seventeenth-century literature.

ROBERT WILCHER is Senior Lecturer in English at the University of Birmingham. His teaching and research interests lie in the sixteenth and seventeenth centuries, with particular emphasis on the literature of the English Revolution. His publications include *Andrew Marvell* (Cambridge: Cambridge University Press, 1985), *Andrew Marvell: Selected Poetry and Prose* (London: Methuen, 1986) and articles on Shakespeare, Milton, Vaughan, Marvell, Quarles and *Eikon Basilike*.

HELEN WILCOX is Professor of English at the University of Groningen. She has published widely on early modern English literature, especially on women's writing and devotional texts. Forthcoming books include the Longmans Annotated Poems edition of George Herbert, and *Women and Literature in Britain, 1500-1700* (Cambridge: Cambridge University Press).

R.V. YOUNG, Jr., is Professor of English at North Carolina State University at Raleigh. Together with M. Thomas Hester he is co-editor of the *John Donne Journal*. In addition to numerous essays and articles on seventeenth-century poetry he has published *Richard Crashaw and the Spanish Golden Age* (New Haven: Yale University Press, 1982).

INDEX OF WORKS BY GEORGE HERBERT